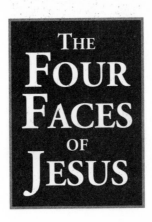

# The FOUR FACES OF JESUS

*Four Gospel Writers*

*Four Unique Perspectives*

*Four Personal Encounters*

*ONE COMPLETE PICTURE*

## ROBERT K. MCIVER

**Pacific Press® Publishing Association**

Nampa, Idaho

Oshawa, Ontario, Canada

For the girls who light up my life:
Susan, Althea, and Skye

Edited by B. Russell Holt
Designed by Michelle C. Petz
Cover art by Sue Rother

McIver, Robert K. (Robert Kerry) 1953-
  The four faces of Jesus : four Gospel writers, four unique perspectives, four
personal encounters, one complete picture / Robert K. McIver.
  p. cm.
Includes index
ISBN 0-8163-1722-4 (pbk.)
  1. Bible. N.T. Gospels—Introductions. I. Title.

BS2555.2 .M385 2000
226'.06—dc21
99-045762

00 01 02 03 04 • 5 4 3 2 1

# CONTENTS

PREFACE

In one way or another, I have been studying and explaining the Gospels most of my adult life—first as an interested layman, then as a church pastor, and for a number of years, as a college teacher. They have formed the basis of my own study and research—both for my master's thesis and my doctoral dissertation, as well as for many of my subsequent academic publications. This book is the result of that lifelong experience with the Gospels.

I have written with the typical church member in mind. No specialized knowledge of New Testament backgrounds or familiarity with Greek has been assumed, nor will the reader find ponderous footnotes. Yet, I hope the reader will find some of the more interesting and useful discoveries of modern scholarship on the Gospels.

I would like to offer sincere thanks to a large number of people who have helped me along the way in the development of this book. First, many thanks to Norm Young, Ray Roennfeldt, Don Hansen, Mike Brownhill, David Theile, and Beatrice Neall, all of whom have read earlier drafts of all or parts of this manuscript and provided invaluable feedback. My thanks, likewise, to the Avondale College students of my Gospels A classes of 1994 to 1998 and the 1995 class in New Testament Faith and Literature who were the first "guinea pigs" on whom I tried the book. My thanks also to Griggs University who, by asking me to prepare a course titled "Jesus and the Gospels," gave me the impetus to begin this project, and also to the readers at Griggs University (especially Bertram Melbourne from its affiliated campus, Columbia Union College, and Herbert Keisler, from the Biblical Research Institute).

Furthermore, a big "Thank you" to my teachers, both those who taught me in the classroom and those whose books have been invaluable. All writers stand on the shoulders of those who have gone before, yet the semipopular nature of this book has precluded me from documenting my indebtedness to different authors. Indeed, it has been both scary and exhilarating to leave behind the protective ranks of footnotes and the canvassing of different possibilities that my academic training has taught me to value. I will have to content myself with this general "Thank you" to all those who have assisted in the development of my understanding of the Gospels.

I should point out that New Testament citations in this book are either translated by myself or quoted from the Revised Standard Version or the New Revised Standard Version.

Many readers will be interested to know that there is a list of suggestions for further reading for most of the chapters in this book available on the internet at the following address: www.avondale.edu.au under the name of the author in the list of theology faculty members.

Robert K. McIver

Part 1

# THE GOSPEL OF MATTHEW

# CHAPTER ONE

# The Matthean Perspective

## WHY FOUR GOSPELS?

Why does the New Testament have four Gospels instead of only one? The reasons the early church kept the four Gospels are lost to us today, although it is not unlikely that they arose in four different geographical regions under the sponsorship of either a prominent disciple or church leader. Why we keep all four of them today is another matter.

The four Gospels have been in the Bible for nearly two thousand years now, and it would take a brave person to suggest that one or more of them was redundant. But there is more to it than that. While the four Gospels have a good deal in common, each is distinctive in what it says about Jesus. Together, they provide four different views of Him and the meaning of His life and ministry. Just as we can get a better understanding of even recent events if we talk to more than one witness, likewise, we will better understand Jesus if we have more than one perspective. The four Gospels provide a four-dimensional view.

To obtain this enhanced view of Jesus, though, we must first take time to examine each Gospel individually to find out what it is saying. For many Christians, this will be something new. The Gospels are bound together in our Bibles as the opening part of the New Testament, and this makes it easy to treat them as a single, unified work. If some detail is missing in Matthew's description of a certain healing, then it might be in Mark. So most sermons and much Christian writing treat the Gospels as four parts of the same work. Sure, the four are dealing with the life of the same individual, but treating them as a whole makes it all too easy to overlook the unique contribution that each makes to our overall understanding of Jesus.

In this book we will first look at each Gospel independently of the others. This way, the special perspective that each provides will be apparent. And after seeing the unique view of each Gospel, we will be in a better position to take the wider perspective. In part 6 of this book, we will be able to view Jesus from the viewpoint offered by the four Gospels combined.

In what order should we study the four Gospels? We will see in part 4 that there was wide consensus at one time about which Gospel was written first, but that consensus has disappeared. Otherwise, we might have started with Mark. Instead, we will study them in the order in which they are found in the New Testament. So this book begins by looking in detail at the Gospel of Matthew.

## WHAT DOES MATTHEW HAVE IN COMMON WITH THE OTHER GOSPELS?

Since there are four Gospels, it is possible to compare them. When we do so, some interesting things emerge. We find that Matthew, Mark, and Luke are very similar but that John is made up mainly of materials that are not found in the other three. Thus, it is most natural to compare Matthew with Mark and Luke. Doing so reveals, for example, that they all three share the same basic outline of Jesus' ministry, beginning with His baptism by John the Baptist in the river Jordan, His use of Capernaum as the center of His public ministry, His teaching and healing ministry, His trip to Jerusalem, His confrontation with the religious leadership there (including driving the money-changers from the temple precincts), and His death and resurrection. In particular, we find that Matthew's sequence of events is very close to that of Mark's—right down to the order in which even minor details of incidents take place.

Most notably, though, Matthew's Gospel shares with the other three a conviction that the most important part of Jesus' life and ministry revolves around His death and resurrection. Chronologically speaking, the Gospels give disproportionate space to the events of the last week of Jesus' life—His betrayal, trial, crucifixion, and resurrection. In my Greek New Testament, seventeen of the 117 pages in Matthew, 15 percent of the total, are devoted to these final events. Thus, Matthew shares the conviction of the other Gospels that although Jesus is a great teacher, He is much more than that. His life can be understood only in terms of His suffering, death, and resurrection. These have changed history. Further, the resurrected Jesus is to return to this world to finalize His victory over the devil, sin, and death.

### WHAT IS DISTINCTIVE ABOUT MATTHEW?

It is the *differences* between Matthew and the other Gospels that reveal Matthew's unique character. Of course, all writing involves a process of selection, and the Gospels are not exempt from this rule. Indeed, John's Gospel goes so far as to comment on this fact with the rather despairing words: "But there are also many other things that Jesus did; if every one of them were written down, I suppose that the world itself could not contain the books that would be written" (John 21:25). All the Gospel writers knew more of Jesus and His teachings than they could fit in a scroll, so they had to select the most important things to write down. What would cause one Gospel writer to choose to include something the others did not? Surely, it must be because he was more interested in that particular fact or item than the others. This interest could be a personal interest or it could be one that arose out of the circumstances of the particular group of Christians that the writer was associated with. If there was a particular need in the community, then the aspects of Jesus' teaching and ministry that related to that need would take on a higher priority.

Admittedly, not all the differences between the different Gospel accounts need to be explained in terms of deliberate policy. Church tradition holds that two of the Gospel writers were eyewitnesses of Jesus' life; they may have been present at some events and not others.[1] But even so, they could not have been present during *everything* that is recorded in their Gospels. They would have had access to other eyewitnesses and even to some written accounts (see Luke 1:1, 2), but not necessarily the same eyewitnesses and writings as the other Gospel writers. So some of the differences between the Gospels would have arisen from the different sources of information available to a particular writer.

How can we know whether the unique material in Matthew is there because of historical accident or the specific interest of the writer and his community, not to speak of inspiration? The issue of inspiration will be explored more fully in chapter 21. At this point, though, it is sufficient to point out that, according to Luke 1:1-3, a significant research aspect was involved in Luke's Gospel in the way he gathered materials and emphasized his use of eyewitnesses and sources. Since this is the case for at least one of the Gospels, the question of deliberate choice or historical accident remains. It is best answered by actually examining the unique material. If there doesn't appear to be a pattern showing that this material serves a particular interest or point of view, then perhaps its presence should be largely explained as an accident of history—the sources that happened to be available to the writer. But if there are common themes, then this would indicate that the writer has purposely selected this material to meet his specific interests and those of his community. Furthermore, these singular interests will be what gives the Gospel its distinctive perspective on Jesus.

## PROMINENT THEMES IN THE MATERIAL UNIQUE TO MATTHEW'S GOSPEL

When we examine the material unique to Matthew, several prominent themes stand out, showing that it does reflect the interests of the writer and his community. These themes include several of Jesus' teachings concerning community discipline, sayings about who to regard as true prophets and warnings against false prophets, mention of Christian scribes, parables dealing with the mixed nature of the community, and sayings concerning the role of Peter. These all relate in one way or another to *the community of believers.*[2]

A second group of unique sayings clusters around matters related to *Jews and Gentiles* and their relationship to the saved community. These include sayings initially limiting the disciples' missionary activity to the Jews only (but which later expand it to include all Gentiles), a number of sayings relating to controversies between Jesus and the scribes and Pharisees, and the recounting of several incidents that would have special relevance to Jews.[3]

A third group relates to *the law* and such associated matters as righteousness, forgiveness, prayer, and practical injunctions.[4] A fourth group concerns *the end of the age* (eschatology). These sayings speak either of the closeness or the delay of the Second Coming or about judgment. Furthermore, there is a considerable interest in the kingdom of heaven.[5]

This list does not exhaust the themes found in the material that is unique to Matthew,[6] but these four are among the most prominent. Further, they are themes that are also pronounced in another unique feature of Matthew's Gospel—*the five discourses.* In these are gathered five large blocks of Jesus' teaching:

Matt. 5–7—the Sermon on the Mount
Matt. 10—the missionary discourse
Matt. 13—parables of the kingdom of heaven
Matt. 18—matters of community discipline
Matt. 24–25—signs of the end of the age

A significant section of the Sermon on the Mount deals with the law; the missionary discourse is intimately tied up with the matter of Jews and Gentiles and their relationship to the community of the saved; both the parables of the kingdom and the discourse on community discipline relate to the community of believers; and the last discourse deals directly with matters concerning the end of the age.

In summary, the uniqueness of these five blocks of material in comparison with the other Gospels, as well as their relationship to interests that are clearly of importance to Matthew, make them the most appropriate parts of the Gospel on which to focus if we want to know Matthew's distinctive understanding of Jesus. Indeed, only two of the subsequent chapters in this section will cover materials outside these discourses— the chapter dealing with the healing miracles of Jesus (Matthew 8, 9) and the chapter on Matthew's understanding of Sabbath. The first of these is about material found in that section of the Gospel which varies most from the sequence of events as found in Mark; the second deals with an important aspect of law, something that we have already seen is of special importance in the Gospel of Matthew. But before we look at those chapters, we will consider part of the first discourse, the Sermon on the Mount, and explore what Matthew 5 has to say about the Christian and the law.

---

1. None of the Gospels states the name of its author. The titles, "According to Matthew," "According to Mark," etc., were added later. Early church tradition has it that the Matthew and John, who were two of the twelve disciples of Jesus, wrote the Gospels attributed to their names. According to this tradition, Mark and Luke were not disciples. Rather, Mark was the interpreter of Peter, while Luke was the companion of Paul. Luke himself tells us that he got his information from other eyewitnesses (Luke 1:2, 3), which implies that he was not an eyewitness to most of the events recorded in his Gospel. In Acts (a book written by the same author as the Gospel of Luke) the writer uses the pronoun "we" in several chapters, strongly implying that he was an eyewitness of the events recorded in those sections of Acts, even if he was not present during the events recorded in his Gospel. How credible are the traditional identifications of the four Gospel writers? The internal evidence of the four Gospels is not inconsistent with these suggestions, but neither is there enough evidence to be really sure they are right.
2. Community discipline: Matt. 18:10, 14-20, 28-31; true and false prophets: Matt. 7:15, 21-23; 10:41; 24:10-12, 14; Christian scribes: Matt. 13:51, 52; the mixed nature of the community: Matt. 13:24-30, 3-43, 47-50; 25:1-13; Peter: Matt. 14:28-31; 16:17-19; 17:24-27. Cf. also Matt. 18:3, 4, 23-35; 19:28b; 21:43; 23:8-10; 28:16-20.
3. Mission to ethnic Jews: Matt. 10:5b, 6, 23; 15:23, 24; expanded mission: Matt. 24:14; 28:16-20; [scribes and] Pharisees: Matt. 5:20; 15:12, 13; 16:12; 23:1-3, 5, 8-10, 15, 16-22, 27, 28, 32, 33); incidents relevant particularly to Jews: Matt. 5:33-37; 6:1-4, 16-18; 9:27-31; 17:24-27; 19:28b; 21:14-17; 21:43.
4. Law: Matt. 5:17, 19, 20, 21-24, 27, 28; 7:21-23; 12:5-7, 11; 15:12, 13, 41; 21:28-32); righteousness: Matt. 3:14, 15; 5:10; 5:20; 10:41; forgiveness: Matt.

6:15; 18:21, 22, 23-35; prayer: Matt. 6:5-8, 10b; 18:19, 20; practical injunctions: Matt. 5:4, 5, 7-10, 14, 16, 21-24, 27, 28, 33-37, 41; 6:1-4, 16-18.

5. Closeness or delay of Second Coming: Matt. 10:23; 16:3; 25:1-13; judgment: Matt. 12:36, 37; 16:27; 18:23-35; 19:28b; 24:10-12, 14; 25:31-46; kingdom of heaven: Matt. 13:24-30; 36-52; 16:19; 17:24-27; 18:3, 4; 18:23-35; 19:12; 19:28b; 20:1-16; 21:14-17, 43; 25:1-13.

6. Other themes include several references to geographic location (Matt. 2:1, 5, 6, 13-15, 19-23; 4:13-16), to healing (Matt. 9:32-35; 15:29-31); to an interest in the miraculous and spirit beings (Matt. 1:18-25; 26:52-54; 27:19, 52, 53, 62-66; 28:2-4, 9, 10); to John the Baptist (Matt. 11:14; 17:13); and to the fulfillment of prophecy (Matt. 1:18-25; 2:1-12, 16-18, 19-23; 4:13-16; 8:17; 21:14-17). The texts cited in the previous footnotes, together with Matt. 1:18-25; 2:1-12; 2:13-15; 2:16-18; 7:6; 10:5b, 6; 11:1; 13:35, 53; 14:33; 19:1a; 20:1-16; 21:28-32; 23:5; 24:10-12, 14; 26:1; 27:24, 25, 62-66; and 28:11-15 comprise a complete listing of the material unique to Matthew.

CHAPTER TWO

# Jesus and the Law in Matthew (Matt. 5:17-48); or the Things We Know for Sure but Wish We Didn't

On what basis do Christians decide to observe one Old Testament law while ignoring another? For example, why do Christians think it a sin to disobey the commandment against committing adultery but do not consider it a sin to disobey the command to circumcise their male children? Why do they feel they must observe the rule against bearing false witness but feel free to disregard the command to consider as unclean a house or clothes with mold? It is not as though circumcision and the distinction between clean and unclean were unimportant in the Old Testament. Circumcision was a sign of the covenant between God and His chosen people (Gen. 17:9-14); it was not something that could be thrown aside without due consideration. The concept of clean and unclean dominated the lives of God's people in the Old Testament; it hardly seems to affect modern Christians. Clearly, Christian practice has changed, but on what basis has this change taken place?

This question is all the more urgent because Christians include the Old Testament in their Bible. Indeed, for almost the first hundred years of Christianity, the Old Testament *was* the Christian Bible. And here is the rub: The Bible is authoritative for Christians. In particular, even though the Christian Bible now also includes the New Testament, the Old Testament, together with its laws, is still authoritative for Christians in some

16

way. How should Christians approach Old Testament law? Moreover, how can all these regulations be dealt with in a systematic manner?

This issue is one of the special interests of Matthew's Gospel. In fact, Matthew found it so important that he placed a discussion of law toward the beginning of his first systematic presentation of Jesus' teaching—the discourse of Matthew 5–7. Although it is by no means the only treatment of law in the Gospel, the material gathered in Matthew 5:17-48 is perhaps the most comprehensive. In this chapter, we will concentrate primarily on these verses, taking first the general statement of principle in 5:17-20. Then we will look at the specific examples provided in the text that show how these principles work out in practice. Finally, we will use the insights gained from these verses to draw some conclusions about the wider issue of how Christians should apply Old Testament laws to their lives today.

## GENERAL STATEMENT (MATT. 5:17-20)

Several books and many articles have been written on just these few verses. This illustrates both how important these verses are for the wider interpretation of the Gospel and the fact that they contain some difficult points of interpretation. Nevertheless, several things clearly emerge from these verses. Indeed, it is this very clarity that causes interpreters such difficulty in understanding the passage in the context of Matthew's whole Gospel.

First, there is an insistence that Christians are obligated to observe the *whole* law:

> "Do not think that I have come to destroy the law or the prophets . . . until heaven and earth pass away not even the smallest letter in the law, or even a hook on one of the letters[1] will be changed until all things take place. Whoever loosens one of the least of these commandments . . . will be called least in the kingdom of heaven" (Matt. 5:17-19).

Here is the problem for Christian interpreters. No compromise is allowed. The Christian is obligated to keep the *whole* law.

# The Four Faces of Jesus

Several of the examples given in the rest of the chapter underline this uncomfortable position, although not the first two. They are taken from the Ten Commandments: " 'You shall not murder' " and " 'You shall not commit adultery,' " (Matt. 5:12, 27). If we read only this far in Matthew 5, we might suggest that the law to which Jesus is referring when He insists that nothing is to be changed is the Ten Commandments. In that case, Christians would be obliged to continue to observe these ten but could ignore the other laws of the Old Testament.

Indeed, the Ten Commandments do stand out as very important in the Old Testament. They were given at the time when God made His covenant with Israel (Exod. 20:1-17; Deut. 5:1-21), and Christians have always had a deep respect for them.[2] They likewise played a significant part in the theology of Martin Luther. He divided Old Testament law into two parts: a moral part (the Ten Commandments) and a ceremonial part (the laws of sacrifices). For Luther, and other Christians from earliest times to this day, the distinction between the moral and ceremonial law provided the best explanation of how to understand the Old Testament law—the Christian is obliged to keep the moral law but not the ceremonial law.

Yet no matter how appropriate this distinction might be as a way to understand some aspects of a Christian's relationship to law, it does not work for Matthew 5:17-48, because Jesus' next three examples are taken from what Luther would classify as ceremonial law: " 'Whoever divorces his wife, let him give her a bill of divorcement,' " " 'Do not make false oaths, but give back to the Lord your oath,' " and " 'An eye for an eye, a tooth for a tooth' " (Matt. 5:31, 33, 38). Not only this, the phrase " 'You shall love your neighbor, but hate your enemy' " (Matt. 5:43) is not actually found in the Old Testament at all! The command to "love your neighbor" is there (Lev. 19:18), but the corresponding "hate your enemy" is found only by implication (Ps. 139:21, 22; Deut. 23:2-6).[3] So, by the examples he chooses, Jesus is emphasizing that *all* law is still binding on Christians, even those laws that Christians appear to have discarded!

The second point to emerge clearly from Matthew 5:17-20 is that the way Christians will keep the law is different from the way that might be expected of them. Jesus did not come to destroy the law; He came to fulfill it (Matt. 5:17). Fulfilling the law is quite different from observing it. Certainly, in fulfilling the law one will still observe it, but fulfilling the law is related more to its inner nature than to the detailed observance of its particulars.

Third, the way Christians keep the law will be superior to that of the Pharisees: " 'Unless your righteousness far exceeds that of the scribes and Pharisees, you will certainly not enter into the kingdom of heaven' " (Matt. 5:20). In some manner, the way the Christian observes the law is both in direct contrast with that of the scribes and Pharisees and is also superior to their manner of observance.

Now, this is uncomfortable, because the first-century Pharisees kept the law very scrupulously. They were concerned not to break any part of the law and had worked out in great detail how this might be accomplished. How could a Christian keep the law "better" than the Pharisees? That is explained in the examples that follow, although most of us probably would be happier if we didn't understand so clearly what is meant.

## EXAMPLE 1: YOU SHALL NOT MURDER

"You have heard that it was said to those of old, 'Do not murder,' and whoever murders will be answerable in the judgment. But I say to you that anyone who is angry at his brother will be answerable in the judgment" (Matt. 5:21, 22).

I have subtitled this chapter "The Things We Know for Sure but Wish We Didn't." This is a deliberate variation of a famous aphorism attributed to Mark Twain: "It's not the things I don't understand in the Bible that worry me; its the things I do understand." I earn my living by teaching the New Testament, and in some of my lectures my students and I wrestle with one or another of the parts of the New Testament that are hard to understand. But in this chapter we have a whole series of clear teachings from Jesus Himself that are easy to understand but that we sometimes wish were more obscure and open to reinterpretation. There is no getting around it. Jesus said that when Christians read the command, "Do not murder," they are to understand "Do not get angry." Now, I put it to you that it is easier to keep the first version of the command than the second. Not too many people are guilty of murder, but just about everyone is guilty of anger at one time or another and, normally, more often than that!

It is entertaining to read the various commentators on these verses. You can almost guarantee they will make a reference to Ephesians 4:26, which says "Be angry, and sin not." They also normally cite the example of Jesus Himself as He drove the money-changers from the temple (Matt. 21:12-17). Both of these points are true, but citing them nevertheless points to the fact that at the heart of these interpretations is the belief that Jesus didn't mean what He said in Matthew 5:21, 22. My students also have this same reaction: "Jesus couldn't have really meant that," they often say. "It's impossible!"

But to interpret these verses in a way that lessens the impact of what Jesus said is to miss their point. Jesus is being deliberately provocative. He is showing how radical are the demands He makes on His followers. Christians will keep the law in a way that is *better* than the law observance of the Pharisees. They should not even get angry!

The way Jesus interprets the law against murder illustrates several things about His understanding of law that will recur in the later examples. First, He makes the law more rigorous, not less rigorous. Second, He internalizes the law. The difference between murder and hate is that one is an external act, while the other is an internal, emotional state. Third, by changing the focus of the law, He transforms it. In the language of verse 17, He "fulfills" the law.

## EXAMPLE 2: DO NOT COMMIT ADULTERY

"You have heard that it was said, 'Do not commit adultery.' But I tell you that whoever looks at a woman to lust after her has already committed adultery in his heart" (Matt. 5:27).

As in the previous example, we wish we didn't understand the meaning of His words, those of us who are males, anyway. Research into male sexuality has shown that men between the ages of thirty-five and forty think of sex more than six times an hour! Younger men do so more often, although between the ages of forty and fifty it drops to twice an hour and further drops to once an hour between fifty and sixty. When men dream of sexual activity, it is rarely with their own spouses, and this is often true also of their daydreaming.[4] So if males intend to take Jesus' words seriously, they have a real problem!

There may be more adulterers than murderers in the world, yet it is still possible for most men to reasonably expect that they will be able to refrain from committing adultery. But how many men can realistically say that they expect to go through life without one improper lustful thought?

As with the law about murder, Jesus has again made the requirements of the law more stringent. He again concentrates on an internal state of mind rather than an external act. Further, by changing the focus of the law, He has transformed it.

### EXAMPLE 3: THE BILL OF DIVORCEMENT

"And it was said, 'Whoever divorces his wife should give her a bill of divorcement.' But I say to you that anyone who divorces his wife on grounds other than sexual immorality, makes her to be an adulterer, and whoever marries one who is divorced commits adultery" (Matt. 5:31, 32).

The provisions cited by Jesus, and given in Deuteronomy 24:1-4, probably worked for the benefit of the women involved, although modern readers might not realize this. It was difficult for a woman to exist in that iron-age society without being in a state of marriage.[5] Thus if her husband should divorce her, she was particularly vulnerable if he did not provide her with legal evidence that she was free to remarry. Thus the certificate of divorce was for her protection.

This, then, was the background of the law in Deuteronomy. Among Jewish circles in New Testament times it appears that this provision was discussed with some interest to determine the proper grounds for divorce.[6] One group thought that only sexual impropriety provided grounds for divorce. Another group had a much freer interpretation of the phrase in Deuteronomy 24:1, "she does not please him because he finds something objectionable about her." They thought that if his wife spoiled his meal or if he found somebody more attractive, it might be grounds for divorce.[7] Mind you, in the first century this discussion was somewhat academic, because divorce was very rare. Arranged marriages, the exchange of bride price and dowry, and the odium attached to it made divorce very unlikely.

Apparently Jesus agreed with those who had a strict interpretation of the grounds for divorce. According to Him, it was possible only in the case of *porneia* (Matt. 5:32). The Greek word *porneia*, which is translated as sexual immorality, or fornication, has a range of meanings. It is used to describe adultery (Rev. 2:21[8]), incest (1 Cor. 5:1), homosexuality (Jude 7), and using the services of a prostitute (1 Cor. 6:13, 15-18). In other words, *porneia* is used of sexual impropriety in general.

Unfortunately, this verse has been used to try to ascertain the specific legitimate grounds for divorce. It does speak of divorce, but as an exception. It was Jesus' intention that married couples stay married. Sure, there were cases where the marriage could not be saved, but that is not the import of Jesus' words. He is saying that if one properly reads the law about giving the divorced woman a bill of divorcement, it is really a command not to divorce at all.

This is a sensitive issue in contemporary Christian circles, at least in the Western world, where divorce has become so common. In the wider society, one in three marriages ends in divorce, and in many Christian communities the rate of divorce approaches this figure. The Christian community needs to extend the healing and forgiveness offered by Christ, but His message still needs to be heard. Marriage is something a Christian regards as permanent. Sometimes this is not possible, but it is the Christian ideal and should also be the Christian norm.

Does the third example differ from the first two examples? Like them, does it show that Jesus makes the law more stringent, looks to its essential nature, and in some way transforms it? It is true to say that one who does not get angry will not murder and one who does not lust will not commit adultery. But will the one who does not divorce write a bill of divorcement? By transforming the law into a prohibition against divorce, Jesus has dramatically changed it. But it is a moot point whether He has abrogated the law. Rather, what He says supersedes it. As with the previous two examples, He has taken the essential meaning of the law and made it more stringent. So stringent, in fact, that the previous law becomes redundant.

## EXAMPLE 4: OATHS

"Again you have heard that it was said to those of old, 'Do not swear falsely, but give back to the Lord your oaths.' But I say to you do not swear at all. . . . Let your words be 'yes, yes,' or 'no, no' " (Matt. 5:33-37).

Oaths were important in the ancient world. The one taking the oath invoked a curse on himself in the event of nonperformance of the contract, thus making the divinity a partner in the agreement. In a time when just about everyone believed in gods, such contracts would not be broken lightly. Mind you, then as now, business deals could go sour, so there was great interest in which oaths could be broken and which ones needed to be kept. Jesus points out the foolishness of some of the distinctions that had been made. Indeed, He goes so far as to forbid oaths altogether—a Christian's response should be "yes" or "no" (Matt. 5:37). In other words, a Christian's word is his bond. It should be more binding than a contract based on an oath, more binding than a modern contract.

This was illustrated for me recently while watching a TV documentary about the way Hong Kong money is being used to buy real estate in Melbourne, Australia. The cameras were present at a real estate deal involving a large building complex located in the heart of the central business district. The deal was worth in the region of $100 million. But the cameras were there not only because of the amount of money involved but for another unusual element. The Hong Kong businessman refused to do business through lawyers, on the basis that he didn't trust anyone who wouldn't keep his word without being forced to do so by a legal contract! Thus a deal worth millions of dollars was consummated on the basis of a handshake. It struck me at the time that that businessman had a reputation to which Christians should aspire. When he gave his word, he meant it. So much so that extraordinary sums of money were settled on the basis of his word alone.

In the matter of oaths, as with His pronouncement about the bill of divorcement, Jesus has extended the provisions of the law in a way which, while consistent with its essential components, radically transforms it. The law has become much more rigorous.

## EXAMPLE 5: RETALIATION

"You have heard that it was said, 'An eye for an eye, and a tooth for a tooth.' But I say to you, do not resist evil; but whoever strikes you on your right cheek turn the other to him . . ." (Matt. 5:38, 39).

If the reaction of my students is any gauge of wider Christian opinion, the common response to this verse—even more so than to Jesus' saying about anger—is that He didn't really mean what He said. How can we possibly live any kind of life in which we do not resist evil?

I must confess, I also find this saying hard to implement in my own life. Indeed, it is but one more part of this chapter that we wish we didn't understand. Jesus is perfectly clear, both in what He says and in His own example—evil should not be resisted. His own actions during his arrest, trial, and crucifixion were consistent with this principle (see Matt. 26:51, 52). He did not resist evil and prevented His disciples from attempting to do so.

The "eye for an eye" principle is found in Exodus 21:24, Leviticus 24:20, and Deuteronomy 19:21. According to this law, if someone injures a person's eye, then he should have the same injury inflicted on his eye. When a modern state cuts off a thief's hand, there is widespread horror at such a mutilating punishment; the same would be true, if not more so, if eyes were put out and bones broken as part of the judicial process. Yet, in the Iron-Age society in which these laws were first enacted, such a provision was, in fact, a *limita-*

*tion* on the kind of recompense that could be exacted. No *more* than an eye could be demanded if an eye was injured; no *more* than a tooth if a tooth was lost. In a society without a regular police force and without easy access to the royal courts, this provision laid a necessary restriction on the kind of rough justice that could be dealt out and that could so quickly degenerate into an ugly vendetta and an escalating number of deaths.

With the increasing sophistication of society, better law enforcement, and the development of a money economy, the notion of putting out an eye came to be considered a rather brutal form of punishment, and a fine was generally imposed instead. This development took place prior to the writing of the New Testament and remains the practice in most societies today.

Again, Jesus' treatment of this law captures its essential intent and makes it more rigorous. The law had been put in place to mitigate the concept of revenge, but Jesus insists that the concept of revenge be abandoned altogether, along with all thoughts of resisting evil. He interprets the law in a way that so transforms it that the original provision is almost lost.

### EXAMPLE 6: LOVE OF NEIGHBOR

"You have heard that it was said, 'Love your neighbor and hate your enemy.' But I say to you, love your enemy and pray for those who persecute you" (Matt. 5:43, 44).

If we are only to love our neighbor, this might leave us free to despise those whom we do not consider to be our neighbors. Jesus expands the command in Leviticus 19:18 by including everyone as our neighbor, especially our enemies. As Jesus points out, even the heathen love those who love them. The real test is: Can we do as God does—can we love those who hate us? In this way, Jesus has intensified the law by expanding its compass to include everyone.

### YOU SHALL BE PERFECT

"Therefore, you should be perfect as your heavenly father is perfect" (Matt. 5:48).

# The Four Faces of Jesus

The section of teaching on law is rounded off by what must be the most terrifying command in the whole of Scripture—to be as perfect as God is perfect! Sure, one can point out that the word *teleios*, translated as "perfect," can equally well be translated as "mature" or "complete." Outside of the Bible it is used to describe achievement at different stages of learning, as well as full-grown or mature animals or people. But none of these possibilities really helps to make this saying of Jesus less terrifying. How can we be as "perfect" or "mature" or "complete" or as "competent" as God? This is just not possible for any human, yet that is exactly what Jesus demands of His followers.

It is perhaps for this reason that the sayings about the law in Matthew 5:17-48 are prefaced by the beatitudes in Matthew 5:3-12. Although these sayings are usually called "The Beatitudes," that isn't a terribly meaningful description for most people. Nor is "blessed" a really adequate translation of the underlying Greek word *makarios*. The closest English equivalent of this word is "happy." Thus, we should read Matthew 5:3 and the following verses as "Happy are the poor in spirit . . . ," "Happy are those that mourn . . . ," etc. These sentences then become quite extraordinary—How can we be happy if we are poor in spirit and if we mourn? But that is just the point that Jesus is making. There is a deliberate juxtaposition of apparently opposite things—happiness and poverty, happiness and mourning. Clearly, Jesus isn't talking about your regular, ordinary happiness; He's talking about something much deeper than the frivolous feeling one gets laughing at a good joke, not that it is bad to laugh at the right time. The happiness Jesus speaks of is a deep-seated joy that permeates a person's life—although He does point to some unexpected sources of that joy.

The first "happiness" belongs to those who are "poor in spirit, because theirs is the kingdom of heaven" (Matt. 5:3). It is a specific kind of poverty that makes one fit for heaven—a poverty of *spirit*.[9] Those who belong to the kingdom of heaven do not consider themselves to be rich in spirit. On the contrary, they are keenly aware of their spiritual deficiencies. This does not mean that they have given up in despair, because they still hunger and thirst for righteousness (Matt. 5:6).

# Jesus and the Law in Matthew

A little imagination brings home the power the image of hunger and thirst would have had for Matthew's first readers. Even under Roman rule, famines were not unknown in Palestine and hunger was a fact of life. Most families would have stark memories of times when food was scarce. Moreover, anyone who had traveled in Palestine would have had some firsthand experience with real thirst. While the coastlands are well watered, there are commonly traveled stretches where water is scarce indeed. Dehydration was a common problem. Jesus was talking to those who knew about real hunger and real thirst. He said happiness belongs to those who hunger after righteousness like starving people hunger for food. Happiness belongs to those who long for righteousness like those dying of thirst in the desert long for water. Such will be satisfied. But their righteousness is a righteousness that is always arriving but never arrived. At no stage will they consider themselves to be rich in spirit. Jesus places extraordinary and well nigh impossible demands not only on our behavior but also on our motives. But the Christian longs for this kind of righteousness, a righteousness that begins with our motivation and results in a pattern of behavior that is within the most demanding interpretation of the law.

Is this a despairing view of Christian maturity? What of the expectation of Christian growth that we find in the New Testament? Should not the behavior of a Christian be substantially different from that of the non-Christian? If Christian life is based on the clear recognition that the requirements of God cannot possibly be met, what does this mean about the New Testament's demand in other places that the Christian should live a blameless life?

Perhaps this dilemma can be solved by separating how Christians view themselves from how others view them. As Christians come closer to God, they themselves become increasingly aware of God's holiness and their own inadequacies. Their personal growth is tied to their increasing dependence on the righteousness of God. However, from the perspectives of others viewing their life, as they come closer to God and become more dependent on God's grace, their whole life is transformed. Others will see great differences in their life. But from within, the Christian longs to be as perfect as God, with the same kind of intensity as the starving hunger for food and one dying of thirst longs for water.

### THEN HOW SHOULD A CHRISTIAN UNDERSTAND THE OLD TESTAMENT LAW?

Has Matthew 5:17-48 answered the questions with which this chapter began? Do we now know why Christians observe some of the Old Testament law and not other parts of it?

Well, yes and no. Yes, we do have some good guidance as to how Jesus wanted his followers to relate to the Old Testament law. But No, some of the details have been left to us to work out.

Matthew 5:17-48 gives an unequivocal answer to the question of which parts of the Old Testament law Christians should observe: They keep the *whole* Old Testament law. But it is equally true to say that the law Christians keep is quite different from the law of the Old Testament. The Christian's relationship to them has been transformed by the coming of Jesus. This transformation involves the drawing out of the inner intent of the original law and moving the focus from the prohibition of certain behaviors to the motivation for those behaviors. The Christian has pure motives as well as impeccable behavior. It is in this way that their righteousness will be greater than the righteousness of the scribes and Pharisees.

The passage we have been looking at outlines the principle that the law remains, although the Christian's relationship to it has been transformed by the coming of Jesus. It then goes on to give six examples of how this is so. Each illustrates in its own way how the Christian keeps the inner intent of the law, while developing a new freedom. This is all very well, but in two of the examples—the requirement regarding a certificate of divorcement and the rule of an eye for an eye—Jesus has so transformed our relationship to the law that little remains of the original command. How then is a Christian to approach other laws in the Old Testament about which Jesus has not specifically spoken? He has deliberately refrained from giving a specific list of rulings on each provision. Rather, we are given a set of model solutions, and we are expected to look at the rest of the law from a similar perspective. Its inner meaning retains its validity, but what that inner meaning is, is left to individual Christians and their communities.

The rest of the New Testament gives a similar picture of Old Testament law. Paul, for example, even though he strongly highlights the inadequacies of law as a means of salvation, still says that the law is just and holy and good (Rom. 7:12). The law still reveals God's will for Christians, but the Christian keeps the law in the newness of the spirit, not the oldness of the letter (Rom. 7:6; 2 Cor. 3:6). Like Jesus, though, Paul does not spell out exactly what he means by the newness of the Spirit. Some change is indicated, but what we get are some principles and some examples. The rest is left for each Christian and the community to work out.

For both Paul and Jesus, the principle of love is the door through which the Christian will approach any thought of keeping the law (Matt. 22:34-40; Rom. 13:8-10). Beyond this principle, there are some specific examples that are given to show how it works. The earliest Christians had to decide a large number of issues. For example, they decided that actual circumcision was no longer obligatory; the circumcision of a Christian was an inner circumcision of the heart (Rom. 2:28, 29). Further, in actual practice, Christians still retained some of the features of Old Testament food laws; in particular, they decided to abstain from meat offered to idols (Acts 15:29; 1 Cor. 8:1-13) and from eating meat from strangled animals (Acts 15:29).

Regarding sacrifices, though, the evidence is less clear. The earliest Christians met daily in the temple (Acts 2:46). Even though this does not imply that they offered sacrifices, it does show that the temple retained a very important place in their thinking. Even late in his ministry, Paul was willing to become part of a dedication ritual centered on the temple, which involved giving offerings and slaughtering sacrifices (Acts 21:23-26). The book of Hebrews, however, reveals another strong current in early Christian thought. According to Hebrews, the earthly sanctuary was but a pale imitation of the real sanctuary in heaven (Heb. 8:5). In this sanctuary, Christians have a better high priest (Jesus), a better sacrifice (His death on the cross), and better access to God. Quite clearly, the better sanctuary and sacrifice has removed the need of the old sanctuary and sacrifices, and Christians ceased to retain any real interest in the sacrifices offered at the temple in Jerusalem, especially after its destruction in A.D. 70.

This does not exhaust the specific examples of Christian practice we can observe in the New Testament, but it does show some of the kinds of practices that grew up among Christians. Once again, the practices of the earliest Christians do not give us a *complete* list of how they understood the different Old Testament laws. They provide further examples but not a complete commentary dealing with each law. This is both frustrating and exhilarating. It is frustrating because it is quite hard to know exactly how Jesus would interpret some laws. But it is exhilarating, because Christians are given the responsibility of making the will of God real in their own lives. Christianity is forward looking. It can handle new challenges and circumstances because it works from general principles, not a set of rigid predefined laws. It seeks to know God's will in the present circumstance and to interpret that by the principles of denying self and loving others. To live as a Christian is future oriented, flexible, and exciting. Perhaps that is what Paul meant when he said the Christian is free from law. Not that the Christian will wish to act contrary to the revealed will of God but that the Christian has the somewhat scary freedom to seek to apply God's will afresh in the challenges that arise from each day's activities.

---

1. The Greek words in Matthew 5:18 translated "jot" and "tittle" in the KJV are *iōta* and *keraia*. The *ita* is the smallest letter of the Greek alphabet. The *keraia*, or "horn," appears to be a reference to a small projection that distinguishes two Hebrew or Aramaic letters.

2. According to the New Testament, this respect for the Ten Commandments goes back to Jesus Himself. Jesus quotes some of the Ten Commandments to the rich young ruler (Mark 10:19). Furthermore, the Ten Commandments are either quoted or alluded to several times in the New Testament (Rom. 13:9; Eph. 6:2).

3. The closest parallel I am aware of is from the first injunction of the "Community Rule" found among the Dead Sea Scrolls. In the translation of Geza Vermes,

the Community Rule begins: "The Master shall teach the saints to live [according to] the Book of the Community Rule, that they may seek God with a whole heart and soul, and do what is good and right before Him as He commanded by the hand of Moses and all His servants the Prophets; that they may love all that He has chosen and hate all that He has rejected . . ." *(The Dead Sea Scrolls in English,* 2nd ed. [Harmondsworth: Pelican, 1975], 72). The Dead Sea community was probably a group of Essenes, and as there is no explicit reference to the Essenes anywhere else in Matthew's Gospel, it seems unlikely that Jesus would have been citing them in this verse.

4. Joyce Brothers, *What Every Woman Should Know About Men* (New York: Simon & Schuster, 1981), 140, 141.

5. The period from the conquest of Canaan by the twelve tribes to the end of the monarchy corresponds with what the archaeologists label as the Iron Age, and the laws of the Old Testament date to this time period, even though there are parts of the Old Testament that were written later (e.g., prophets like Zechariah wrote after the Jews returned from the exile, in the Persian period). Tamar provides a good example of the position of an unmarried female, although she comes from the time of the patriarchs, who lived at a slightly earlier age than the Iron Age. On the death of her second husband, she was sent back to her father's household to wait until a younger brother of her second husband became of marriageable age (Gen. 38:11). Naomi provides a further example. She took great pains to provide a husband for Ruth. The common Old Testament command to protect the fatherless and the widows has its basis in their vulnerable position in society.

6. The evidence that exists comes from later Rabbinic documents that report that the matter was discussed by rabbis earlier than, or contemporary with, Jesus, as well as by later rabbis. It is uncertain how accurately these earlier discussions are reported, although the probability is good that there is some substance to the record.

7. *m Git,* 9:10.

8. In Revelation 2:21 *porneia* is used in parallel with *moicheia,* a word that has the strict meaning of adultery.

9. Notice that Luke 6:20 merely says "happy are the poor." As we shall see later (chap. 15), the economically poor are one of Luke's interests.

CHAPTER THREE

# The Healing Miracles As Understood by Matthew (Matt. 8, 9)

**THE PLACE OF MATTHEW 8, 9 IN THE WIDER SCHEME OF THINGS MATTHEAN**

Just about everything in Matthew's Gospel is in the same order as we find it in Mark. This is true even for the sequence of details that make up larger events. Matthew 4:23–13:58, though, stands out as different from the rest of the Gospel in this respect; the order of the material in this passage is quite different from the order in which it is found in both Mark and Luke. Such a difference is strong evidence that Matthew has deliberately shifted the order of the elements that make up these verses. This makes the significance of Matthew 4:23 and 9:25 unmistakable. Let's compare these two verses, while noting the contents of the intervening chapters:

> Matt. 4:23, "And he [Jesus] went about in the whole of Galilee, teaching in their synagogues and preaching the gospel of the kingdom and healing all illness and all sickness in the people."
> Matt. 5-7, Jesus as teacher
> Matt. 8, 9, Jesus as healer

# The Healing Miracles As Understood by Matthew

Matt. 9:35, "And Jesus went about in all the towns and villages teaching in their synagogues and preaching the gospel of the kingdom and healing all illnesses and all sicknesses."

Thus Matthew 4:23 and 9:35 form a deliberate frame for the intervening chapters. These verses state that Jesus' activities were threefold—teaching, preaching, and healing. Matthew then provides us with typical examples of Jesus' teaching (Matt. 5-7, the Sermon on the Mount) and healing (Matt. 8, 9). Interestingly enough, immediately after these insights into Jesus' teaching and healing, the disciples are told to go out, likewise teaching and healing (Matt. 10:1, 7). Their message, like that of Jesus, was the proclamation that the kingdom of God was near (cf. Matt. 4:17; 10:7). In a word, the disciples' mission was to be a continuation of the mission of Jesus Himself.

## WHAT IS THE MESSAGE CONVEYED BY THE HEADINGS?

From what has been already said, it is clear that Matthew deliberately brought together the miracle stories of chapters 8 and 9. Furthermore, he has shaped the stories both by his selection and by the way he presents them. We can see how this is so by comparing Matthew's accounts with those of Mark and Luke.[1] Generally speaking, he reports events in a way that highlights the centrality of Jesus and the necessity of faith.

The first miracle story, the healing of the paralytic in Matthew 9:1-8, provides an excellent illustration of Matthew's narrative technique. It is instructive to compare the beginning of Matthew's account with how the same story is told in the Gospel of Mark.

> And getting into the boat he crossed over and came to his own town. And behold they brought to him a paralytic lying on a sleeping pallet. And when he saw their faith, Jesus said to the paralytic, "Take heart, child, your sins are forgiven" (Matt. 9:1, 2).

> And when he had again crossed to Capernaum, after some days it was heard that he was at home. And many gathered to-

gether so that there was no room, not even towards the door, and he spoke the word to them. And they came bringing a paralytic to him carried by four men,[2] and because they were not able to make their way to him through the crowd, they dug through the roof above where he was, and when they had completed the hole they lowered the sleeping pallet on which the paralytic was lying. And when Jesus saw their faith he said to the paralytic, "Child, your sins are forgiven" (Mark 2:1-5).

The way Mark introduces this healing miracle is full of human interest. The four men digging through the roof is a dramatic action that sets the imagination alight. How easy it is to reconstruct the scene, especially if we consider the wretched state of one who was paralyzed in the first century and add to this scene information made available from the work of archaeologists digging in the very village in which this incident occurred.

Without modern health care, the paralytic would soon develop bedsores from having to lie without moving for long periods of time. Untreated bedsores quickly form gaping wounds full of rotting flesh that have a smell all their own. The only "good" thing about first-century conditions would be that these sores would soon become infected with maggots, which tend to eat the decaying flesh and leave behind the healthy flesh. Even so, the bedsore would remain an open wound, and the patient would be smelled long before he could be seen! The condition of any first-century paralytic was indeed unenviable!

Mark's text doesn't state whether the paralytic or his four friends initiated the visit to Jesus, but the surging crowd at the door of the room where Jesus was teaching seemed to rule out all possibility of reaching Jesus for healing. Their urgency, however, took them up the outside stairs, which led to the roof, and they began to dig through it.

With the help of archaeology, we can actually form a very clear picture of the background of this scene. Italian archaeologists have been digging at Capernaum for decades and suspect that in their work they have found the actual house in which Jesus was sitting at the time of this incident.[3] If they have not actually found the very house, then it is one very much like it.

From the archeological remains, it appears that the walls of the houses in Capernaum were built of rough basalt stones around open courtyards. Their roofs were formed over a structure of branches laid between the walls, supported in the larger rooms by pillars. Earth and clay was tamped down over these branches. Sometimes the roofs were flat, although the ones at Capernaum appear to have been at a slight slope, which would allow the water to run off more efficiently. In summer it can get very hot in Capernaum, so the roof would be a popular place to be at the end of a hot day, and stairs were provided to give access to it.

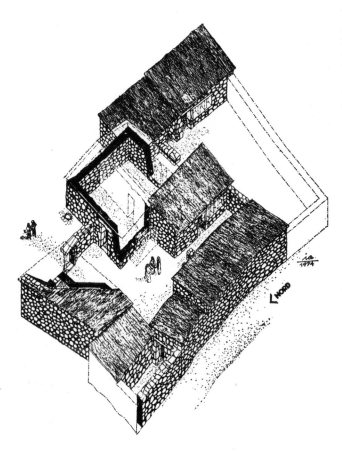

This background information makes the scene described in Mark come alive. Picture this: Jesus is seated in the small room surrounded by

His listeners. A number of people pack the courtyard and listen intently to hear what is being said inside. Suddenly, those inside see the roof over them begin to crumble; bits of dirt and dead branches fall onto the floor. Anyone underneath the spot hurriedly moves aside and makes room beneath. The sky becomes visible through a hole that appears in the roof and rapidly expands. After some activity, the paralytic is finally lowered into the room, and the smell of his bedsores permeate it. Silence and stillness reign where a moment before there had been frenzied activity. Jesus looks intensely at the paralytic and says, "Child, your sins are forgiven."

This is a remarkable story, dramatically described in Mark. Yet almost all of this detail is completely missing in Matthew's account. Matthew reduces the healing to only its essential elements—a paralytic is brought for healing, Jesus sees "their,"[4] faith and tells the paralytic that his sins are forgiven. In Matthew's Gospel, there is no mention of the need to dig up the roof of a house to gain access to Jesus—the very thing that gives the story its unique interest. But doing so does change the focus of the story, highlighting as it does the central link between Jesus' ability to heal and His ability to forgive sins.

Nor is this the only time that Matthew's version omits interesting, but unessential, details of the various healing miracles. In Mark 1:29, 30 we read that Jesus, together with James and John, went to the house of Simon [Peter] and Andrew after attending the synagogue. When they arrived, they discovered that Peter's mother-in-law was ill, so Jesus healed her, even though it was the Sabbath. By way of contrast, we read in Matthew 8:14, "And when Jesus came to the house of Peter, he saw Peter's mother-in-law lying down and fevered." Matthew omits the fact that Peter shared ownership of the house with Andrew and that James and John were present, apparently because these details were not essential to the central action of the healing. Reducing the number of characters in the account has the effect of highlighting those that are left. Thus, Matthew focuses the action on Jesus and those around Him. Another example of this same thing is found when we compare Mark 10:46 to Matthew 20:29-

34. Mark recounts that the disciples were present when the blind man was healed, but Matthew doesn't mention this fact.

The healing of the woman with a flow of blood, as recounted in Matthew 9:20-22 and Mark 5:25-34, not only illustrates Matthew's tendency to highlight the centrality of Jesus by eliminating unnecessary details and participants but also provides an example of how Matthew's Gospel stresses the necessity of faith if healing is to take place. In Mark the sequence of events is: the woman comes up behind Jesus and touches Him; she is then healed; Jesus stops and asks who touched Him; the woman confesses; and Jesus assures her that her faith has healed her. Jesus' insistence on identifying the woman and His subsequent remarks show that her faith was the most important factor. The sequence of events in Matthew 9:20-22 highlights this centrality of faith even further.

> And behold, a woman with a twelve-year flow of blood came up behind [him] in order to touch the hem of his garment; for she said, "If only I touch his garment, I will be healed." And Jesus turned around and when he saw her he said, "Take heart, daughter, your faith has healed you." And she was healed from that hour (Matt. 9:20-22).

In Matthew, Jesus tells the woman that her faith is the basis of her healing *before* she is healed. This is all the more notable because of the similarity between Matthew and Mark in the sequence of even small details. It has the effect of giving added stress to something present also in Mark's account—the necessity of faith.

This theme is also present in two other places in Matthew where it is absent in Mark. For example, when the disciples ask why they were unable to heal the demon-possessed boy (Mark 9:29), Jesus replies it was because they had failed to pray. In the parallel account in Matthew 17:20, Jesus tells them their failure is due to a lack of faith. Likewise, in Matthew 15:28 Jesus tells the Canaanite woman that He grants her request because of her faith, a statement that is missing from the parallel passage of Mark 7:24-30.

# The Four Faces of Jesus

## SUMMING UP

Matthew 4:23–9:35 clearly indicates the deliberate arrangement of materials by each Gospel writer. First, Matthew gathers representative samples of Jesus' teaching in the Sermon on the Mount. Then he puts together several representative healings (see Matt. 8, 9), reporting these in a way that brings out tendencies apparent also in accounts of the same event as given by other Gospel writers. In particular, he shapes these healing stories to highlight the centrality of Jesus and the necessity of faith before healing can occur. This latter aspect is particularly significant, because the very language used for healing indicates a link between healing and salvation. So, just as faith is necessary for healing, it also is necessary for salvation.[5]

---

1. Aside from the healing of the centurion's servant (Matt. 8:5-13; cf. John 4:43-54), John does not record any of the miracles or healings recorded in Matthew 8, 9. Therefore it is not possible to include John's Gospel in this comparison.

2. I have translated this relatively literally so that the roundabout style of this passage can be seen more clearly in the English.

3. Stanislao Lofredo, *Rediscovering Capharnaum* (Gerusalemme: Edizioni Custodia Terra Santa, 1986) [available to tourists at gate of Capharnaum], 51-57. See also James E. Strange and Hershel Shanks, "Has the House Where Jesus Stayed in Capernaum Been Found? Italian Archaeologists Believe They Have Uncovered St. Peter's Home," *Biblical Archaeological Review* 8/6 (Nov/Dec 1982): 26-37. The diagram of how the archaeologists have reconstructed this house, which appears here, is taken from Lofredo, *Capharnaum*, 53.

4. Interestingly enough, even though Matthew has omitted all reference to the four men carrying the paralytic, he has retained this plural pronoun, which implies that it was the faith of all of them—the paralytic *and* his companions—that was the basis of the subsequent healing.

5. This is something that can be explored further with profit and is a theme we will take up again in chapters 12 and 20.

# CHAPTER FOUR

# Four Scary Things Jesus Said About the Sabbath in Matthew 12:1-14

### SOME SCARY THINGS ARE FUN, BUT OTHERS . . .

Not all scary things are unpleasant. Take roller-coaster rides, for example. It's a bit embarrassing to admit, but I don't like heights. This means that I find all roller-coaster rides scary. Nevertheless, I like some roller-coaster rides and not others. When we took our children to Disneyland some years ago, we found a ride there called Thunder Mountain. This ride is designed to give kids a big thrill, and although adults also get a thrill from it, the ride is not designed to scare adults very much. Our youngest child, Skye, was just tall enough to be allowed onto this ride. We got in a cart that was supposed to represent a mining rail car and strapped ourselves in. The car went up a ramp, and then suddenly we began to drop. The cart went faster and faster. We suddenly went around a corner that threatened to throw us out, but eventually we made it to the bottom and got out. Now, although I *was* a little scared, I actually enjoyed that roller coaster enough to ride it several times!

At Disneyland there is a second roller coaster, Space Mountain, but this one is *not* designed for kids! This one is designed to scare thrill seekers. And these thrill seekers had better be in good health, or so the signs seem to indicate: "Do not go on this ride if you have a bad back or you have a heart problem." In some perverse sort of way, this sign, repeated at close intervals all the way up to the entrance, actually made the ride look more interesting to me. My two girls, obviously, couldn't go on it, but my wife was kind and took them for an ice cream while I went on the ride.

Let me tell you what happened. Most of the people in the line were athletic-looking teenagers who appeared to be having a ball. When I got to the front of the line, it turned out that I was to sit in the very front of the front car. I thought nothing of it at the time. I climbed aboard, and the attendant strapped me in. Now, the attendant was quite serious with these straps. I got a belt over each shoulder. Even then, despite these signs and the screams I could hear through the doors, I wasn't really worried.

The ride began. We went through some doors and into darkness. This was a "space" ride, and all I could see at first were artificial stars and some shadows moving around. I could hear, however, and the screaming was much louder inside the doors. A chain engaged the car and pulled us higher. Suddenly we dropped! I'll just say that the next few minutes were among the most frightening of my whole life. The car jerked to the right. The car dropped, apparently faster than gravity could pull, and I surged upwards against the straps. Then it swerved; the car went up; then it dropped. The ride went on and on. Sitting in the front, I had nothing by which to predict where the thing was going to take me next. I didn't know what was going on. I hadn't really gotten a good hold on anything in the car, so here I was, being thrown about in the dark, jerked in directions I couldn't predict, and falling at horribly unpredictable intervals. I was too scared to scream!

The ride finally ended, and I must admit that I staggered away from the machine a bit wobbly around the knees. Fortunately, it was a long walk out, so by the time I got back to my wife and the girls, I thought I had recovered. I casually said to Susan, "Wow, you've got to try that! Why don't you let me look after the girls while you have a go."

She took one look at me and said, "You've got to be kidding!"

Now what has all this to do with what Jesus said and did on the

Sabbath? Quite a bit, really, because roller-coaster rides and walking up dark staircases at night are not the only things that can frighten us. Even some ideas can be very frightening, especially when they deal with things that are important to us. As we explore Matthew 12:1-14, my hope is that even though the ideas are a bit scary, they might be scary in the way Thunder Mountain was scary—an exciting exploration of interesting ideas; not scary like Space Mountain—too scary to be interesting, let alone fun!

### THE INCIDENT IN THE WHEAT FIELD

Matthew 12:1-7 tells of a controversy between Jesus and the Pharisees. One Sabbath, as Jesus and His disciples were walking through a wheat field, they plucked some heads of grain, rubbed them between their hands to get rid of the husks, blew the husks away, and ate the grain that was left. The Pharisees immediately challenged Jesus on this. Surely, what the disciples were doing was work, and you should not work on the Sabbath.

Strictly speaking, the Pharisees were right. When the disciples plucked the grain, it was reaping. When they rubbed it between their hands to get rid of the outside husks, it was threshing. When they blew these husks away, it was winnowing.

But Jesus defended His disciples and gave four arguments. First, He cited the example of David. David and his men were fleeing for their lives, and they were hungry. So they went into the tabernacle and ate the shewbread. Now they were not priests and should not have done this. But like the disciples, David and his men were hungry, and this overrode the prohibition.

Jesus then mentions the actions of priests on the Sabbath. They actually do more work on that day than they do on other days. Normally this would be wrong, but the fact that it is done in the temple makes it all right. But according to Jesus, He is greater than the temple, so this makes right what his disciples have done, even though normally they should not have done it.

Jesus then quotes Hosea 6:6, in which God says "I do not want

41

animal sacrifices, but kindness." Clearly, in Jesus' view, the Pharisees had missed the point. They were wanting sacrifice when they should have been much more interested in mercy. The disciples were hungry, and they should have been shown kindness. In fact, the disciples were guilt-less, so Jesus says in verse 7.

Finally Jesus said, "The Son of Man is Lord of the Sabbath." The Son of Man is one of Jesus' favorite descriptions of Himself, and so here He is claiming to have authority over the Sabbath. If He finds nothing wrong in the disciples' behavior, then they have done nothing wrong.

Now, I want you to notice what Jesus did *not* say. He didn't say the disciples were doing something trivial and therefore dismiss the accusations of the Pharisees. He admitted they were doing something wrong but said their actions were still justified because they were doing something else that should be done. The first two arguments He presents both make this point.

The first scary thing Jesus said about the Sabbath, then, is this:

*Sometimes in life you are faced with a choice between two different things. If you do either one, you will be breaking the law that says you shouldn't do it. Sometimes two things we should do are in conflict, and to do either means that we will do something else we shouldn't.*

This is scary, because we all want to do what is right. But life is complicated, and sometimes it isn't easy to know what is the right thing to do. Let me give an illustration that married men will find familiar. Your wife comes home from shopping and has just bought a new dress she wants to show you. She goes to the trouble of getting changed and asks, "What do you think of it, dear?"

Well, if you like the dress, that's not a problem. But what about those times when you don't like it? What do you say then?

You have a lot of conflicting things to consider. You love your wife, so you don't want to say anything that will make her feel bad about herself. It's important to be kind. How can you be kind and say what you really think? Further, the dress has been paid for; it's not as though it can be easily taken back; are you really going to make your wife feel terrible every time she puts it on? Shouldn't you rather make the best out of a bad job?

## Four Scary Things Jesus Said About the Sabbath

But wait a minute. Aren't good marriages based on trust and honesty? Surely you should tell the truth!

What should you do? The answer is not easy.

Mind you, not all of life's decisions are hard. Sometimes we have a clear choice. At other times, we have to choose between two things that are both good. But life has an awkward habit of frequently throwing up hard decisions. Sometimes we have to make choices like the one David faced—a choice that will mean we must do something we would not want to do under other circumstances. It's scary that Jesus didn't promise us a way out. There is no guarantee that the decisions of life will suddenly become clear because we are Christians. No, we have to make some hard decisions. But what principles do we use to decide? Well, that's another scary thing—in fact, it's the second scary thing Jesus said about the Sabbath:

*Jesus said that human need, any human need, takes precedence over the Sabbath.* Is this scary? Sure it is. What is left? If the Sabbath can be ignored for trivial matters, what about substantial matters?

The next story in Matthew 12 makes it even worse. Matthew 12:9-14 recounts the healing of a man with a withered hand. But his was a chronic, not an acute, condition. There was no urgency at all about the condition, only that the man had a need and that Jesus saw to that need immediately. The man would not have been worse the next day. And compared to the long history that had led to the atrophy of his hand, waiting one more day wouldn't have added anything to the man's discomfort. But Jesus healed him on the Sabbath, because he had a need.

It is clear that any human need takes precedence over the Sabbath. But does this mean that Jesus was abandoning the Sabbath altogether? If any human need takes precedence over the Sabbath, does this mean that the day is emptied of significance?

No. In fact, quite the opposite. Jesus and His opponents were arguing about *how* the Sabbath should be kept, not *whether* it should be kept. These arguments show not that Jesus wanted to drop the Sabbath but that He wanted to free the Sabbath from its burdensome restrictions. This was so important to Him that He provoked hostile and dangerous

43

confrontations with the Pharisees.

This leads us to the third scary thing about what Jesus said and did on the Sabbath: *Sometimes we have to stand against regularly accepted community standards regarding Sabbath keeping.* Jesus stood against His community. This is very scary, because we don't like acting alone against the desires of everybody else. In fact, it's often foolish to do so, because our community helps us understand what Sabbath keeping is all about. We often have difficulty defending the exact details of what we do or don't do on Sabbath. Just try explaining why you consider going for a walk along the beach a great activity for Sabbath but not swimming in the water you're walking beside! Why do we feel one activity is in harmony with the Sabbath but not the other? The way we observe Sabbath is often dependent on the community's experience of Sabbath observance, and although an individual's decisions may seem arbitrary, they combine to make a larger profile that is significant and meaningful.

But there is a danger in this. The danger is that the community will not retain a clear focus on the real meaning of Sabbath and allow its real meaning to get lost in a whole series of trivial distinctions. I think that this is the complaint Jesus had with the Pharisees. They were very concerned to observe the Sabbath, and rightly so. But Jesus accused them of missing the main point: The Sabbath was made for man, not man for the Sabbath. They had missed the point that the Sabbath is a day for meeting our needs, not something to be burdened with a whole list of things we shouldn't do. They had forgotten that mercy is more important than sacrifice.

Today, we need to make the Sabbath our own and ask, "How is it relevant to us?" In asking such questions, it is all too easy to turn our backs on the community's experience. But despite this danger, every generation, and every individual in that generation, needs to ask the important question, "What is the relevance of the Sabbath to me?" We need to change, because circumstances and society changes. But such changes are not easy. Jesus' example shows that sometimes asking this question will bring us into direct conflict with accepted community norms. And this leads us to the fourth scary thing Jesus said and did on the Sabbath.

# Four Scary Things Jesus Said About the Sabbath

*He never gave us a list of things we should or shouldn't do on the Sabbath. He gave us only general principles.*

## PRINCIPLES OF SABBATH OBSERVANCE

It would be so much easier if Jesus had been more specific. What exactly did He consider to be work that should not be done on the Sabbath—especially as He felt free to teach, preach, and heal on the Sabbath? What exactly would He think about all the myriad questions that keep cropping up today regarding proper Sabbath observance?

We wish He had been more precise. But Jesus steadfastly refused to do more than to clearly reject the Pharisees' approach of carefully listing what can and cannot be done on the Sabbath. He gave some general principles, but they were very general. For example, in Mark 2:27 He said, "The sabbath was made for man, not man for the sabbath." If the Sabbath was made for humankind, then we should enjoy our Sabbath keeping. If there is something about how we keep it that is not to our benefit, especially our spiritual benefit, we should change it. If the day is full of burdensome restrictions, that should be changed.

Closely allied with this principle is another one that Jesus highlighted several times: People's needs are primary. People come first in Sabbath keeping. If someone is ill, then we should help them, even if we need to do things that we would not otherwise do. None of us would hesitate to go on the Sabbath to the pharmacy to get a doctor's prescription filled if one of our children became ill. I have done it myself, even though it felt awkward because it involved the passing of money. The problem is that Jesus didn't give us a lot of help in determining how to act in such situations (or in many others that arise). When does this principle of helping others become less important than what it does to our own Sabbath observance? We need to remember that it is all too easy to lose the distinction between this special Sabbath day and other days.

This brings us to a related principle of Sabbath observance we find elsewhere in the Bible: The Sabbath is holy. *Holy* means "separated from other things." In other words, the Sabbath is to be different from other days. How different? The Bible says not to work on the Sabbath. So, clearly, we will cease our normal occupations. But what do these include? We are not told. We have to work it out ourselves. It is rather nice to have one day a week in which I do not sit down in the evening to watch TV. But the Bible nowhere speaks about TV. A TV-free day is something the community has discovered—without television, the Sabbath is different from other days.

The Bible also gives us the principle of Sabbath worship. Sabbath is the day above all other days in which we set aside time for fellowship with God. We come together on this day to think of Him, what He has done for us, and the differences this makes in our lives. It is a day of fellowship with other believers. A day in which our work does not fill to bursting every spare moment of every day. It is a day we can meet with others, including our families. During the rest of the week it is hard to keep ahead of what needs to be done. Work, maintenance, study, exercise, all conspire to make us semistrangers to each other at times. But the Sabbath is free from many of these commitments, and it is a day where, with a little effort, we can build the bonds within the family.

## SUMMING UP

None of these aspects of Sabbath keeping is too specific, though, is it? None of the scary aspects of what Jesus did and said have gone away. Sometimes, we will still have to choose between two courses of action, so that if we do either one, we will have to do something we would not otherwise have chosen to do. We will sometimes have to stand against long-established community standards. We will have to venture out to make decisions based on principles, not rules. It will be left to us to learn how to apply the principles of putting people first, of worship—and still make the day different.

Yes, this is scary. In some respects, living the life of a Christian is living on the edge. But it is also an exciting life of freedom in Christ. The Christian is one who is open to the future. Scary? Sure. But I hope for you it is not as scary as riding on Space Mountain at Disneyland was for me. I hope it is scary like Thunder Mountain. Just scary enough to give an edge to your life. Scary enough to be great fun.

CHAPTER FIVE

# The Study of Parables

**THEY DON'T PREACH IT LIKE THIS ANYMORE**

The parables of Jesus have long been favorites of preachers and congregations alike, so we have many examples of how they have been understood through the centuries. In many ways, these old sermons show how different we are from our spiritual ancestors. These differences sometimes make their interpretations of parables fascinating to read. Take, for example, this famous interpretation of the parable of the Good Samaritan by Augustine:[1]

> **A certain man went down from Jerusalem to Jericho;** Adam himself is meant; **Jerusalem** is the heavenly city of peace, from whose blessedness Adam fell; **Jericho** means the moon, and signifies our mortality, because it is born, waxes, wanes, and dies. **Thieves** are the devil and his angels. **Who stripped him,** namely, of his immortality; **and beat him,** by persuading him to sin; **and left him half-dead,** because in so far as man can understand and know God, he lives, but in so far as he is wasted and oppressed by sin, he is dead; he is therefore called **half-dead.** The **priest and Levite** who saw him and passed by, signify the priesthood

and ministry of the **Old Testament**, which could profit nothing for salvation. **Samaritan** means Guardian, and therefore the Lord Himself is signified by this name. The **binding** of wounds is the restraint of sin. **Oil** is the comfort of good hope; **wine** the exhortation to work with fervent spirit. The **beast** is the flesh in which He designed to come to us. The being **set upon the beast** is belief in the incarnation of Christ. The **inn** is the Church, where travelers returning to their heavenly country are refreshed after pilgrimage. The **morrow** is after the resurrection of the Lord. The **two pence** are either the two precepts of love, or the promise of this life and that which is to come. The **innkeeper** is the Apostle [Paul], the supererogatory [extra] payment is either his counsel of celibacy, or the fact that he worked with his own hands lest he should be a burden to any of the weaker brethren when the Gospel was new, though it was lawful for him "to live by the Gospel."[2]

Augustine's interpretation of the parable has a certain horrible fascination. Without needing to think too closely about it, we know it is wrong and that much of what is said toward the end of the parable is fanciful and too strongly influenced by Augustine's theology. But there remain parts of the parable Augustine interpreted as they still are in some modern sermons. If the last part of his interpretation is so clearly inappropriate, how can we know that the earlier parts are not inappropriate as well? This question leads us to an important issue: How should parables be interpreted?

In order to gain a historical perspective, this chapter approaches the question by first looking at how parables have been interpreted in the past. Then we will turn to the positive task of developing appropriate principles that may lay the foundation for the sound interpretation of parables.

## ALLEGORY, ALLEGORY EVERYWHERE

From the second to the nineteenth centuries, allegory was the predominant method used to interpret the parables. Augustine's exposition of Jesus' parable of the Good Samaritan is an excellent example of allegorical interpretation. In his interpretation, each element has its meaning:

a man=Adam
Jerusalem=heavenly city
Jericho=mortality
the thieves=the devil and his angels

The key to the allegorical method of interpretation is that each element of the parable represents something else.

The Christian church did not invent allegorical interpretation; it already existed in traditions of the educated Greeks. After all, the stories the Greeks told about their own gods involved extremely barbaric behavior in which the gods schemed, committed sexual indiscretions, and sometimes murdered their own families. Under the softening influence of allegory, however, these atrocities became symbols representing much more noble ideals. Indeed, many parts of the Old Testament had already been interpreted using allegory.[3] As with the myths about the Greek gods, allegorical interpretation of the Old Testament proved the best way to handle some of its more troubling aspects.

Using allegory as a way to understand the parables was natural to the early church. Not only did the difficulties in the text disappear, but even apparently irrelevant details took on a deeper Christian significance. Furthermore, congregations, both ancient and modern, love parables when they are interpreted as an allegory.

Yet, using allegory to understand the parables has some rather disastrous consequences. First, allegorical interpretation normally does violence to the meaning of the parable as a whole. While each detail becomes meaningful, the coherent message of the parable is lost.

Second, an allegorical interpretation entirely ignores the historical situation in which the parables were first given. They belonged to Jesus' ministry and, as such, had a real purpose, both in the immediate debate between Jesus and His opponents and as a valuable teaching tool. But an allegorical interpretation treats the parables as timeless, with a meaning applicable to any situation.

Third, allegorical interpretations are somewhat arbitrary. This can be amply illustrated from Augustine's interpretation of the parable of the Good Samaritan given above. For example, on what basis does Augustine say that the oil with which the Samaritan anointed the man's wounds represents the comfort of good hope and that the wine represents an exhortation to work with fervent spirit? Both of these interpretations are fine moral messages, but how do they arise from the parable? Indeed, if we compare one allegorical interpretation of a parable with another, we will find a wide variety of suggestions for what the various elements represent. Without some coherent basis for identifying what the elements of a parable represent, such applications are often completely arbitrary. This fact spelled the end of the allegorical approach to the parables, at least in the scholarly community. Adolf Jülicher, a nineteenth-century German scholar, is the man whose name is associated with this change in approach to interpretation.

## JÜLICHER AND THE END OF AN ERA OF INTERPRETATION

Some writings mark a turning point in thinking, and Adolf Jülicher's 1888 book *Die Gleichnisreden Jesu* (*The Parables of Jesus*) is one such book. It is all the more remarkable that this book was instrumental in changing a method of approach that had nearly 1,800 years of practice behind it.

In volume 1 of his book, Jülicher set out an extended history of how each of the parables had been interpreted. In doing so, he highlighted the inadequacies of the allegorical method so clearly that no reputable scholar since has tried to defend it. Indeed, just comparing the different interpretations of the parable of the Good Samaritan that have been given through the years would convince almost anyone that the allegorical method of interpretation is unfair to the parable. A better method is to apply the principles developed later in this chapter. We will do this in part 3, when we look at the Gospel of Luke.[4] But first, what has been the result of Jülicher's work?

Jülicher's legacy, as far as the interpretation of parables is concerned, is both positive and negative. It is positive in that he decisively freed the parables from the allegorical method and allowed them to be read with fresh eyes. Some of the other consequences of his work, however, have been negative by providing too narrow a definition of what a parable should be.

Jülicher took the work of the Greek philosopher, Aristotle, as his starting point for defining parables. Aristotle had used the distinction between a simile and a metaphor to explain the difference between parables and allegories. A simile compares something with something else, using the words *like* or *as*. The bad schoolboy joke, "Your teeth are like stars; they come out at night," is a simile. It uses the word *like* to make a comparison between teeth and stars. If, however, the same schoolboy tells his friend that he "is nothing but a clumsy cow," he is using a metaphor. In a metaphor, we say something *is* something else; not that it is *like* something else.

According to Aristotle, an allegory is but a series of extended metaphors. Each element of the story is said to be something, but actually represents something else. A parable, on the other hand, makes a comparison. It is like an extended simile, and like the simile, a parable makes only one point of comparison.

Volume 2 of Jülicher's work, published some years later, was not nearly as well received as volume 1. In volume 2 he got around to giving his own interpretations of the parables, and the single points of comparison he found in them seemed to be general moral truths more in keeping with nineteenth-century German liberal thinking than with the times in which Jesus lived and taught. For example, Jülicher saw the point of the parable of the prodigal son (Luke 15:11-32) as "an elevated revelation over a fundamental question of religion; namely, 'Dare the God of righteousness accept sinners in grace?' " According to Jülicher, the parable of the unjust steward (Luke 16:1-8) has the meaning that the "determined use of the present is a prerequisite for a happy future." He sees the parable of the talents (Matt. 25:1-14) as showing the principle that "reward is only earned by performance."[5] Jesus' life and teachings were radical enough to end in His betrayal and death. But as Jülicher understands them, Jesus' teaching would have caused a surfeit of boredom in His listeners, not alarm.

So Jülicher's interpretations didn't take root, even though his basic insight—that parables have only one point of comparison—became scholarly orthodoxy. This insight, while quite helpful as a way to approach some of the parables, actually proved a problem with others, particularly those in Matthew 13 and their parallels in Mark 4 and Luke 8, because Jesus accompanies two of the longer parables in Matthew 13 with an interpretation the majority of scholarly opinion has discarded as not actually the authentic words of Jesus. This was particularly true through the middle part of this century, when parable research was dominated by the work of C. H. Dodd and Joachim Jeremias.[6]

## PARABLE INTERPRETATION A. J. (AFTER JÜLICHER)

Both Dodd and Jeremias considered the interpretations given in Matthew 13 to be secondary. In other words, they thought the parables came from Jesus, but the interpretation came from the early church. Why? Because scholarly orthodoxy after Jülicher held that parables should have only one point of comparison, and the interpretations provided in Matthew 13 make several comparisons. If a "true parable" has only one point of comparison, then an interpretation which makes more than one point of comparison is treating the parable like an allegory. So, Dodd, Jeremias, and many other later scholars felt the interpretations provided in Matthew 13 did not originate with Jesus, because they did not follow the pattern of a "true parable."

For both Dodd and Jeremias, many of Jesus' parables dealt with the nearness of the coming kingdom and with His call for a decision from His hearers. In saying this, Dodd and Jeremias undoubtedly recovered aspects of the parables that had lain forgotten for centuries and advanced everyone's understanding. So impressive was this work, in fact, that for several decades it appeared that all that remained was to refine the interpretations of the parables that Jeremias had advanced. Yet as with most aspects of scholarly endeavor, this thinking has changed in recent decades.

Today there is a greater willingness to define parables more flexibly. There is an awareness that Jesus' parables arose out of an environment far different from Aristotle's Greek philosophical world where Jülicher found his definition of a parable. The parables arose in Palestine, and the kind of interpretations found in Matthew 13 are not very different from the interpretations the Jewish rabbis provided for some of their parables. Indeed, it is even said that true parables grew only on Jewish soil and that so far they have been found only in the Gospels and in the writings of the rabbis.

With this increasing flexibility, a large number of different ways to approach the parables has blossomed. Some scholars speak of their "multivalent meanings." In other words, they think that a parable can mean different things to different audiences and may mean something new to modern readers than to Jesus' first hearers. Others concentrate on the listener's response to the parable, because the parables were meant to challenge their listeners to accept or reject Jesus. Yet others approach the parables asking the kind of historical questions that concerned Dodd and Jeremias. If anything, modern parable research is marked by a willingness to try new approaches and the disappearance of any one dominant methodology.

### WHAT, THEN, ARE THE PARABLES?

In the face of this new flexibility, it is more than appropriate to go back to basic starting points as we look at the parables. Surely we should pay close attention to what those writing the New Testament considered to be a parable. After all, they were much closer in culture and experience to Jesus than was Aristotle. When we look at what is labeled as a parable in the Gospels, we find that *parable* is a general term that can be used to describe a number of different kinds of things. In fact, it is used for the following:[7]

*1. Proverbs.* The saying in Luke 4:23, "Physician, heal thyself," is labeled a parable, though in English we would call it a proverb.[8]

*2. Metaphors.* The saying in Luke 5:36-38, "New wine is put in new wineskins," which we would call a metaphor, is also described as a parable.

*3. Figurative sayings.* Mark 7:14-17 recounts that after Jesus had said to the crowd, "There is nothing outside of anybody which when it enters them is able to make them unclean," the disciples asked Jesus to explain the "parable." We would probably classify this as a figurative saying.

*4. Similes or similitudes.*[9] This is the category that Jülicher thought was a true parable. Similes use the word *like* or *as,* and there are a number of parables which are clearly similes or similitudes. Mark 4:30-32 introduces a parable with the words, "To what shall we compare the kingdom of heaven," while Matthew 13:33 begins a parable with the words, "The kingdom of heaven is like . . ." In both these parables, an explicit comparison is made between the kingdom of heaven and something else.

*5. Story parables.* The parable in Luke 14:16-24 takes the form of a story of a king who called for a great banquet. No explicit comparison is made. The parable is provided within a context to which it is expected to make a comment, but aside from that, the example given in the story is expected to be self-explanatory. Perhaps the parable of the Good Samaritan should also be classified as a story parable, but one in which the point is made explicit: "Go and do likewise" (Luke 10:37). The story of the rich fool likewise provides an example of an inappropriate response to good fortune (see Luke 12:16-21).

*6. Allegory.* The parable of the sower, recorded in Matthew 13:1-8, as well as the other Gospels, is provided with an interpretation (vv. 18-23) that makes several points of comparison. This parable is not a full-blown allegory, because not every detail of the parable is given meaning. Whether it should be classified as an allegory is, therefore, a moot point. But the parable naturally breaks into several sections that appear to correspond to a series of points of comparison. Moreover, attempts to find just *one* point of comparison have been largely unsuccessful. This should, at least, alert us to the possibility that a parable may have more than one point of comparison, although it must also be admitted that this is probably the exception rather than the rule.

What, then, should be concluded from this raw data? How should a parable be defined? Certainly, it means something broader than Aristotle's or Jülicher's definition of a parable. It is used, in fact, in a way very like the Hebrew word *mashal*, a word usually translated in the Old Testament as either "proverb" or "parable." One thing is sure: There is no one English term that corresponds to the way the Greek word *parabol* is used in the Gospels. Even so, we should try to form a tentative working definition, inadequate though it may be.

Parables, then, are figures of speech that can become quite elaborate and among which are found several different types; these types include metaphor, simile or similitude, and stories with an explicit message.

## PRINCIPLES OF INTERPRETATION

What does all this actually mean when we come down to interpreting a specific parable?

Our brief survey of parables in the Gospels has shown that not all parables are alike. So perhaps this variety should form the basis for the first principle of good parable interpretation: *Be sensitive to the type of parable being studied.* For example, a story parable should not be interpreted as if it were an allegory. While all the details of the parable make up the total picture presented in the story, not all details will be of equal significance for interpreting the parable. For example, an allegorical interpretation of the parable of the prodigal son would try to provide a separate meaning for the ring the father put on the prodigal's finger and the shoes for his feet. These are but details that give the story substance— not significant items with meanings of their own. This is the whole problem with Augustine's interpretation of the parable of the Good Samaritan. The Good Samaritan is a story parable, not an allegory, and therefore Augustine's allegorical interpretation does violence to its meaning.

Similitudes are a common type of parable. For example, a parable that begins "The kingdom of heaven is *like* . . ." is a simile or similitude. With this type of parable, the principle advocated by Jülicher and used by Dodd and Jeremias—that a parable can have only one point of comparison—is most appropriate. So much so that this might be said to be our second principle of good parable interpretation: *Similitudes are best interpreted by looking for the one point of comparison the parable is making.*

The Four Faces of Jesus

With such parables, it would be most inappropriate to use the approach of allegorical interpretation to try to find a specific meaning for each element of the parable. Mind you, our approach should not be so rigid that we automatically rule out other points of comparison if they arise naturally from the parable itself. On the other hand, we would not necessarily expect to find more than one point of comparison. It is this kind of parable that Jülicher has saved from well-meaning, but misleading, allegorical interpretation.

Third: *We should interpret the parable in a way that is consistent with the parable as a whole.* This is yet another problem with Augustine's interpretation of the parable of the Good Samaritan—he interprets many of the elements that make up this parable in ways that are quite unconnected with the rest of the elements in the story. As a result, the overall coherence of the entire parable is lost. This principle is particularly important, because when major elements of a parable do not fit a particular interpretation, it is a fair indication that the whole interpretation needs rethinking.

Fourth: *We need to interpret the parable in its biblical, historical, and social context.* Even skeptical scholars believe that these parables belong to Jesus' ministry.[10] Parables have their own function that relates to the original situation in which they were given. Often they formed parts of the vehement debate between Jesus and His opponents. The parables were not the mild moral stories envisaged by Jülicher. They were the vehicles that Jesus chose to convey His radical ideas. Further, Jesus lived in a distinctive society, and the more we know about that society, the more the parables make sense. For example, the way seed was sown in the ancient world explains why it ended up on the path as described in the parable of the sower. As we will see in a later chapter, the ring given by the father to the prodigal son had a specific meaning in the ancient world—a meaning that throws light on what the father was actually doing at that time. This historical background can be very useful at times. At other times, the gaps in our knowledge of society in Jesus' day and its customs can make some parables obscure, as in the parable of the dishonest steward found in Luke 16:1-13. No doubt this parable made perfect sense to Jesus' first listeners, but scholars are still debating what particular set of values and customs lies behind the master's commendation of the steward who had just defrauded him.

Fifth: *The interpreter needs to be very cautious of adding an interpretation not warranted by the text* (preachers beware!). This plea arises out of the all-too-attractive temptation to use the parables to make a good point. Augustine's interpretation has a lot of good theology (for his time perhaps). But precisely because of this, it fails as an exposition of the *meaning* of the parable. It imports meanings into the text that are just not there. This is a constant temptation to all speakers who draw on the imagery of the parables. Perhaps we should not criticize too strongly those preachers who fall into this trap in their effort to make the parables more relevant to the needs of their listeners, but neither should we exempt ourselves from a severe self-discipline which refuses to go beyond the meaning inherent in the parable.

It is easy to present these five principles of good parable interpretation as a rigid procedure which, when applied, yields the correct meaning of the parable. But the parables have their own qualities that sometimes appear to transcend the best efforts of scholarship. In particular, they have an emotional impact that even we who live in a different culture can still feel today. Just as knowing about the techniques of poetry or music can enhance our understanding and enjoyment of these artistic expressions, but fall short of fully explaining our emotional responses, so knowing about the principles of interpreting parables helps us understand them better but does not explain them fully. There is that added intangible dimension in them that affects the emotions and calls us to decision. In some ways the parables are both the easiest and the hardest parts of the New Testament. They are so simple a child can find meaning in them, yet they are so profound that they reward us with new insights after many hours of contemplation. *We should not overlook the emotional impact the parable makes on its hearer or reader.* I'm not sure we can call this a principle of good parable interpretation, but it is true that each parable is different. Each needs to be read very carefully. And in the last analysis, each parable calls for a response from us.

# The Four Faces of Jesus

Now that we have been become somewhat sensitized to some of the issues in parable interpretation, let's put these insights to work as we look at Jesus' third discourse in Matthew 13.

---

1. Augustine (A.D. 354-430) was a convert to Christianity who became bishop of Hippo, near Carthage, in North Africa. His extensive writings have been very influential on later Christian thought, both Catholic and Protestant.

2. *Quaestiones Evangeliorum*, II, 19, [slightly abridged] as found in C. H. Dodd's *The Parables of the Kingdom* (London: Fontana, 1935, 1961), 13, 14.

3. A famous example can be found in the writings of Philo of Alexandria. This first-century Jew wrote commentaries on parts of the Old Testament, reinterpreting them to show how they really taught the very things that the best Greek philosophers were teaching. Philo's writings were so well thought of in Christian circles that it was Christians rather than Jews who preserved them.

4. See chapter 16.

5. These examples are taken from the summary given by Robert H. Stein, in his book *An Introduction to the Parables of Jesus* (Philadelphia: Westminster, 1981), 55.

6. C. H. Dodd, *The Parables of the Kingdom* (London: Fontana, 1961 [first published 1935]); Joachim Jeremias, *The Parables of Jesus*, rev. ed. (London: SCM, 1972 [first published in English in 1954]).

7. Stein, *An Introduction to the Parables of Jesus,* 18, 19.

8. Some English translations obscure this by translating the Greek word *parabolē* [parable] as "proverb." Cf. Luke 6:39; Mark 3:23, 24 for further examples of proverbs called "parables."

9. A similitude is an extended or elaborate simile.

10. Like jokes, parables are resistant to change. All the essential parts of a joke need to be remembered to make the joke work, and jokes can travel all around the world, passed on by word of mouth, and still not be essentially changed. Likewise, all the elements of a parable need to be present to make it work. It is therefore highly likely that Jesus' earliest followers remembered His parables pretty much as they were first given. This is why parables have been given particular attention by those who have doubts regarding the accuracy of many of the other sayings attributed to Jesus; in the parables they consider that they are in touch with Jesus' authentic voice.

# CHAPTER SIX

# The Parables of the Kingdom (Matthew 13)

Jesus' third discourse in Matthew (Matt. 13:1-52) is devoted entirely to parables. There is not any difficulty in determining their common theme—the kingdom of heaven.[1] The summaries of Jesus' activities given in Matthew 4:23 and 9:35 both include the statement that He was actively "preaching the gospel of the kingdom" (cf. 4:17). This chapter, therefore, represents what the Gospel writer considered to be the heart of Jesus' preaching.

Parables are fascinating for a variety of reasons. The stories are interesting in themselves, often giving a brief glimpse of everyday life in a culture that is strange to most of us. More importantly, they intrigue us by presenting a mystery for us to solve. We know in advance that each parable conveys a specific message, and we derive not a little enjoyment from working out exactly what that message is. The parables of Matthew 13 share these characteristics. They are interesting in their own right for the glimpses of the ancient world they provide. But there is also a lot of fun to be had trying to work out exactly what they mean.

Two intriguing issues stand out as we look at these parables. First: In what way does the kingdom of heaven they speak of relate to the kingdom that God will set up at the end of the age when He destroys all other kingdoms? (see, for example, Dan. 2:44, 45). Within other parts of the New Testament there is an eager expectation that when Jesus returns from heaven He will inaugurate dramatic changes on the earth. For example, the book of Revelation describes the following events: death destroyed, sinners consumed by fire, the New Jerusalem descending from heaven, and God Himself dwelling on the earth (Rev. 20:11-15; 21:1-4, 11-13, 22-27). If heaven is wherever God dwells, then this means that heaven itself will have come to earth. This indeed is the glorious kingdom that God Himself will set up at the end of the age and that parallels the kingdom of God spoken of in Daniel 2:44, 45. However, the way several of the parables of Matthew 13 speak of the kingdom of heaven appears to be different from the scenario presented in the book of Revelation. So the issue is this: What is the relationship between the future kingdom to be set up by God's direct intervention in human history and the kingdom of heaven spoken of in the parables of Matthew 13?

The second major issue confronting us in these parables of Matthew 13 is the relationship between the kingdom of heaven and the church. Is the kingdom of heaven the same as the church? In other words, if the church grows in number, does the kingdom of heaven also grow? Or is there absolutely no relationship between them?

Only a careful examination of the parables will throw light on these two issues, but sometimes it is useful to know the kind of questions we will be meeting so we can be alert to the need to look for evidence in the text. We will now look at these parables, one at a time, starting with the parable of the sower.

### THE PARABLE OF THE SOWER (MATT. 13:1-9, 18-23)

In the parable of the sower, a farmer goes out to sow some grain. According to farming practices of the time, there were several ways he could do this. A farmer might sow his seed by tying a bag of seed over his shoulder, dipping his hand in it, and scattering it abroad as he walked up and down the field. In this process, some seed would inadvertently fall on parts of the field the farmer did not intend. In the other sowing method, a farmer might tie a bag of seed onto the back of a donkey, make a hole in the bag, and lead the donkey around the field as the seed trickled out. The seed would continue to flow even when the donkey moved over unproductive parts of the field such as the path. Further, there is some debate in the scholarly literature whether seed was sown on ploughed land or whether the seed was just cast over last year's stubble, which had been grazed. This latter method is particularly suited to dry conditions where there is a risk of wind erosion and would explain why some seed was sown amongst the weeds.

No matter the method of sowing, in the parable, seed that fell on different types of ground gave different kinds of harvests. The seed that fell on the path didn't give a harvest at all; it was eaten by the birds.

The seed that fell upon the rocky ground sprang up quickly because the underlying rock allowed the ground to warm more quickly than elsewhere in the field, and the seed would germinate more quickly. But because there was insufficient soil to retain moisture, the plants grown from this particular seed went brown during the summer and then died.

The seed that fell on the parts of the fields where there were a large number of weeds was choked by the weeds and eventually died.

But the seed that fell on receptive soil had a bounteous harvest: some thirtyfold, some sixtyfold, some a hundredfold. Not stated in the parable, but known by experience to nearly all who originally heard the parable, was the fact that such yields are extraordinary. From what evidence is available, it appears that in first-century Palestine one sack of grain used as seed would give a harvest of between four and five sacks. In other words, in a good year, fertile soil would give a fivefold yield. In particularly fertile parts of the Roman Empire, such as Sicily, eightfold yields were occasionally experienced, but such yields were unknown in Palestine.[2]

But what does this parable mean? If we take seriously the principles of good parable interpretation developed in the last chapter, then the first thing to do is to identify what type of parable it is. This question is easier to answer for nearly every other parable in this discourse. The others make an explicit comparison—the kingdom of heaven is *like* . . . That is, they are either similes or similitudes. But this kind of specific comparison is missing from the parable of the sower.

Of course, it's possible to eliminate some unlikely possibilities. For example, the parable of the sower is clearly not a proverb or a figurative saying. But any decision about what type of parable it is has to emerge from a careful examination of the parable itself, along with its biblical context.

In the previous chapter we saw how scholars have challenged the appropriateness of using the biblical context to interpret this parable. In particular, they have raised serious questions from time to time as to whether the interpretation provided in verses 18-23 should be considered authentic. At one time, it was almost a scholarly convention to deny that Jesus could have given such an interpretation. In more recent times, although many would still deny the legitimacy of the interpretation, a number are prepared to allow the possibility that it could be attached to the parable by Jesus. This, together with an increased interest in the meaning of the final text of the Gospel, means that there is much less criticism today of those who use verses 18-23 to explain the parable. Let us consider this interpretation on its merits.

Although the interpretation of verses 18-23 gives a different explanation for each of the various results following the planting of the seed, it has one coherent theme—the various reactions of those who hear the message of the kingdom. As the seeds were snatched by the birds from the path, so the devil snatches the message of the kingdom away from those who do not understand it. The seeds that fell on the rocky ground symbolizes those who appear to receive the message of the kingdom with great gladness. They remain enthusiastic during good times, but when persecution arises, they quickly fall away. The seed that fell among the thorns represents those who, though sincere believers, allow the distractions of everyday life to drive out interest in the kingdom. Finally, the seed that fell on the good ground represents those who hear and understand the word. The results of their lives are as extraordinary as grain that produces a harvest of thirtyfold, sixtyfold, or even one hundredfold.

This interpretation fits the parable in a natural way. The parable's structure is periodic, having several major segments, although each revolves around the single theme of the amount of harvest, with a slightly greater stress on the seed that fell on the good soil. The interpretation also follows this pattern. It has an overall coherency that fits the parable well. Indeed, without Jülicher's constricting definition of a parable as something with only one point of comparison, there is little in the interpretation that might give rise to the idea that it is secondary. In sum, both the parable itself and the interpretation provided indicate that this is a parable with more than one point of comparison. Does this make it an allegory?

Again, it would depend on how an allegory should be defined. It is not a full-blown allegory like *Pilgrim's Progress*, because not every detail represents something else. The four points of comparison are just that—comparisons. So one could make a case for calling this parable a similitude with several points of comparison. I would probably wish to describe the parable in such terms, but I have no quarrel with those who would wish to extend their definition of allegory to include such a parable.

We've examined the historical background of the parable of the sower, identified its type, and looked at an interpretation. Before we leave this parable, though, we should ask if it relates to the two issues that were raised in the introduction to this chapter—the relationship of the kingdom of heaven with the future kingdom at the end of the age and the relationship of the kingdom of heaven to the church.

This parable is only tangentially related to the question of the relationship between the kingdom of heaven with the future kingdom at the end of the age, or the relationship between the kingdom and the church. It has a different focus, dealing with the various reactions of those who hear the word concerning the kingdom (verse 19). But it provides little information regarding the identity of the kingdom. The next parable in Jesus' discourse—the parable of the weeds among the wheat—brings up these issues most urgently.

## THE PARABLE OF THE WEEDS AMONG THE WHEAT (MATT. 13:24-30, 36-43)

There is an interesting background to this parable. The Greek word translated "tares" or "weeds" is *zizania*. This is the bearded darnel, a weed known to us from ancient laws prohibiting just the kind of behavior reported in the parable. As a young plant, bearded darnel looks exactly like wheat. In fact, as it grows, the plant and the grain it produces are nearly impossible to distinguish from wheat until they are mature. Wheat matures to a golden brown color, while the mature bearded darnel is black. Because the two plants could be distinguished only when they were mature, it was customary to leave the separation of the bearded darnel from the wheat until harvest. It was very important to separate them carefully, though, because bearded darnel is a mild hallucinogen. Too much of it causes strange behavior and illness.

As a revenge, it was hard to beat the illicit sowing of bearded darnel. It would slow up your enemy at harvest time, the time when everybody has more to do than can comfortably be fitted into any one day. Not only this, if any bearded darnel did get into the cooking, then its hallucinogenic properties would take a toll on that household.

The story line of the parable closely follows this typical pattern. An enemy sows bearded darnel while the farmer is asleep. The servants report on its presence in the field but are told to leave it until it can easily be distinguished from the rest of the crop, at which time it should be separately gathered and burned.

With this parable, it is easier to apply the first principle of good parable interpretation developed in the last chapter. This parable explicitly begins, "The kingdom of heaven is *like* . . ." (v. 24), thus clearly identifying it as a similitude. There is a likeness between events in the parable and the kingdom of heaven. Yet, as with all good puzzles, the point of the comparison takes a little getting at. *What* in the parable is like the kingdom of heaven? Is it the householder, the crop, the sorting of the bad grain from the good, or the coming of the harvest?

As with the parable of the sower, this parable also comes with an interpretation (vv. 36-43). This interpretation links various elements of the parable to a drama being enacted on a cosmic scale. The one who sows the good seed is the son of man (v. 37). This part of the interpretation is easy to work out, since "the son of man" is one of Jesus' favorite descriptions of Himself. The interpretation goes on to identify the field as the world and the good seed as the sons of the kingdom (v. 38). The enemy is the devil, the harvest is the end of the age, and the harvesters are the angels (v. 39). At the end of the age, the angels will be sent to gather out of the kingdom all causes of sin and all evildoers (v. 41).[3] At this time there will be weeping and gnashing of teeth, but the righteous will shine as the sun in the kingdom of their Father (v. 43).

According to this interpretation, the kingdom of heaven is represented in some ways by the mixed crop. The good seed are the sons of the kingdom, while the bad seed represents those who are evildoers. The point to note, though, is that these evildoers are gathered *out of the kingdom* (v. 41). Does this mean they have been part of the kingdom until this time? At the very least, it means that they have been so closely associated with the kingdom that it has not been possible to distinguish them before the sorting that takes place at the end of the age. Furthermore, where would we find both sons of the kingdom and sons of the evil one so closely associated that it is not possible to tell them apart? Where else but the church? The field may be the world (v. 38), but the crop appears to be the church. Here is a very close association between the kingdom and the church. The presence of a foreign crop among the good seed should perhaps stop us from too easily equating the kingdom of God and the church, but they are certainly very closely associated.

What of the other issue raised in the introduction to this chapter? How should this kingdom be related to the kingdom that God will set up at the end of the age?

In the parable of the weeds, it appears that the kingdom of heaven is present in the world and that it exists before the end of the age spoken of in verse 40. Yet something happens to this kingdom with the coming of the end of the age. After the unrighteous are removed, the righteous are then able to shine as the sun (v. 43). The kingdom might have been present earlier in some way, but there is a difference in the kingdom before and after the sorting process has taken place.

This parable is a similitude. And while we do not insist that a parable have only one point of comparison, it is instructive to ask where the stress of the comparison lies. In both the parable and the interpretation, most attention is given to the need to leave the two different types of people/crops together until the "harvest," at which time the bad will be destroyed and the good gathered. Perhaps the main point of the parable is this: Within the church (or kingdom?) there will be both good and bad right up to the time when Jesus returns. This theme is also taken up in one of the shorter parables appearing later in Matthew 13, the parable of the net.

### THE PARABLE OF THE NET (MATT. 13:47-50)

The background of this parable is most likely to be found in the distinctions of Leviticus 11:9-12, that divide fish into "clean" (suitable for eating) and "unclean" (unsuitable). Thus, a fisherman would need to sort his catch before taking fish to the market.

The parable compares the kingdom of heaven to a fish catcher who casts the net into the sea, bringing in all kinds of fish. Just as the fish catcher sorts the good fish from the bad, so the angels will gather the evil people from the midst of the righteous and cast the evil into the lake of fire.

Few commentators would deny that the church is in view in this parable. The net contains both good and bad, as does the church. Both classes remain together until the end of the age, when the angels will sort one from the other. In other words, the church is not composed only of the righteous; it is a mixture of good and bad Christians and will remain so until the Second Advent. And it will be the angels of God who finally separate the good from the bad (v. 41), not the members of the church community.

But we have not yet come to grips with the hard question regarding this parable. By type, the parable is clearly a simile or similitude—"The kingdom of heaven is like . . ." (v. 47). So the hard question to answer is: The kingdom of heaven is like . . . what? What in the story is being compared to the kingdom of heaven? Is it the net, representing the church? Or is it the end of the age bursting into the present status of affairs? It is not easy to decide, but that is what makes the parable so intriguing!

The main feature of the parable is the presence of two kinds of fish and their sorting out. The interpretation provided in verses 49, 50 concentrates on the process of sorting. Perhaps the comparison being made in this parable is similar to that which we found in the parable of the weeds. Until the end of the age, evildoers are associated with those who belong to the kingdom. Although the kingdom is present throughout the centuries, it undergoes a transformation at the end of the age as the evil ones are removed from it.

## PASTORAL IMPLICATIONS

The parables of the weeds and the net have considerable pastoral and practical implications. One thing seems clear: Within the church there will be a mixture of true followers of God and those who are unsaved. To the human eye it is often difficult to distinguish between the two groups. Indeed, just as there is the danger of mistakenly destroying the good grain in trying to remove the bearded darnel before the harvest, so we should not be too radical in our attempts to remove evil from the church. The need for community discipline is shown by the discourse in Matthew 18 (discussed in the next chapter), and these parables should no doubt be balanced by what is found there. Nevertheless, the parables do make clear that the final task of separating the righteous from the wicked belongs to God and His angels and will not take place before the end of the age.

This should determine our attitudes toward others in the church. The church is the repository of all kinds of people. It may sadden us that some of these have doubtful commitment to Christianity, but it should not surprise us. Neither should we be surprised when the most unlikely of people turn out to be sincere Christians. As Jesus said, He came to call sinners, not the righteous, to repentance (Matt. 9:13). The church is a hospital for sinners, not a showcase for saints. Our dealings with each other in the church should be based on this reality and the example of love that Jesus showed for all sinners, even those of religious pretensions!

## THE PARABLE OF THE TREASURE HIDDEN IN A FIELD
## (MATT. 13:44) AND THE PARABLE OF THE PEARL OF GREAT PRICE
## (MATT. 13:45, 46)

The parable of the treasure introduces a new theme—the discovery of the kingdom. Even though the parable of the treasure hidden in a field is very short, a little imagination shows that this parable provides one of the more entertaining glimpses into the world of first-century Palestine.

Why undiscovered treasure should be hidden in a field is not hard to understand. The wealthy had access to banking services that included such sophistications as international transfer of funds on letters of credit and the like. But such business was done by personal arrangements among the wealthy; most households in first-century Palestine would have had no access to such services. Any surplus wealth would need to be stored in a safe location. Life could end unexpectedly from all sorts of causes; agricultural accidents, sudden disease, and the violence of war, for example, were all relatively common. Thus the knowledge that a considerable amount of wealth was buried in a certain field could easily have died with its owner.

Picture, then, the hired laborer plowing the field. His plow strikes on something. This is not unusual, given the rocky nature of much of the soil, but this particular obstruction is sufficiently different to merit further investigation. He finds the treasure, quickly hides it, and finishes the day's work as though nothing out of the ordinary had happened. When he gets home, he announces to his family that they will be selling all they own—their house, their chickens, their possessions, everything! His wife immediately questions him about what he plans to do with the money. He wants to buy some land about which he has shown no previous interest. She complains, she argues, she weeps, but he is adamant. Everything must be sold, so the land can be purchased. Would he explain why? Probably not, because he would not want any news of his find to leak out.

The second parable in this section—the pearl of great price—also involves someone selling all his possessions. This time the object to be bought is not found by accident. Rather, the merchant has spent his life actively seeking the one perfect pearl. When he finds it, he sells everything to purchase it.

Both these parables begin with the words "The kingdom of heaven is like . . ." (verses 44, 45), so they are similes or similitudes. Because there is very little elaboration of the main point, it is relatively easy to discover the point of comparison in these two parables. It is this: the discovery of something that requires a total commitment of all one's possessions and resources. One person stumbled across the treasure of the kingdom by accident; the other found it after a long and deliberate search. But once found, the kingdom costs both men everything they own. This, then, is the point of comparison.

These parables do throw a subsidiary light on the question of the relationship of the kingdom of heaven with the kingdom coming at the end of the age. Clearly, we can discover the kingdom in the present. There is no need to wait for the end of the age before the kingdom comes into existence. This, in fact, has been one of the common themes of several of the parables in Matthew 13. Now that we have looked at each of these parables, it is probably a good idea to look for other common themes among them and to compare the findings on the kingdom of heaven derived from Matthew 13 with what is said about the kingdom in the rest of Matthew's Gospel.

## THE KINGDOM OF HEAVEN IN MATTHEW

Although Matthew 13:1-50 contains the most concentrated teaching on the kingdom of heaven in the Gospel, the kingdom is a theme that permeates the whole of it. Several other major parables either explicitly begin with the words "The kingdom of heaven is like . . ." or mention the kingdom,[4] and there are a number of other important sayings of Jesus that deal with it. What does the rest of the Gospel have to add to our understanding of the kingdom of God?

In Matthew, several of the sayings involving the kingdom speak of the qualities required for membership—such as humility (18:1-5) and forgiveness of others (18:23-35). On the other hand, the parable of the workers in the vineyard (20:1-16), in which all the workers get the same reward, even those who worked only part of the day, teaches that the kingdom is available because of God's good will. A further saying states that it is hard for the rich to enter the kingdom (19:23). This last declaration introduces an important aspect of the nature of the kingdom: it is something that can be entered. In other words, it is something with boundaries.

There has been a lot of scholarly discussion regarding exactly what is meant by the kingdom of God, and a good number of scholars have concluded that the key concept is that of God's reign. The language of the kingdom, they say, speaks more of God's reign than of the territory over which His reign extends. But one has to ask if this idea is fair to the language we find that speaks of *entering* the kingdom of heaven? Does not such language speak of the kingdom in terms of a territory? Just as the kings of earth have their own territories the devil can show Jesus (4:8), so also God has a territory, a place that can be entered. It is not as though the concept of entering the kingdom of heaven is unique to Matthew 18:23. Such language is used also in Matthew 21:23. Furthermore, there is a clear boundary conceived between the kingdom and that which lies outside it. How else could Peter be entrusted with the *keys* to the kingdom (16:19). If there are keys, it is possible to be "locked out" of the kingdom. To be locked out means that there is a sufficiently well-defined boundary to mark the difference between "in" and "out."

The kingdom of heaven, therefore, implies both reign and territory. Yet this territory is not geographical. The kingdom appears to be made up of people. In particular, it is made up of "the sons of the kingdom" (13:38), "the righteous" (13:43, 49).

Some of the sayings about the kingdom of heaven in the rest of the Gospel relate to issues that have already been discussed. For example, while one saying has a clear reference to a future kingdom of heaven (8:11), another has an equally clear reference to the presence of the kingdom of heaven in the ministry of Jesus: "If I cast out demons by the spirit of God, then the kingdom of God has come upon you" (12:28). There is the same curious dual-time reference elsewhere in the Gospel that we have already observed in Matthew 13. The kingdom is present now but is something still to come. Indeed, John the Baptist, Jesus, and Jesus' disciples all preach that the kingdom "has come near" (3:2; 4:17; 10:7).

How can the kingdom be present already but still to come in the

# The Parables of the Kingdom

future? Perhaps the parables of the weeds and the fish in Matthew 13 can give us the answer. While the kingdom is present in the world before the end of the age, after the evildoers have been taken out of it, it will undergo a change. Its true character will then be revealed. So the kingdom is in the world now, but its full glory will be revealed only at the end of the age.

Is there more information in the rest of the Gospel on how the kingdom relates to the church? Perhaps the threat in Matthew 21:43 is the most relevant: "Because of this I say to you that the kingdom of God will be taken from you and given to a nation bearing its fruits." Spoken as this was to the Jewish religious leaders, this was nothing less than a threat that their nation could lose its covenant status. Who would be recipients of the kingdom is not spelled out, but it is not unlikely that they would be understood in terms of the church. Here is yet another association between the church and the kingdom.

But is the church identical with the kingdom of heaven? Not really. Two of the parables in Matthew 13 underline the presence of evil in the midst of the present kingdom of heaven. It is not until this evil is removed that the kingdom reveals its true nature. Thus, while most members of the kingdom of heaven will be found in the church, not everybody in the church is a member of the kingdom of heaven.

Summing up, then, the results of our thinking about the two issues raised at the beginning of this chapter, we find, first, that in the Gospel of Matthew the kingdom of heaven is present in the person and ministry of Jesus and in the activity of those in the church who are the sons of the kingdom. Yet only with the coming of the end of the age and the removal of the "sons of the evil one" will the kingdom be revealed in its full glory. The present kingdom is but an anticipation of the future kingdom.

Second, there is a close relationship between the kingdom and the church, but the two are not identical, because right to the end of the age the church will be made up of both the sons of the kingdom and the sons of the evil one. Often, from their outward appearances these two groups cannot be distinguished. In fact, only God can really determine who is in each group, and at the end of the age He will send His angels to sort the righteous from those that are evil.

---

1. Of the nine parables in this discourse, seven explicitly include the statement "the kingdom of heaven is like . . ." (Matt. 13:24, 31, 33, 44, 45, 47). Furthermore, if one compares the interpretation of the first parable given in Matthew 13:18 with the parallel passages of Mark 4:14 and Luke 8:11, the word *kingdom* is present in Matthew but absent from the others. The presence of this word links this parable also with the topic of the kingdom of heaven. Note, also, that with only rare exceptions, Matthew consistently uses "kingdom of heaven" instead of "kingdom of God." This is true even of places where the parallel passages in Mark and Luke have the terminology "kingdom of God." This datum, together with the parallel use of the terms in Matthew 19:23, 24 show that the two terms are synonymous. The last parable in this discourse, the very short saying in verse 52, also features the language of the kingdom, because it makes reference to a scribe "instructed in the kingdom of heaven." In sum, all the parables of this chapter are about the kingdom of heaven in some way.

2. The detailed evidence for these figures is given in Robert K. McIver, "One Hundred-Fold Yield—Miraculous or Mundane? Matthew 13:8, 23; Mark 4:8, 20; Luke 8:8," *New Testament Studies* 40 (1994), 606-608.

3. Literally, those who do lawlessness. This is another aspect of Matthew's interest in the law, and his insistence that true Christians observe all the law, which we explored in an earlier chapter.

4. The parable of the unforgiving servant (Matt. 18:23-35), the parable of the workers in the vineyard (20:1-16); and the parable the marriage feast (22:2-14) all begin, "The kingdom of heaven is like . . ." The conclusion derived from the parable of the vineyard and its tenants (21:33-46) is framed in terms of the kingdom (verse 43).

# CHAPTER SEVEN

# The Christian Community and Its Governance (Matthew 18)

Matters to do with church discipline were some of the most unpleasant things I had to be involved in when I was a church pastor. But church discipline is not just something that troubles pastors. It is a topic that can quickly generate vigorous discussion among church members—and a wide range of opinions. On one side are those who think that the Christian church has no right to tell its members that their behavior is wrong or to exclude any member who does not live up to the standards of the church. On the other side are those who vehemently argue that the church must enforce Christian standards among its membership. How can it tolerate those who openly practice sin? Most church members normally fall somewhere in the middle. There are some sins that most everyone considers the church should discipline (e.g. adultery) and others on which they almost all agree the church should *not* act (e.g. pride).

So the fourth discourse in Matthew, dealing as is does with community discipline, is taking up a topic of real interest to church leaders and members alike. Let's consider the contribution that Matthew 18 makes to this issue, before returning to make some general comments on the matter of community discipline in the modern church.

# The Four Faces of Jesus

## THE HEART OF THE FOURTH DISCOURSE: PROCEDURE FOR COMMUNITY DISCIPLINE (MATT. 18:15-17)

"If your brother sins against you, go reprove him, between him and you alone. If he hears you, you have gained your brother. But if he does not hear, take with you one or two more, so that 'out of the mouths of two or three witnesses the matter may be established.' If he disobeys, then tell the church; if he disobeys even the church, he shall be to you as a tax collector and a sinner" (Matt. 18:15-17).

The meaning of this passage is relatively straightforward. If a dispute arises between two members of the community, it should be dealt with between the two parties if this is possible. Otherwise, the party with a grievance should take along two others, who, if matters are not resolved, can then act as witnesses to the dialogue when the matter comes before the whole community. If the individual in the wrong refuses to take the guidance of the community, then he becomes as one outside the community. An interesting feature of this passage is that this is one of only two uses of the word *church* in the four Gospels.[1] In the context of Jesus' ministry, we should understand the word in terms of its Old Testament background. In the Septuagint, the Greek translation of the Old Testament, the word Matthew uses for "church" in his Gospel was used to describe those occasions when the people of God all gathered together at some important occasion.

This short passage in Matthew has some very interesting implications. First, its inclusion in the Gospel may well shed light on the important question of whether the Matthean community—the Christian community among which the Gospel of Matthew was written—had separated from Judaism. We know only a little about this community, so any clues we can get from the text help us to reconstruct a suitable historical background against which to interpret the Gospel. One of the crucial questions is whether the community was still part of Judaism. Did these Christians still worship in the synagogue with their fellow Jews, or had they separated from it by this time?

# The Christian Community and Its Governance (Matthew 18)

At its beginning, of course, Christianity was composed entirely of Jews, who worshiped with their coreligionists in the temple and the synagogues. This changed as non-Jews became Christians and as the leaders of the synagogues excluded Christians. The whole process progressed unevenly. In some places Christians worshiped in the Jewish synagogue for some time. In others, they were forced out very early. Where the Matthean community fits into this scheme of things is important for understanding several significant passages in the Gospel that deal with the relationship between Christians and Jews.

The key passage dealing with community discipline, Matthew 18:15-17, is unique to Matthew. As we will see later, all of Matthew 18 is devoted to the issue of community discipline. Why is there so much interest in community discipline that an entire chapter of the Gospel is devoted to it? Almost certainly because the community had become responsible for the discipline of its own members. Would this be the case if the community were still worshiping in a Jewish synagogue? Unlikely, because the elders of the synagogue would then be responsible for community discipline. So, we conclude that this chapter is evidence that the Matthean community had already made its break with Judaism—slim evidence, perhaps, but the best available in the Gospel. This break was probably fairly recent, because another feature of Matthew's Gospel is its great interest in how the Christian community should relate to Jewish synagogues. Later Christian writings show little interest in this particular issue, for by this time the Christian church had become predominantly Gentile and maintained little sustained contact with Jewish synagogues.

There is a significant omission in Matthew 18:15-17—the lack of any reference to elders. Because most of the first Christians had been regular attendees of synagogues, early Christian worship was influenced greatly by the practices of the synagogue. Synagogues were governed by a board of elders, who were responsible not only for overall community management but also for community discipline. So many early Christian communities also appointed elders to act in leadership roles (Titus 1:5-9; 1 Tim. 3:1-7; Acts 14:23; 20:17, etc.). Under such a style of organization it would have been all but obligatory that elders be involved in any community discipline. In fact, under most circumstances, the elders would have been the ones to take any disciplinary action, not the whole community.

The Matthean community, however, appears to be organized on different lines. On the basis of Matthew 23:8-10, it seems likely that they did have individuals in teaching and leadership roles. These verses remind the community that no one should be called rabbi, father, or teacher. There is little point to such a reminder unless some within the community were actually performing functions that could legitimately demand this kind of recognition. But although some took these roles, they were reminded that they acted only as part of a community under the leadership of Jesus, the risen Lord. There is a basic egalitarianism in the ethos of the Matthean community. Even though some members took teaching and other leadership roles, they all considered themselves equal, with only one leader, Jesus. This is evident in the fact that they did not appear to have elders that ruled their community. The individual members of the community were responsible for initiating any action against another individual.

There are several other interesting implications in this passage, but we will consider only one more—the fact that the Matthean community did reserve the right to exclude some from within its membership. This is all the more significant in light of its view of the church that we saw in the previous chapter of this book when we looked at the parables in Matthew 13. Those parables make it clear that the church would be composed of both righteous and sinners right up to the end of the age. The evildoers would eventually be removed from the church, but this is something that angels did, not humans, and not before the end of the age. Why, then, is the community acting against members? On what grounds does it put them outside of the community? Unfortunately, the text does not make this clear. Elsewhere in the New Testament we find Paul urging the Corinthian community to act against someone who is cohabiting with his father's wife (1 Cor. 5:1). Paul considered this to be a sin that even the heathen would not tolerate and demanded that the

# The Christian Community and Its Governance (Matthew 18)

Christian community at Corinth do something about it. Perhaps this would be the case also in the Matthean community. Perhaps it would act only against someone who persisted in an open sin of some magnitude. The context of Matthew 18 also supports this kind of supposition.

## CAREFUL CONTROLS AGAINST HARSH JUDGMENTS

Any community that acts against one of its individual members faces several real dangers. Often such actions are accompanied by much bitterness. Sometimes people act from base motives such as revenge. This kind of action can spread a chill through the personal relationships of those involved. Furthermore, we all know the kind of individual who would gladly rid the church of nearly everybody and for good reasons, or so he thinks. This kind of spiteful individual can do great damage to a community. Yet, if we read the context provided in Matthew 18, such dangers should be avoided by those calling themselves Christians.

First, the provisions of Matthew 18:15-17 create a strong obligation for due process. They provide for no mob action. The process outlined here is a long and considered process that involves face-to-face dialogue between the principal parties, witnesses, and an appeal to a wider body for counsel.

Second, the Christian community is bound to act within the parameters set by heaven. As verse 18 says, "What you bind on earth will have been bound in heaven, what you loose on earth will have been loosed in heaven." The tenses indicate that actions taken on earth reflect actions that have previously taken place in heaven.[2] In other words, the community cannot act in any other way than God acts. This is further underlined by the parable on forgiveness, which brings us to the next point.

Third, the parable of the unforgiving servant (Matt.18:21-35) is placed directly after the saying that gives directions for community discipline. In other words, this parable is intended to provide the context in which to take disciplinary action. Moreover, it is probably one of the most sobering parts of the New Testament.

In the parable, two servants owe debts. The principal character owes his master a debt impossible to pay and in turn is owed a debt by one of

The Four Faces of Jesus

his fellow servants. The Greek word *aphiēmi* means to forgive both a slight and a financial debt. It is used in the parable when the master "forgives" the debt of the servant who could not pay. Elsewhere in the New Testament the word is used of God forgiving us our sins.

In the parable, even though his master has let him off his massive debt ("forgiven" him), the principal character refuses to "forgive" his fellow servant his tiny debt. This is such an injustice it is reported to the master, who throws the miscreant into jail. The parable is introduced by Jesus' command to "forgive" seventy times seven and concludes with the observation, "So also will my heavenly Father do to you if each of you does not forgive his brother from his heart" (v. 35).

There is a terrible obligation on Christians. Since God has forgiven us so much, we are then obligated to forgive others. But what has this to do with community discipline? A great deal. Action is initiated by an individual. This individual is obligated to be as forgiving of others as God has been of him or her. The community is under obligation to be as forgiving as God. The interaction between its members is based on forgiveness. Thus community discipline can have been only a very rare event that was enforced in cases of extraordinary persistence and magnitude.

Neither should the parable immediately before Matthew 18:15-17 be ignored. In Luke 15:1-7 Jesus tells the parable of the lost sheep to illustrate God's seeking of the sinner. Here in Matthew 18:10-14 He tells the same parable, or one very much like it, to illustrate the community's search for one of its members who has strayed (v. 12). The shepherd leaves the flock to go seeking the one who has strayed. The ninety-nine sheep are put at risk, while an all-out effort is made to recover the one who is lost.

The parable of the straying sheep is a remarkable introduction to the concept of community discipline. The community will put itself at risk in an effort to recover one who is straying. The community will act by means of due process and careful deliberation. Most important, it will act as God acts, forgiving us seventy times seven occasions!

# The Christian Community and Its Governance (Matthew 18)

## SOME REFLECTIONS ON COMMUNITY DISCIPLINE IN MODERN CHRISTIAN CHURCHES

Several aspects of Matthew 18 have a remarkable relevance to modern Christian communities. The parable of the unforgiving servant provides a salutary reminder of how Christians should act toward each other—with an attitude of forgiveness. Indeed, the community will seek the good of the one who is straying, even to the extent of putting itself at risk.

Further, in conflict situations, Christian communities will act with due process. The essential first step of this due process is one individual talking to another. I can illustrate the importance of this first step from my own experience, both as a pastor and a teacher. Some church members think of their pastor as a kind of large dog they can order to attack people. Likewise, as a teacher of Bible in a Christian college, I have some of my students come up to report something to me and then demand, "What are *you* going to do about it?" It didn't take me long to learn to ask in response, "Have you spoken to the individual concerned?" Most often the answer is no, mainly because they wish to avoid open confrontation. But this is not the way of Jesus. He said that the individual should be approached first.

If the individual approach fails, then each different community will have developed its own form of due process. If nothing else, Matthew 18:15-17 surely stresses that this due process should be adhered to carefully so that each stage is well thought through. Initially, an attempt should be made to resolve the matter in as small a group as possible, but if this breaks down, then as wide a consultation as is possible should be undertaken.

On what kind of things should the Christian community act? Matthew 18 is not specific, and if what we have said in an earlier chapter about Jesus and the law is correct,[3] then the Christian community is responsible for taking the principles of Christian living and applying them to the specific circumstances in which it finds itself. The community would then be responsible for deciding which issues are of such importance that action needs to be taken. In any event, the community would not act hastily or for trivial matters. At times the community will act, but it is important for the whole community to be sure that when it does so, it is for very important issues. Unfortunately, the reality of church life often falls far short of this ideal because there is continual pressure to become judgmental over less important things, and there are good sociological reasons for doing so.

Sociologists tell us that a society defines itself by what it excludes. The laws of a society provide boundaries of acceptable behavior. If you step outside of those boundaries, then you cease to be part of the community. Some conservative Christian communities place great stress on their members' deportment and appearance. For example, should members wear jewelry? Should the community allow makeup? These issues then come to define the community. You can tell somebody who belongs just by looking at the way he or she dresses. The danger in this, though, is that debate about these issues will hide the real nature of the community. This is especially true as the community expands into different cultures. It may fit the North American culture to prohibit jewelry on women, for example, but how does this requirement fit in a place like India where jewelry takes on quite a different role in society? As the membership of Christian communities becomes better educated and more sophisticated, it rightly begins to demand that greater stress be placed on more important issues. Of course, a Christian's beliefs will affect behavior and deportment, but community discipline should be reserved for only matters of central importance.

What are these important issues? Take, for example, the following questions: What does it mean to be a Christian? Should Christians all believe in God? Do they need to believe that Jesus is the Son of God? Do they need to believe He rose from the dead? These are all live issues in the Christian churches today and, to my way of thinking, lie very close to the heart of Christianity.

I am responsible for helping my community think through what is absolutely essential to Christianity and what can be left to the individual's choice. If I take the lead of Christ, then I will give a wide

80

latitude to those around me, but sometimes I will have to personally confront somebody. I hope I make sure it is over something important when I do so!

---

1. Greek, *ekklēsia*. This word is found frequently in the epistles of the New Testament, and it appears that the early church mainly used this term, rather than the term *synagogue*, to describe its meetings. The other occurrence of this word in the Gospels is Matthew 16:18.

2. The tenses involved are both future perfect periphrastics. The perfect tense speaks of something that has happened in the past that has effects in the present. In a future perfect periphrastic construction, this basic scheme is complicated a bit, but the point still stands: What happens on earth should reflect something that has already happened in heaven.

3. See chapter 2.

CHAPTER EIGHT

# The Discourse on the End of the Age (Matthew 24, 25)

**SOMEBODY, SOMEWHERE WILL BE SAYING THIS**

This year, somewhere a group of Christians will be saying with great certainty that this will be the year Jesus returns. This is true of the year in which I write these words, and it will be true no matter what year you actually read them. Such individuals will come equipped with charts listing dates and showing how prophecies point unerringly to "this year" as the very year that the world as we know it will end. In most years, the number of such groups is quite small, but at times throughout the history of the Christian church such expectations have been widespread. The approach of the year 1000 saw many predict that this year would be the one in which time would end, as did the approach of the year 1666. A large number of North American Christians accepted William Miller's prediction that Jesus would return sometime during 1843-1844.[1] In more recent times, conservative Christians groups have seized on such events as the rare 1981 alignment of all the planets as the harbinger of the end. The world media featured the expectation of a Korean group that Jesus would return on October 29, 1992. You can be sure that the future will bring equally confident predictions of the year that Jesus will return.

Are all these groups merely deluded fanatics, or have they recaptured something authentic from the New Testament that is missing today from much of Christianity? Christian hope is centered on the return of Jesus to deal decisively with the problem of sin and to usher in the new age in which righteousness will rule. But does this hope grow dim without the expectation that Jesus is coming back *soon*? Furthermore, how can one keep this expectation of Jesus' soon return in light of the fact that He made that promise nearly 2,000 years ago?

These are issues that confront Christians today, and they are the very issues that Matthew 24 addresses. How can we know that the return of Jesus is near? What should be our response since He has not come as soon as we expected? These two questions dominate Matthew 24, 25.

## THE QUESTION(S) OF THE DISCIPLES

"As he was leaving the temple, his disciples came to show him the buildings of the temple. He said to them, 'Do you see all these things? Truly I tell you that there will not be left one stone upon another stone which will not be thrown down.' When he sat on the Mount of Olives the disciples came to him privately and said, 'Tell us, when shall these things be and what is the sign of your coming and the end of the age' " (Matt. 24:1-3).

It isn't surprising that the disciples would be impressed at the buildings of the temple. Its reconstruction, begun in the reign of Herod the Great, and continuing during the lifetime of Jesus, was completed only shortly before A.D. 70, at which time the temple was burned as the Romans took the city.

Although nothing remains standing today of the actual building of the second temple, archaeologists' findings have gone a long way to show how magnificent the structure was. The construction of the surrounding wall was impressive enough in its own right. Where the temple's western wall once stood, several very large stones have been discovered, including one which measures forty-six by ten by ten feet and is estimated to weigh 415 tons. By comparison, the largest megalith at Stonehenge weighs forty tons, and the blocks of the Egyptian pyramids weigh fifteen tons.

Other temple blocks thirty-nine feet (350 tons) and thirty-six feet in length (325 tons) also have been found.[2]

The temple itself was surrounded by a portico with very large pillars. The first-century Jewish historian Josephus waxes eloquent about them, claiming that it would take three men to reach around them.[3] The pillars discovered by archaeologists are not quite this large, but it would take two men to reach around them.

The temple itself was a magnificent building of white marble, dominating the city of Jerusalem. When completed, the temple complex rivaled any in the ancient world. Little wonder that the disciples were impressed by it. Jesus, though, predicted that not one stone of it would be left upon another, and such was the case. When the Romans took Jerusalem in A.D. 70, the temple was burned. After the second Jewish revolt in A.D. 135, the Romans expelled all the Jews from the city of Jerusalem and made a systematic attempt to level the temple site.

But, of course, this was future in the disciples' day, and at a convenient opportunity they asked Jesus to explain further what He meant about the temple being cast down. The way they asked the question was important: "When shall these things be [i.e., the destruction of the temple], and what will be the sign of your coming and the end of the age." They can be forgiven for mistakenly thinking that the destruction of the temple of Jerusalem could be understood only in terms of the end of this age and the setting up of the kingdom of God. Such is the picture presented in such Old Testament passages as Zechariah 14.

Subsequent events have shown that the disciples were mistaken in this belief. Nevertheless, Jesus answered their question as they asked it. His answer mingled events surrounding the destruction of Jerusalem with events surrounding the end of the age. In some ways, the destruction of Jerusalem was a preview of what would happen on a global scale at the end of the age.

## SIGNS OF HIS COMING THAT ARE NOT NECESSARILY SIGNS OF THE END

Jesus begins His answer to the disciples by listing some of the possible signs of the end. He mentions false christs that will deceive many, wars and rumors of war, famines, and earthquakes. Then He specifically says, "Watch, don't be troubled; for these things must be, but the end is not yet. . . . All these things are the beginning of the birth pangs" (Matt. 24:6, 8). So wars, famines, and earthquakes are *not* signs of the end. Instead, they are but the beginnings of the birth pangs.

Now that I am a father, I understand more about the image of birth pangs. Before the baby is actually born, there are a number of false alarms. In these, the uterus of the mother-to-be begins to contract in a kind of dry run for the real thing. These are called Braxton-Hicks contractions and are not really even the beginnings of the birth pangs. Once labor starts, though, the birth pangs mount in intensity, and finally a baby is born. But the process is not as fast as I had imagined before the actual event. Labors of eighteen hours are not unusual, although few are allowed to proceed past twenty-four hours these days. But there is a certain inevitability about labor. Once it really starts, it keeps going until there is a resolution. It is this, no doubt, that made the onset of labor such an appropriate illustration of the relationship of wars, famines, and earthquakes to the end of the age. They are the beginning of a process that will keep going until resolution. But they are not actual signs of the very end, only the signs that the end has begun. The signs of the very end are found in what Jesus describes next.

## THE REAL SIGNS

According to Matthew 24:9-14, the spread of the gospel will be accompanied by an increasing tide of persecution but will eventually go throughout the whole world as a witness to all nations, "and then shall the end come" (v. 14). This, then, is the first great sign of the end—the gospel going to all the world.

Matthew 24:15, 16 continues thus: "Therefore, when you see the abomination of desolation spoken of by Daniel the prophet standing in the holy place (let the reader understand), then those in Judaea should flee to the mountains. . . ." Here, then, is the second great sign of the end—"the abomination of desolation spoken of by Daniel the prophet."

What is meant by the term "abomination of desolation?" Modern translations often phrase this as "desolating sacrilege," and although that wording loses something of the mystery of the more traditional translation, it does convey a sense of the underlying concept. A holy place is desecrated and, as a result, is left abandoned. In Jewish thought, the introduction of idols into the temple would bring about this kind of desecration.

The terminology "desolating sacrilege" is found in Daniel 9:27, 11:31, and 12:11. In Daniel 9:27 the desolating sacrilege appears in the temple toward the end of the "seventy weeks" that have been allocated to the people and city (Dan. 9:24). In Daniel 11:31 the regular sacrifices of the temple are interrupted and replaced by an abomination that makes desolate. Daniel 12:11 likewise speaks of the interruption of the regular offerings of the temple and the setting up of a desolating sacrilege. All three references speak of an interruption of the temple sacrifices and the setting up of an "abomination of desolation."

Perhaps the closest New Testament parallel to this kind of imagery is found in Revelation 13. This chapter describes the deception of a sea beast and a land beast that utter blasphemies against God and deceive the whole world. They set up an image to the beast in the temple and try to compel everyone on earth to worship that image. Those who resist are put to death, and an economic boycott is enforced against those who do not accept the mark of the beast. Thus is pictured a worldwide convulsion over religious issues, during which those who do not wish to participate in apostate religious practices experience severe religious persecution. Matthew 24:15-22 likewise pictures severe persecution followed by a time of trouble "greater than that experienced since the foundation of the world" (v. 21).

To sum it up: There are two particular signs that the end is very close: the gospel going to all nations and a worldwide confrontation over religious practices.

## DATE SETTING

The relationship between these signs and specific dates are clearly set out in Matthew 24:32-44. The signs are likened to a fig tree. When the branches of the fig become "tender," this is a sign that summer is near.

# The Discourse on the End of the Age (Matthew 24, 25)

" 'So also you, when you see all these things, know that it is near, at the very doors' " (v. 33). The signs are given so Christians may know that the end is near. They will be able to tell that the end of the age is *very* close. But, the exact day nobody knows, not the angels, not even the Son (v. 36). It will be like the time of the Flood. People were busy with the everyday round of events, and the Flood was a surprise when it came. So the " 'coming of the Son of Man' " will be a surprise as well.

Matthew 24:36 spells the end of every attempt to set an exact date for the return of Jesus. Thus those who predicted His coming in the year 1000 or 1666 or 1844 or 1992 were *wrong* in doing this. Jesus said, specifically, that the exact time will *not* be known. However, Christians can still know that it will be soon. What this means is illustrated by the following two parables—the parable of the faithful and unfaithful servants and the parable of the ten maidens.

## THE PROBLEM OF THE DELAY

"Who then is the faithful and wise slave, who the master puts in charge of the household slaves to give them food at the right time? Happy is that servant who his master will find doing so when he comes. For truly I tell you that he will put him in charge over all his possessions. But if that evil slave says in his heart, 'My master delays,' and begins to beat his fellow slaves, eating and drinking with the drunkards, the master of that slave will come at a day when he does not expect, and at an hour he does not know, and will cut him in half, and his portion will be with the hypocrites. There will be weeping and gnashing of teeth" (Matt. 24:45-51).

There is a difference between the two slaves. This difference does not lie in the fact that they do not expect their master to return. No, they both expect it. The difference is that the evil slave lives his life on the assumption that the return will be delayed. On the other hand, the faithful slave, although he also does not know when his master will return, lives his life on the assumption that it could be at any time. These are

87

two different reactions to the same set of circumstances, a set of circumstances shared by Christians.

The Christian, likewise, does not know when his Master will return. He can either live his life on the assumption that the coming will be delayed or he can live his life on the assumption that Jesus could return at any time.

The well-known parable of the ten maidens (Matt. 25:1-13) also shares this theme of delay and unexpected return. Ten young women go out to greet a bridegroom. A short delay would be expected, because with arranged marriages it was customary to have some last-minute haggling over the details of the bride's price or dowry. Even so, this particular wedding had more than the usual delay. As they waited, all the young women went to sleep. When the bridegroom came, they all awoke but five of them did not have any more oil for their lamps and as a consequence were locked out of the wedding celebrations.

Again, both groups in the parable expect the bridegroom, but there is a difference between them. The wise maidens had made provision for the possibility that his coming would be delayed. They had extra oil for their lamp. The foolish virgins were not able to cope with the delay. So in contrast to the evil servant of the previous parable, who lived his life in the expectation that his master's return would be delayed, these girls live their lives in the expectation that there will be no delay. So when delay occurs, their resources are not adequate to meet it.

Thus, the two parables make the same point but from opposite directions. The delay of the Master's coming is common to both. Two dangers flow from this delay. One is that the believer will assume that it will be an indefinite delay. The other is that the believer is so attuned to the Master's soon return that his Christianity collapses when Jesus does not return as soon as expected. The believer's faith is so tied to a dramatic reversal of the present world that it withers and dies if left in the present world by the delay of Jesus' coming.

The concept of delay is not present in the other two parables in Matthew 25; however, both deal with the conduct of individuals while the master is absent. The parable of the five, two, and one talents (vv. 14-

30), addresses the issue of faithfulness in the use of the resources granted while the master is absent. The parable of the judgment (vv. 31-45) speaks of the final reckoning that will be given to all, a judgment based on how each has responded to the " 'least of these my brethren' " (vv. 40, 45).

## HOW SHOULD WE ACT?

The twin parables of Matthew 24:45–25:13 have great cogency for Christians today. Like the figures in these parables, Christians of today have experienced a delay in their Master's return. Perhaps those who spend their time setting new dates for the return of Jesus are like the foolish maidens—they have made no provision for the possibility that Jesus' return might be delayed. But I suspect that this is not the problem most Christians have. Most Christians today are probably better represented by the servant who says "My master is delayed." The belief that Jesus will return is alive, because it is so prominent in the New Testament. But the passing centuries have eroded the urgency of this belief. The temptation for us today is to live life on the assumption that Jesus is coming back—but not any time soon.

Life can be lived in a way that is quite independent of any belief in Jesus' return. But this way of living is exactly what Jesus was attacking in the discourse of Matthew 24, 25. He points out that this world is on an inevitable path that will end in His return to bring judgment to the earth. Evil will be blotted out, and good will reign. More than this, He has given signs by which we can know that this process has begun. It is as inevitable as the birth of a child once labor has started. A time is coming—a time of great trouble—during which everyone will be forced to choose sides in the struggle between good and evil. Good will emerge triumphant from this struggle. Christians must live in the light of the reality of all this; how they conduct their lives is affected by the knowledge that someday all will be called to account. They take seriously the fact that their goals lie in the future. Not that this excuses them from using to the best of their ability the resources granted to them here. But such a knowledge brings a new perspective of themselves and their duty.

The Jesus that we meet in Matthew 24, 25 is like the Jesus we meet elsewhere in the Gospels—a very disturbing individual who challenges our perceptions of reality. He tells us to be ready " 'because you do not know the hour when the Son of Man comes' " (Matt. 25:44).

---

1. Initially, Miller thought the date would be 1843, but further study convinced him and his followers that the correct date was October 22, 1844.
2. Murray Stein, "How Herod Moved Gigantic Blocks to Construct Temple Mount," *Biblical Archaeological Review* 7 (May/June 1981): 42-46.
3. *Antiquities,* 15:411-416.

Part 2

# THE GOSPEL OF MARK

CHAPTER NINE

# Mark's Introduction to the Story of Jesus

## HOW TO GET STARTED (MARK 1:1-3)

Students producing essays, journalists writing columns, authors writing books, and playwrights writing plays all share a common problem—how to get started. Each particular genre has its own challenges and ways of meeting them. In narrative accounts the problem revolves around how to introduce the main characters in such a way as to introduce the major themes of the work at the same time. One technique often used in plays is to delay the appearance of the main character. This both raises the expectation of the listener or reader and gives an opportunity to allow others to say things about the main character that would be difficult to say with him or her present.

Some of these literary considerations are evident in the opening of Mark's Gospel. Jesus Himself does not appear until John the Baptist has been allowed to speak about Him. John himself is no insignificant herald, and this boosts the importance of the One whom he announces. Right from the first, John is introduced as one who fulfills the prophecy of Malachi 3:1 and Isaiah 40:3. He is the one making ready the way of the Lord. Yet, important though John is, and even though everyone is flocking to him to receive his baptism of repentance, John announces that One is coming who is much greater even than he. John baptizes with water, but the One who comes will baptize with the Holy Spirit (Mark 1:1-8).

When Jesus appears, in verse 9, a miraculous sign and a voice from heaven confirm what has already been said about Him. As He is baptized, the Spirit descends upon Him in the form of a dove, and a voice from heaven proclaims " 'You are my beloved son, I am very pleased with you' " (v. 11). In this way, John's testimony and the miraculous events connected with Jesus' baptism have prepared the reader to recognize something extraordinary in Jesus. This is no ordinary man. He is One especially endowed with the Holy Spirit. Furthermore, right from the outset, heaven itself proclaims that Jesus is the Son of God.

The same care that has characterized the choice of material for the opening verses of Mark's Gospel is also shown in the selection of the first incidents that are described from Jesus' ministry.[1] Each incident is carefully chosen to demonstrate a key point about Jesus that will be further developed in the Gospel—Jesus is the preacher of the nearness of the kingdom, He calls disciples, He wins the victory over unclean spirits, He brings healing. The centrality of the Cross, so important to the overall message of the Gospel, is also introduced with the motif of the Messianic secret in the dialogue between Jesus and the demons (Mark 1:24, 25), but this development will be the subject of a subsequent chapter.

## JESUS PREACHES THAT THE KINGDOM OF GOD IS NEAR (MARK 1:14, 15)

After the arrest of John, Jesus came into Galilee preaching the gospel of God, saying, " 'The time is fulfilled, and the kingdom of God has drawn near; repent and believe in the gospel' " (Mark 1:14, 15).

Not only are these words the very first words uttered by Jesus in Mark's Gospel, they are said to be a summary of His preaching. These two factors mean that they are very important clues to how the rest of the Gospel should be read.

The reference to time carries a prophetic weight, as does the mention of the kingdom of God. The idea of God as a king is found frequently in the Old Testament (e.g., 1 Sam. 12:12; Ps. 5:2, 10:16, 74:12; 95:3; Isa. 6:5; Jer. 8:19, etc.,) and the associated thought that He has a kingdom is not unknown there either (Ps. 47:7; 103:19). But to announce that God's kingdom is drawing near implies that something dramatically different will occur within the historical realm.

Daniel, in the Old Testament, associates this kind of thought with God's kingdom. For example, in chapter 2, Daniel outlines the future of the world in terms of four components of a great image, which represent four kingdoms. But in the days of the last fragments of the last kingdom, a stone will smash the image into pieces and then will grow to fill the whole earth. As Daniel explains, this stone represents the time when "the God of heaven will set up a kingdom that shall never be destroyed. . . . It shall crush all these kingdoms and bring them to an end, and it shall stand forever" (Dan. 2:44). Here Daniel associates the kingdom of God with the destruction of all earthly kingdoms. In this scheme of things, there is a dramatic break between this age and the age to come. When Jesus announced that the kingdom of God was near, He likely had in mind the kind of kingdom of God Daniel 2 presents. In other words, Jesus' ministry marked the nearness of the dramatic transition between this age and the age to come. The reader might even suspect that Jesus Himself could be the catalyst that would bring about this change. The possibility has been introduced, and subsequent events narrated in the Gospel will either bear this out or show how the saying about the kingdom should be understood in other ways. But in any event, right from the outset Mark's Gospel characterizes the preaching and ministry of Jesus with the expectation that events are moving toward the climax of earth's history.

## JESUS IS THE ONE WHO CALLS DISCIPLES TO FOLLOW HIM (MARK 1:16-20)

The next incident narrated in the Gospel shows that Jesus demands of individual humans that they follow Him. He sees Simon (Peter) and Andrew casting nets into the water and says to them, " 'Follow after me, and I will make you fishers of men' " (Mark 1:17). They immediately abandon their nets and follow Jesus. He then finds James and John and calls them, and they leave their father with the boats and follow Him.

Although it is more than likely that Jesus had had some prior contact with His first disciples,[2] this is the first time in the Gospel of Mark that Jesus meets these men. This makes the incident all the more dramatic. Jesus comes to them while they are busily engaged in their everyday occupation and challenges them to abandon all that they have been doing so far in life, committing themselves entirely to Him and to His service. "Come follow me" is nothing less than a radical demand that takes precedence over everything in their lives—their work, even their family (they left their father with the boats, v. 20).

At this point, modern readers find themselves in the same situation as the ancient reader. In Mark's Gospel, Jesus comes also to us and demands that we follow Him. As it did with Peter, Andrew, James, and John, this is a demand that takes precedence over all else in our lives. Jesus demands of us nothing less than total commitment.

I have personally felt the strength and radical nature of Jesus' demand in my life. It came to me as I was studying for a mathematics degree in preparation to become a high school teacher. Once the realization of Jesus' demand hit me, I spent a lot of energy exploring the exact implications it would have for my life. Should I abandon my teaching career and go into full-time gospel ministry? Should I become a Christian teacher of mathematics and serve the Lord where He had called me? I would have liked a direct message from heaven, but none was forthcoming. As is so often the case, however, I really didn't need one, because I already knew what I should be doing, although it took some years for me to act on it.

The time that stands out in my mind, though, is when we finally made the break and decided to sell our possessions and go study theology. I say "we," because I was married by this time and had spent nearly four years as a math teacher. I resigned from my job so that I could train to become a full-time gospel minister. This meant not only changing my job but changing countries. And so we sold our "ownership flat" (called a "duplex" in some countries), our furniture, and most everything else we had gathered together, packed all our possessions in a few cartons and trunks, and moved. Our home was very simple, but we had seen it built from the foundation up. We had worked hard to establish the lawn and gardens; we had planted fruit trees and had not yet harvested any fruit from them. I was sad to be driving away. I was very conscious that I was facing an unknown, uncertain future. What would God have in mind for me?

I have not regretted the choice. I have enjoyed studying Scripture and theology and have loved the challenge of working first as a church pastor, then as a lecturer, then as a Ph.D. student, and now once again as a lecturer. Every new phase of my working life has brought different challenges, but they all have been exciting. Even now, I don't know what the future holds for me. But if I look back on where my walk with God has taken me, if the future is anything like the past, I know that it will be fulfilling and challenging.

## JESUS IS THE ONE WHO HAS DEFEATED THE EVIL SPIRITS (MARK 1:21-28)

The next incident Mark recounts from Jesus' ministry is His healing of a man with an unclean spirit in the synagogue on the Sabbath. This story brings together several themes that Mark's Gospel subsequently explores further.

We live in a society that has inherited a mechanistic understanding of the universe, so we may tend not to realize that perhaps the most important of Mark's themes regarding Jesus' ministry is that Jesus has overcome the evil spirits. Evil spirits are very prominent in the Gospel of Mark. They take possession of humans and talk through them (Mark 1:24; 3:11; 5:7-9), they can tear them [with convulsions] and almost take their lives by throwing them into the fire (Mark 9:18;[3] cf. 1:23). They can endow humans with near supernatural strength so they cannot even be confined by chains. They can cause men to live among the tombs of the dead, to cry out, and to cut themselves (Mark 5:2-5). Evil spirits were considered responsible for some diseases such as an inability to speak or hear (Mark 9:17, 25).

# The Four Faces of Jesus

In other words, the world of Mark's Gospel was a world that was dominated by the powers of the spirit world. But not all of these spirit powers were evil. The angels of God represented good. They were in a constant struggle with the powers of evil. Often it appeared that the evil spirits were gaining the supremacy. But the message of Mark's Gospel is that Jesus has conquered these evil spirits. His followers have authority over them (Mark 6:7), and their power has been broken.

However, this is not the only theme that emerges in Mark. The spirit that Jesus casts out is described as an *unclean* spirit. As will emerge in the next chapter, the issue of cleanness is taken up by Jesus, who is the One who by His touch can make the unclean clean. Further, it should be noted that this incident took place on the Sabbath. Jesus' actions on the Sabbath are one with His wider actions in challenging the way the Old Testament laws were observed. This has already been explored in the chapter dealing with Matthew 5:17-48, but this theme is also present in Mark's Gospel.

## JESUS IS THE ONE WHO BRINGS HEALING (MARK 1:29-34)

After the incident in the synagogue, Jesus goes to Peter's house and finds Peter's mother-in-law ill. Jesus heals her, and she is restored and able to serve Him and His disciples. That Jesus brings healing is a theme taken up several times throughout the Gospel. This theme will be explored in greater depth in the next chapter dealing with Mark 5.

## JESUS IS THE ONE WHO HAS WIDE HORIZONS OF MINISTRY (MARK 1:35-39)

"And when he got up very early in the morning, he went out and came to a deserted place where he began to pray. And Simon and those with him searched for Jesus, and when they found him they said, 'Everyone seeks you.' And he replied, 'Let us go elsewhere, into the neighboring market towns, so that I can also preach there; it was for this reason I came out' " (Mark 1:35-38).

In Mark, Jesus' ministry is not restricted to any one location. He is the One who moves on to preach in other villages. His message is urgent; He and His disciples have to tell everyone that can be reached.

# Mark's Introduction to the Story of Jesus

## THE STAGE IS SET

The summary statement of Mark 1:39—"and he [Jesus] went preaching in their synagogues and casting out demons in the whole of Galilee"—marks the end of the initial presentation of Jesus. The stage has been set and the readers' expectations aroused. They see Jesus as the unique Son of God, specially endowed by the Holy Spirit, going about proclaiming the nearness of the coming kingdom of God, calling individuals to follow Him, triumphing over the evil spirits, healing the sick, and proclaiming the message in ever-widening circles.

---

1. The temptations of Jesus, which follow the baptism chronologically and which are given considerable attention in both Matthew and Luke, are covered in but two verses in Mark. This has the effect that more stress is given to subsequent events than is the case in the Gospels of Matthew and Luke.

2. Luke 5:1-11 gives a fuller account of the incident and places it later in Jesus' ministry, which allows time for the first disciples to have had some exposure to Jesus and His teachings.

3. There is something different about the boy described in Mark 9:14-29 that marks his case as different from normal spirit possession. The symptoms described could be that of epilepsy, a condition known in the ancient world and ascribed to demon possession. Jesus may have recognized the epilepsy, and although He didn't challenge the father's belief that the problem was caused by spirit possession, He quietly pointed out the difference to His disciples. While this is a possibility, there is not enough information given to be certain that this is the correct interpretation of the incident.

CHAPTER TEN

# Clean and Unclean, in Mark 5

**SOMETHING FROM THEIR HERITAGE FORGOTTEN BY CHRISTIANS**

In practical terms, one of the biggest differences between modern Orthodox Jews and Christians of any persuasion is Judaism's adherence to the distinctions between clean and unclean. If my students represent an accurate indication of wider Christianity, most Christians have forgotten this aspect of their religious roots within Judaism. But because the issue of clean and unclean greatly affected the day-to-day activities of first-century Jews, early Christians were still keenly aware of this aspect of their religious heritage—and the relationship of Jesus to it. Mark 5 explores this relationship in some detail, but before we turn to that chapter, we need to take some time to remind ourselves of the background against which Jesus' actions took place.

**UNCLEAN, CLEAN, AND HOLY IN THE OLD TESTAMENT**

It was no accident that the innermost part of the Old Testament temple was called the Holy of Holies. This is because God manifested Himself there, and God is holy in the greatest degree. Indeed, from one perspective, it is possible to view the system of washings and sacrifices that characterize the worship in the temple as a way of ensuring that it was safe to approach divinity. One could approach God if one was in a state of cleanness. But if there was any defilement, then one would die (Exod. 28:43; Lev. 10:8-10). A number of things could cause this state of uncleanness—touching a dead body (Lev. 11:39), giving birth (Lev. 12:2-5), contracting a skin disease (Lev. 13:2-37, 45, 46), bodily discharges in both men and women (Lev. 15:1-30), and touching somebody or something that is already unclean (Lev. 15:5-12, 20-24; 11:31-38). In particular, sin would cause uncleanness.[1]

Not only people, but clothes and houses could also become unclean (Lev. 13:47-59; 14:33-57). Because of their unique position close to God, the priests had to be particularly careful not to contract contagion. They were permitted to attend the funerals of only their immediate family members, and the high priest who had to go into the holy of holies once a year was not permitted to attend even these funerals (Lev. 21:1-4, 11).

The "natural" state of humans was to be clean, but because it was so easy to become contaminated, it was no small matter to remain in a state of cleanness. If one did become unclean, there were various provisions for cleansing, depending on the seriousness of the contamination. Sometimes remaining outside the camp until nightfall and then washing was prescribed, but other types of uncleanness involved certain sacrifices, as well as washing.

## THE PHARISEES

In Jesus' day, those who belonged to the Pharisees had the commendable aim of observing every detail of the law. So, of necessity, a great part of their concerns would be tied up with the matter of "clean" and "unclean." Although predominantly a lay organization, the Pharisees adopted the stringent rules concerning purity that were imposed upon priests in the Old Testament. Avoiding contamination required continuous attention, and the Pharisees were scrupulous in avoiding contact with things and people who could convey uncleanness.

## CLEAN AND UNCLEAN, IN MARK 5

This first-century background makes us sensitive to the fact that most everything in Mark 5 is concerned with the issue of Jesus' relationship to the unclean. First, in verse 2 He is met by a man with an unclean spirit. Verse 9 explains that this unclean spirit is in fact many spirits. Eventually they end up taking control of a herd of pigs, the *sine qua non* of unclean animals. From there, Jesus goes to the house of a dead girl, where on the way he is touched by a woman with a flow of blood. Both the dead girl and the woman with the flow of blood were unclean, and by Old Testament law anything or anyone touching them would also be unclean. But the touch of Jesus made the unclean clean. With this broad framework in mind, let us look again at these familiar stories.

## THE GERASENE DEMONIAC

The behavior of the demoniac at Gerasa was extraordinary by any measure. Dwelling among tombs, crying out day and night, and cutting oneself with stones (Mark 5:3-5) is not within a normal range of behaviors, no matter how broadly these are defined. Little wonder that attempts had been made to restrain him, although his supernatural strength enabled him to break any chains or fetters. As soon as he saw Jesus, he rushed up to Him, although the words he speaks are those of the unclean spirits that have taken control of him. The unclean spirits immediately began to bargain with Jesus, asking first that they not be sent out of the region (v. 10) and then that they might be sent into the nearby herd of pigs. Given permission to do this, the unclean spirits entered the pigs, whereupon the whole herd of some 2,000 rushed off a cliff and drowned in the Sea of Galilee (vv. 11-13).

This had the effect not only of ridding the possessed man of the unclean spirits but the immediate neighborhood of its unclean animals. Mark's theme of Jesus' control over the unclean spirits has already been featured in the previous chapter so needs little further elaboration. But it is true that Mark 5:1-20 shows that the ministry of Jesus brings whole neighborhoods release from unclean spirits and other matters of uncleanness.

The herdsmen hurried to inform those in the nearby city of the destruction of the pigs. Next follows one of the most poignant moments in the whole Gospel. The townspeople and those working in the fields all hurried to see for themselves what had happened. "And they came to Jesus and when they saw the one who had been demon possessed sitting clothed and in his right mind . . . they were afraid. And those who saw what had happened explained to the people about the demon possessed man and the pigs. *And they began to beg him to leave their district"* (vv. 15-17, emphasis supplied). This is an unexpected reaction. The local inhabitants saw the miraculous change in the demon-possessed man and recognized the power of Jesus over the unclean. As a result, they were fearful. What they were fearful of is not spelled out explicitly in the text, but certainly they did not wish for any more change. They had become comfortable with the local unclean spirits and were unprepared to meet the cost of their eradication. Jesus moved on, leaving behind the healed man as living testimony to what He could do for the region.

THE WOMAN WITH THE FLOW OF BLOOD

The situation of the woman with the flow of blood was unenviable. By Old Testament law, not only was she unclean, anything that she sat on, lay on, wore, and cooked with was unclean, too, as was anybody who touched her (Lev. 15:19-27). Nor could normal marital relations take place while she suffered from the condition. This had been her lot for twelve years. She had spent all her money on the remedies available to her, but instead of getting better, she got worse (v. 25). Hearing that Jesus was in the neighborhood, she thought that if she could touch only the edge of His garment, she would be healed. She *did* touch His garment and was healed.

At the touch, Jesus stopped and inquired who had touched Him (v. 30). The disciples explained that in a crowd it is all to easy to be jostled, but the woman knew of what Jesus asked and came forward to explain what had happened to her, at which point Jesus said, " 'Daughter, your belief has saved/healed you; go in peace and be healed from your affliction' " (v. 34). In getting the woman to come forward, Jesus challenged one possible interpretation of how she had been healed—the magical interpretation, that there was something inherent in Jesus that was available to all those who might touch him. On the contrary, the woman had not been healed because of any magical property within Jesus but because she had belief (faith) that she would be healed. Faith was the key to her healing.

At this point, the translator of Mark becomes frustrated, and the English reader misses a double entendre of the text. The word translated "healed" in verse 34 has two meanings, one is "to heal" and the other is "to save." The underlying Greek word is the one used for salvation in the New Testament. Thus the woman not only has been *healed* by her faith, she has also been *saved* by her faith. Further, this reveals an important aspect of Jesus' healing miracles—they not only were miracles of healing, they were also positive demonstrations of Jesus' ability to save. Faith, the basis of the woman's healing, was also the basis of her salvation. Believing that Jesus is able to save is what brings salvation to anyone, even one who has been desperately seeking salvation for twelve years and has spent her all in the endeavor. Faith in Jesus brings salvation to the most desperate.

## Jairus's daughter

Just as belief was the basis for the healing of the woman with the flow of blood, so belief was what Jesus commanded of Jairus when news reached the father that his daughter had died (v. 36). The belief demanded of Jairus was greater than just believing that Jesus could heal the sick. This ruler of the synagogue was asked to believe that Jesus had power over death itself.

When Jesus arrived at Jarius's house, He explained to the mourners that the girl was not dead but only slept and needed to be awakened (v. 39; cf. John 11:11). Jesus went into the room where the body lay, grasped it by the hand, and said, "Talitha Koum," an Aramaic phrase meaning "Child, I tell you, arise" (v. 41). She arose, as if from sleep.

Jesus deliberately touched the dead body. By Old Testament law, a dead body is unclean, and anything that touches it becomes unclean (Num. 19:11, 16). But instead of making Jesus unclean, His touch caused the dead body to come to life! Likewise, when the woman with the flow of blood touched Jesus, He should have become unclean. Instead, the unclean woman became clean. These incidents in Mark 5 show that Jesus is the One who comes to drive out the uncleanness from a region, that His very touch brings cleanness to the unclean.

---

1. The removal of sins on the Day of Atonement is described in Leviticus 16:19 as removing the uncleannesses of the people of Israel.

CHAPTER ELEVEN

# The Messianic Secret in Mark

## WHY STUDY WILLIAM WREDE'S IDEAS?

In most fields of academic study, certain books stand out as land-marks of important advances in understanding. German scholar William Wrede's 1901 book on the Messianic secret in the Gospel of Mark is one such work.[1] At the time of its publication, it caused shock waves in scholarly circles, the effects of which can be felt to this day. Indeed, no serious work on the Gospel of Mark is carried out without some interaction with this famous study, even though today few scholars would understand Mark in exactly the same way that Wrede did.

Not only is Wrede's work interesting because it is of historical interest, but it also introduces us to a method of investigating the Gospels that has dominated university-based research for more than a century and that has influenced most commentaries written on the Gospels. Furthermore, Wrede's ideas introduce one of the important keys to the interpretation of the Gospel—the Messianic secret. All scholars, even those who disagree with Wrede, agree that this concept is an important key to Mark's theology. For all these reasons, then, it is worthwhile to look at Wrede's understanding of Mark, even though it is somewhat alien to most Christians when they first meet it.

# The Four Faces of Jesus

## WILLIAM WREDE'S CONCLUSIONS CONCERNING THE SECRET

At the turn of the century, many of William Wrede's fellow German scholars were becoming uncomfortable with the view of Jesus that had come to dominate nineteenth-century scholarship on the Gospels. Biblical studies had not been immune from the scientific rationalism that characterized nineteenth-century intellectual activity. Although there had been a good deal of interest in Jesus' life, there had been a willingness to strip away from the Gospel account all that was considered to be legendary. For example, the prophecies about the end of the world were attributed to somebody other than Jesus,[2] and few scholars believed that the miracles recorded in the Gospels actually happened. Out of the residue of "authentic" material, scholars reconstructed a picture of Jesus as a man who brought a moral earnestness to the problems of everyday life. A man rather like the upright, middle-class, educated, nineteenth-century Germans who were writing books on the life of Jesus![3]

Wrede began by criticizing the methods of interpretation used by his predecessors, which had led them to these conclusions. He accused them of being far too arbitrary in their selection of evidence—deleting the bits of the Gospel accounts they didn't like and accepting the rest. If such things as miracles and predictions of the end of the world were not credible (and Wrede did not believe that they were), then neither were the other materials associated with them in the Gospels. In particular, if demons did not actually speak through those they possess, then no credibility should be given to what they said about Jesus. This observation led to the heart of Wrede's thesis. He noted that it was the demons who first introduced the idea of the Messianic secret in Mark's Gospel (Mark 1:24; 5:7). It was they who proclaimed Jesus to be the Messiah, but who were silenced. Furthermore, in the Gospel as a whole there is a distinctive pattern—each time Jesus is recognized as the Messiah before the crucifixion, He gives a stern command not to tell this to others.

Why would Jesus try to prevent others from calling Him the Messiah? Wrede's explanation is that just as the demons were not historically factual, neither was their recognition of Jesus as Messiah. In fact, according to Wrede, Jesus was not recognized as the Messiah in His own lifetime. It was only after Pentecost that others recognized Him as Messiah. When early Christians proclaimed Jesus as Messiah, their listeners who remembered Jesus would say, "Wait a minute. Why do you say Jesus is the Messiah when He never said that of Himself?" The Christians would reply that Jesus did say that of Himself, but He swore His hearers to secrecy until after the Resurrection. In other words, according to Wrede, the "Messianic secret" was invented by the early church to explain why Jesus had not claimed to be the Messiah while He was alive.

## CRITIQUE OF WREDE

Most Christians meeting these ideas for the first time are quite disturbed about what Wrede said regarding the historical accuracy of the Gospel accounts. They are downright dismayed that such skepticism is often typical of university-based scholarship on the Gospels. As a result, they tend to reject outright what Wrede has to say.

Indeed, if you believe that miracles can happen and that the accounts of the Gospels are historically sound, then the whole basis of Wrede's reconstruction disappears. However, it is worth recounting his ideas in an introductory book such as this so readers might be alerted to the basic historical skepticism that forms the foundation for much of what they might read in scholarly books. The danger is that they will so distrust what they read that they will overlook some genuine insights into the Gospels that such research can bring.

Wrede's seminal work on the Messianic secret is a case in point. Even though he is wrong in his basic approach and wrong in many of the details of what he says,[4] he has asked an important question—What is the function of this pattern that we can observe in Mark, that Jesus does not permit others to proclaim Him as the Messiah? If Wrede's answer to this question is inadequate, then the search for a better solution should significantly advance everyone's understanding of the Gospel of Mark.

## IF WREDE IS WRONG, WHAT IS THE EXPLANATION OF THE SECRECY MOTIF?

Probably the best place to begin a study of the secrecy motif in Mark is Mark 8:27–9:1. This important passage is prefaced by an account of a healing (8:22-26) that is unique to the Gospel of Mark. One can understand why the other Gospels do not record this particular healing because, on a superficial reading, Jesus didn't get the healing right the first time. A blind man is led to Jesus, who takes him outside of the village. Jesus thereupon spits on his eyes and places his hand on him, and the man partially recovers his sight. He sees men, but they look like trees walking around (v. 24). Jesus then places His hands on the man's eyes again. This time he is fully healed and can see clearly. The disciples are rather like this man before he was touched a second time, as will be seen in the passage that follows. They have seen Jesus, but they do not yet see Him clearly; they do not yet understand (Mark 8:21). What is missing is that they do not understand that Jesus must suffer.

In verse 27 Jesus asks His disciples about public opinion of Himself. Who do others think He is? They reply that some say He is a resurrected John the Baptist, others that He is Elijah, still others that He is a prophet. When Jesus asks His disciples who they think He is, they reply that He is the Christ (the Greek form of the Hebrew term "Messiah"). Whereupon, Jesus demands that they tell nobody of this (v. 30). Why is Jesus so insistent that others should not be told that His disciples think He is the Messiah? Perhaps what He talks of next provides the reason.

Jesus immediately begins to teach His disciples that it was necessary that He (the Son of Man) should suffer; be rejected by the elders, chief priests, and scribes; be put to death; and rise on the third day (v. 31). Peter's reaction is revealing. He takes Jesus aside and begins to rebuke Him, whereupon Jesus rounds on Peter and says, " 'Get behind me, Satan, because you are not thinking the things of God, but the things of man' " (vv. 32, 33). Here, perhaps, was the root of Jesus' prohibition to those who wanted to proclaim Him as the Messiah. It was true that He was the Christ, but Jesus' own understanding of the Christ included the concept of suffering, a concept rejected by even those closest to Him.

Although it is not possible to be sure, it appears that the disciples' concept of the Messiah was of one who would come and conquer by use of force. Indeed, it is quite possible to read many of the

Old Testament prophecies in this light (Isa. 9:6, 7; 11:1-5; 63:1-6). Popular imagination was fueled by the feats of the Maccabees. These were Jewish leaders who had rebelled against their Seleucid rulers at a time of religious persecution and who had successfully driven them out of Palestine. Their successors had ruled Palestine until the coming of the Romans. Many in Jesus' day were looking for a leader who would repeat the success of the Maccabes, but this time in a revolt against the Romans. There were groups in Palestine agitating revolt against Rome, and armed insurrection against Rome did indeed break out in A.D. 66 and 135, although it ultimately proved unsuccessful. The second of these revolts tapped into the very Messianic expectation that Jesus appears to be fighting. It was led by Simon bar Kochbar, who was recognized as the Messiah by some of the prominent Jewish rabbis. It was a potent mix—religious expectation of a divine deliverer mixed with the political goal of throwing off Roman rule. Even so, it ultimately proved disastrous for the nation.

In Jesus' opinion, though, these kinds of Messianic expectations missed the point. For Him, the concept of Messiahship was inextricably linked with the concept of suffering. This was in marked contrast to the popular understanding of the Messiah, and, therefore, until after the events of the Cross, the disciples would continue to be like the man who had only partially recovered his sight. They saw that Jesus was the Messiah, but they did not yet properly understand what this meant.

This is true of other concepts in the Gospel of Mark as well. Just as the disciples would not properly understand the Messiahship of Jesus until after His death and resurrection, so they would not understand the Transfiguration until that time. The account of the Transfiguration immediately follows the passage that we have just been studying. Jesus took three disciples up to a mountain and was changed before them so that His garments became shining white. Elijah and Moses appeared with him (Mark 9:2-4). While they returned from this event, the disciples were warned not to speak of it until after the Son of Man was raised from the dead (v. 9). They did not understand the reference to the resurrection of the Son of Man (v. 10), and one cannot blame them for this before the event. Like the Messiahship of Jesus, the Transfiguration could not be understood apart from the Cross and the Resurrection. Indeed, one of the central insights of Mark's whole Gospel is that Jesus Himself cannot be understood apart from His death and resurrection, but that is a theme that will be more fully explored in the next chapter.

## SUMMING UP

William Wrede brought the theme of secrecy in Mark to the attention of readers of that Gospel, and even though few today accept his conclusions about this theme, he has highlighted one of the important aspects of the Gospel—that Jesus could not be publicly revealed as the Messiah until after His death and resurrection, because His concept of the Messiah was that of a Messiah who suffers. His disciples and those they talked to were looking for a Messiah who would push the armies of Rome out of Palestine. Only after the Cross were they able to properly understand what Jesus meant when He called Himself the Messiah. Indeed, for Mark, Jesus Himself cannot be properly understood apart from the Cross.

---

1. William Wrede, *Das Messiasgeheimnis in den Evangelien. Zugliech ein Beitrag zum Verständnis des Markusevangeliums* (Göttingen: Vandenhoek & Ruprecht, 1901 [& 1963]); translated *The Messianic Secret* (Cambridge: Clark, 1971).

2. Mark 13 (which parallels Matthew 24, which has already been covered in chapter 7) was called the little apocalypse and was widely thought to have been composed by an anonymous early Christian, not Jesus.

3. The remark of G. Tyrrell, when he said, "The Christ that Harnack sees, looking back through nineteen centuries of Catholic darkness, as only the reflection of a liberal Protestant face seen at the bottom of a deep well," has been widely quoted. G. Tyrrell, *Christianity at the Cross-Roads* (London, 1904), 44, as cited by Robert Grant and David Tracy, *A Short History of the Interpretation of the Bible*, 2d ed. (Philadelphia: Fortress, 1984), 197, n. 30.

4. For example, several scholars have challenged Wrede's assertion that the Messianic secret is associated with demons. Indeed, the demons in Mark 1:24; 5:7 do not recognize Jesus as the Messiah but as the Son of God. The most extended discussion of the Messianic secret, that of Mark 8:27–9:1, takes place in a context that does not contain any reference to demons at all!

CHAPTER TWELVE

# The Message of Mark

**THE BIGGER PICTURE**

In some ways the Gospels are like multifaceted jewels; there are many different ways of looking at them, and each brings its own reward. So far we have looked at Mark from several different perspectives. At times we have examined details as small as the meaning of an individual word, but we have been mainly dealing with the incidents that make up one or more chapters of the Gospel. Now, though, we will step back a few paces to take in the perspective of the whole Gospel, dealing primarily with what the Gospel has to say about three facets—Jesus, discipleship, and the kingdom.

First, what does it say about Jesus?

## *JESUS*

**THE REALLY HUMAN JESUS**

The Jesus who strides through the Gospel of Mark is fully human. Although the Gospel begins with the ministry of John the Baptist and does not recount any of the stories of Jesus' birth or early childhood, this does not mean that the Jesus of Mark has unknown origins. He hails from Nazareth. When He returns to His hometown, He is known as the builder; the son of Mary; and the brother of James, Joses, Judas, and

Simon. He also has sisters (Mark 6:1-3).

Although many miracles surround Jesus, these all take place among real people, in real places, during known times. He begins in Nazareth, is baptized in the river Jordan, and then goes to Capernaum, where He makes His home (Mark 2:1[1]). He teaches and heals in the synagogue in Capernaum (Mark 1:21). His activities take Him around the Sea of Galilee (Mark 3:7; 5:1), to the regions of Tyre (Mark 7:24), to Caesarea Philippi (Mark 8:27), and finally to Jerusalem (Mark 11:1) where He meets His death. He is heard by, and affects, a wide range of people within and without Palestine, including such notables as Herod Antipas, tetrarch of Galilee and Peraea (Mark 6:14), and Pilate, procurator of Judea (Mark 15:2). All these are real places and historical people. Jesus is no mythical visitor from another world at some indeterminate time. His life and ministry have a historical background that is realistically portrayed. It has extraordinary elements within it, but it is portrayed as the life and ministry of a real man, living in real circumstances.

Furthermore, Jesus exhibits typically human emotional responses to the situations in which He finds Himself. He is moved with compassion at the plight of a leper and reaches out His hand to touch him (Mark 1:41). He becomes angry at the hardness of heart that would lead the Pharisees to bring a cripple to the synagogue on Sabbath just to see if His compassion would cause Him to heal the man on that day (Mark 3:5). He marvels at the unbelief of the people of His hometown (Mark 6:6). He has compassion on the hunger of the crowd (Mark 8:2). He looks upon the proud young man who can claim to have kept all the commandments of God—and He loves him (Mark 10:21). He becomes very distressed in Gethsemane as He contemplates the ordeal that awaits Him (Mark 14:33). He cries out in despair on the cross because He feels forsaken by God (Mark 15:34).

In sum, the Jesus portrayed by Mark is fully human.

## JESUS, THE SON OF GOD

Yet in Mark's Gospel there is something different about the man Jesus. The very first sentence informs the reader[2] that Jesus is the Christ, the Son of God (Mark 1:1).[3] Jesus is announced by a forerunner, John the Baptist, who himself is acting in fulfillment of Isaiah's prophecy (Mark 1:2). John announces Jesus as One who is greater than he is.

The first time Jesus appears in the Gospel is at His baptism. Even before He speaks, the heavens open and the heavenly voice says "You are my beloved son, I am very pleased with you" (Mark 1:11). The demons proclaim Jesus as the holy one of God (Mark 1:24), and at the moment of His death, a Roman centurion can recognize that Jesus is a Son of God (Mark 15:39).

The very actions of Jesus reveal that there is something extraordinary about Him. He heals the sick (Mark 1:29-34), cleanses lepers with a touch (Mark 1:40-43), enables quadriplegics to walk (Mark 2:1-12), restores withered limbs (Mark 3:1, 5), restores hearing to the deaf (Mark 7:32-35) and sight to the blind (Mark 8:22-25; 10:46-52). He can multiply five loaves and two fishes to feed a crowd of five thousand (Mark 6:30-44). He walks on the water (Mark 6:45-52). He raises the dead to life (Mark 5:35-43). He exercises authority over the spirit world. Although they are His enemies, demons recognize Him and obey Him (Mark 1:23-26; 5:2-14). He changes into a bright, shining being before the frightened eyes of three of His disciples and talks with Elijah and Moses (Mark 9:2-4). None of these are the actions of a mere human.

The claims Jesus makes of Himself also point beyond what might be expected of a human. For example, He claims the right to forgive sins, something both He and His enemies recognize is a prerogative of God alone (Mark 2:5-8). In claiming to forgive sins, Jesus applies to Himself the title "Son of Man." As the Son of Man, He also claims authority over the Sabbath (Mark 2:28) and claims that His death is the essential aspect of the forgiveness of sin (Mark 10:45). At His trial, when pressed to say whether or not He is the Christ, Jesus says that His accusers will see the Son of Man coming in the clouds (Mark 14:62). However this verse may be understood, it must surely mean that Jesus is claiming extraordinary things for Himself. He will be sitting at the right hand of power when He returns from heaven!

A further claim arises as Jesus celebrates the Passover with His disciples. He takes the wine and says, "This is my blood of the covenant which is poured out for many" (Mark 14:23-24). This language is reminiscent of events at Mount Sinai recorded in the Old Testament. At that time, when God had come down to give His law and to enter into a covenant with Israel, Moses took some of the blood of the sacrifices, threw it on the congregation, and said "Behold the blood of the covenant which the Lord has made with you" (Exod. 24:8). Jesus uses His own blood as the basis of a new covenant, which He Himself would make with His people. In doing this, he appropriates the moment when God made a covenant between Himself and His people at Mt. Sinai, which is again nothing short of extraordinary.

In sum, the Gospel of Mark proclaims Jesus as the Son of God. It introduces Him as the Son of God, it shows others acknowledging Him as the Son of God, it shows Him acting and speaking in a way that points beyond humanity and toward the fact that God was manifest in Him. For Mark, Jesus is the Son of God in a way totally unique to Himself.

## THE HEALING MIRACLES AS A PARABLE OF SALVATION

One of the more prominent activities of Jesus in the Gospel of Mark is healing the sick. The fact that Jesus performs these miracles points both to who He is and to His ability to save. For example, in the dialogue between Jesus and the Pharisees regarding whether He is able to forgive sins (something only God can do), Jesus asks, " 'What is easier, to say to the paralytic, "Your sins are forgiven," or to say "Rise, take up your mat and walk" '? But so that you know that the Son of Man has authority to forgive sins upon earth . . . He said to the paralytic, 'Rise, take up your mat, and go to your house' " (Mark 2:9-11). The physical miracle demonstrated that Jesus has the power He claimed—the power to forgive sins.

Another aspect of the healing miracles grows out of the dual meaning contained in the Greek word for "healing." In the chapter dealing with the concepts of clean and unclean in Mark 5, we saw that the Greek verb *sōzō* means both "to heal" and "to save."[4] Thus, when the woman

114

with the flow of blood said to herself, "If I but touch the hem of his garment, I will be healed," she could equally have been saying, "If I but touch the hem of his garment, I will be saved" (Mark 5:28). When Jesus said to her, "Your faith has *healed* you," He was saying at the same time, "Your faith has *saved* you." Thus the healings of Jesus are but parables of His ability to save humans from their sins. That He restores sick bodies shows that He can restore sinful humans. Just as Jesus is the source of healing, He is also the source of salvation.

### JESUS THE TEACHER

Compared to Matthew and Luke, Mark records less of Jesus' actual teachings. Interestingly enough, however, Mark's Gospel uses the verb "to teach" slightly more often than do the other Gospels. Since Mark is shorter than the other Gospels, this shows that Mark portrays Jesus as teacher considerably more frequently than do the other Gospels. Jesus is said to be teaching in Mark 1:21, 22; 2:13; 4:1, 2; 5:2, 6, 34; 7:7; 8:31; 9:31; 10:1; 11:17; 12:14; 12:35; 14:49 and is called teacher in Mark 4:38; 5:35; 9:17; 9:38; 10:17, 20, 35; 12:14, 19, 32; 13:1.[5] He is called Rabbi by the disciples twice (Mark 9:5; 11:21), or three times if we count Judas's salutation at the betrayal (Mark 14:45).[6]

The fact that Mark reveals less about the content of Jesus' teaching gives greater emphasis to what he actually does say about it. The Gospel begins the account of Jesus' ministry by summarizing His activity in the following words: "Jesus came to Galilee preaching the kingdom of God, saying, 'The time is fulfilled and the kingdom of God is near. Repent, and believe the gospel' " (Mark 1:14). This programmatic summary of Jesus' teachings reveals that He spoke about the following: (a) the fulfillment of time prophecies; (b) the nearness of the kingdom of God; and (c) repentance and belief. Several of these themes recur in the teachings that are recorded of Jesus.

The two longest accounts of Jesus' teachings are found in Mark 4 and 13. Mark 4 is devoted largely to parables. The first, the parable of the seed, shows the reaction of different people to the "word" (Mark 4:13-20). Some reject it, some neglect it, but in others it multiplies and bears spectacular fruitage. The next two parables—sowing seed (Mark 4:26-29) and mustard seed (Mark 4:30-32)—deal with the kingdom of God. The kingdom, Jesus says, is like sown seed. It grows naturally until ready for harvest. Also, the kingdom is like mustard seed; it begins small but grows large.

The second major block of Jesus' teaching, recorded in Mark 13, deals with the signs of the accomplishment of all things. There will be terrible strife on the earth. The believers will suffer. The Son of Man will return on the clouds of heaven. Jesus here portrays Himself as the major actor in this great cosmic drama. Jesus' preaching about time and the closeness of the kingdom further reveals His importance.

The other notable aspect of Jesus' teaching in Mark is His teaching that the Son of Man, the Messiah, must suffer (Mark 8:31-38; 9:31; 10:32-34). The disciples were particularly resistant to this aspect of Jesus' teaching, but it constituted one of its essential components.

### JESUS CANNOT BE UNDERSTOOD APART FROM THE CROSS

Perhaps the single most important message of Mark is that Jesus cannot be understood apart from the Cross. Even the amount of space the Gospel devotes to the events surrounding the crucifixion highlight this fact. While it is probably an exaggeration to call the Gospel of Mark a passion narrative with an extended introduction, it is true that slightly more than one-fifth of the Gospel is devoted to describing the events of the last two days of Jesus' life—and a not inconsiderable amount of the rest of the Gospel also deals with the meaning of the passion.

The importance of Jesus' passion is highlighted by the emphasis given to the so-called "Messianic secret" in Mark. As we have seen in a previous chapter,[7] Jesus insisted that although He was the Messiah, His messiahship could not be adequately understood apart from His suffering, death, and resurrection. Neither could the Transfiguration, which Jesus insisted should also be kept secret until after the Resurrection (Mark 9:9).

In other words, the essence of Jesus—His messiahship, His divinity—could not be proclaimed by the disciples before the Cross because they could not really understand Jesus until after the Cross. In fact, in the Gospel of Mark, Jesus cannot be understood apart from His suffering and death.

## DISCIPLESHIP

### "FOLLOW ME"

In the Gospel of Mark, Jesus begins calling His disciples as soon as He embarks on His public ministry. He comes upon two fishermen working beside Lake Galilee and abruptly says to them, " 'Come, follow me' " (Mark 1:17). They immediately respond by leaving all behind them—their boats, their nets, everything. He then calls James and John. They also leave everything and follow Jesus. They are not told where they are going, although they are told what they will do. They will become fishers of men.

This is perhaps the essence of discipleship in Mark. Jesus finds people at their work and challenges them to leave everything and follow Him. This challenge is not to be undertaken lightly. Those who follow Jesus must be prepared to live, and even to die, like their Master. " 'If any wish to follow behind me, let them deny themselves and take up their cross and follow me' " (Mark 8:34). All disciples of Jesus are to follow Him in the path of unselfish, unappreciated service. They will be betrayed to the courts; they will be beaten in the synagogues; brothers will betray brothers to death, and fathers their children. The disciples of Jesus will be hated by everybody (Mark 13:9-13).

Although Jesus demands that His disciples give up everything and be prepared to pay any price, the cost is worthwhile. When Peter says "Look, we have left everything and followed you," Jesus replies, "Truly I tell you, nobody has left house or brothers, or sisters, or mothers, or fathers, or children, or fields for my sake or the sake of the Gospel, who will not receive a hundred times in houses, brothers, sisters, mothers, children, and fields, in this age and the age to come" (Mark 10:28-30). The disciples might have left houses and family, but they were to be received into larger households and have a larger family. Jesus dramatically explains this point when His own family comes to visit Him. They stand outside demanding to see Him because they are His family. Instead of going outside, He tells those around Him that *they* are His family: " 'Who is my mother and my brothers?' And, as he looked at those sitting surrounding him, he said, 'Behold my mother and my brothers. For whoever does the will of God is my brother and sister and mother' " (Mark 3:33-35). The family of Jesus' disciples is a close family. Disciples leave everything, but even in this world, they gain everything. They join a wider, but closer, family. Their parents, brothers, and sisters are their fellow disciples. Jesus demands everything. His followers receive in return one hundredfold of what they have given up, and heaven to boot! But this does not mean that they understand Jesus immediately on becoming His disciples.

## THEY SEE, BUT PEOPLE LOOK LIKE TREES WALKING

When Jesus first restored sight to the blind man at Bethsaida, he could not see clearly. He saw men, but they looked like trees walking (Mark 8:22-26). In many ways, the disciples were like this partially-healed blind man. They saw the real meaning of Jesus, but dimly.

Peter, for example, is only partially correct in his understanding that Jesus is Messiah (Mark 8:24-34). Jesus is indeed the Messiah, but not the kind of Messiah Peter is expecting. He is a suffering Messiah. Peter was seeing Jesus, but like the blind man, he was not seeing quite correctly. He was only dimly perceiving who Jesus really was.

This is true of the disciples throughout the Gospel of Mark. They perceive some aspects of Jesus, but others they fail to understand. Every time Jesus speaks of His approaching suffering, the disciples either reject what He says outright (Mark 8:31-33) or misunderstand it and talk about it in worried tones to each other because they are afraid to ask Jesus what He means (Mark 9:9, 10, 31, 32; 10:32-34). The disciples were not able to include the notion of suffering and death in their concept of Jesus.

The request of James and John to sit on either side of Jesus when He came into His glory (Mark 10:35-45) is yet a further example of this inability to see clearly. Jesus had just told them that He was about to suffer and die (Mark 10:32-34), and their immediate response is to ask Him for these preferred positions. Jesus asks them if they are able to drink the same cup as He will drink (Mark 10:38). In other words, are they prepared to suffer as Jesus will suffer?

Other actions of the disciples likewise show that they do not fully understand Jesus and His call to discipleship. Peter tells His Master that he will die with Him if necessary (Mark 14:27-31). Indeed, at the arrest of Jesus, Peter shows better than average courage and superior initiative. The other disciples all scatter, but not Peter. He follows his Lord to see how things will turn out. He is even able to position himself in the courtyard of the high priest. But once there, he finds that the course he has chosen is not one where he can confess his Lord. In fact, as Jesus had predicted, Peter ends up vehemently denying his Lord (Mark 14:66-72).

The portrayal of the disciples in the Gospel of Mark shows not only their commitment but also their misunderstandings. These were real people. They had left their all to follow Jesus, but in their walk they often stumbled. They particularly faltered when it came to Jesus' suffering and death. This is what they found hardest to understand. Indeed, this is the part of the imitation of Jesus they found most difficult to implement in their own lives, as do we.

## " 'LORD, I BELIEVE; PLEASE HELP MY UNBELIEF' "

In the initial summary of Jesus' preaching, given in Mark 1:14, Jesus challenges His hearers to repent and to *believe* the Gospel. The words translated "belief" and "faith" come from the same Greek word. Faith, or belief, is one of the key motifs of Mark's whole Gospel, as it was in Jesus' teaching as recorded in all the Gospels.

Belief is the essential prerequisite for healing. It is in response to the paralytic's belief (and that of those who brought him) that Jesus restored him to health (Mark 2:5). When the woman with the flow of blood touched Jesus and was healed, Jesus, surrounded and jostled by the crowd, asked who had touched Him, thus requiring that the woman reveal herself. This caused her great distress, but Jesus wished to underline the fact that it was her faith that had healed/saved her (Mark 5:34). Jesus also assures the father of the boy with the unclean spirit that healing is possible only if he has faith (Mark 9:23).

The Four Faces of Jesus

Belief is also something Jesus urged upon His disciples. The disciples were astonished that Jesus was able to curse a tree and the next day it was dead (Mark 11:12-14, 20-25). Jesus told His disciples to have faith. Whatever they asked for, they would receive, if only they had belief/faith (Mark 11:24).

Disciples need faith, but it can be ambiguous faith. The cry of the demon-possessed boy's father is the cry of the faithful in Mark: " 'Lord, I believe; help my unbelief' " (Mark 9:24). This man has adequate faith, as demonstrated in the healing of his child. But his is an uncertain faith at best. He believes, but at the same time he doubts. He even needs Jesus' help to believe properly. In Mark, the faith of the disciple is the faith of one who believes and yet is also unbelieving. There is no certainty, only faith. The faithful make a choice based on inadequate evidence and partial conviction. They choose to believe in Jesus, and they cry to Him to help their unbelief.

## KINGDOM

### THE NEARNESS OF THE END

From the beginning of His ministry, Jesus proclaimed, " 'The kingdom of God has come [very] near' " (Mark 1:15). The urgency of the nearness of the end of time permeates much of the ministry of Jesus. The kingdom of God is a looming presence. This reality undergirds Jesus' demands for total commitment by His followers. The kingdom is like grain that is growing. It has almost reached the time of harvest. With the appearance of the mature fruit will come the time of the harvest (Mark 4:26-28). Jesus even told His listeners that some of them would live to see the kingdom come in power (Mark 9:1). The coming of the end would be signaled by wars, earthquakes, persecution of Jesus' followers, and the great religious cataclysm foretold by Daniel the prophet. The exact hour may not be known, but it is near (Mark 13:1-36).

### JESUS, THE TURNING POINT OF HISTORY

The central aspect of Jesus' message about the coming kingdom of God is that Jesus Himself is the key actor in the whole drama. It is the persecution of His disciples, the preaching of the gospel concerning Himself, and the religious cataclysm surrounding His rejection that precipitates the end, while the coming of the Son of Man in the clouds signals the end of all things (Mark 13:9-12, 14, 24-27). Jesus had a clear sense of His own destiny and of His central importance in God's dealings with humanity. His death was the ransom for the sins of many (Mark 10:45). Jesus is the central focus of the drama of the salvation of sinful humanity. His life, ministry, death, and resurrection form the single most important event in the history of the world. He is the One who will usher in the kingdom of heaven.

### WHAT DOES IT ALL MEAN?

The Gospel of Mark announces itself to be "The Gospel [good news] about Jesus Christ, Son of God," and indeed it is. This Gospel portrays the man Jesus as the central point in the history of humankind and the world. He is the one crucial player in God's plan to save the world from the destruction brought about by sin. He is truly human, but more than this, He is the Son of God Himself, who has come to earth in order to suffer, die, and rise again on the third day. He is the One who comes demanding full commitment. He comes to each of us, whatever we are doing, and insists, "Come, follow Me." According to Mark's Gospel, our response is the most important decision we will ever make. The response is not based on absolute certainty; it is based on faith—the kind of faith that cries out, " 'Lord, I believe; help my unbelief.' "

---

1. "He returned to Capernaum, and after some days it was known that he was *at home* [*en oikō*]."

2. Actually, like all ancient literature, Mark was meant to be listened to, not read. Those who read, always read aloud. See Paul J. Achtemeier's, "*Onme Verbum Sonat*: The New Testament and the Oral Environment of Late Western Antiquity," *Journal of Biblical Literature* 109 (1990), 3-27, where some of the relevant ancient texts are discussed.

3. The phrase "Son of God" is omitted in some important manuscripts. It's regarded as only a "C" reading in the United Bible Societies' Greek New Testament (a reading they think is original but cannot be sure). If it is not original in Mark

The Four Faces of Jesus

1:1, the concept is still introduced very early in the Gospel (Mark 1:11).

4. See chapter 10.

5. The KJV consistently translates *didaskalos* as "master" throughout Mark and for most of the other occurrences of the word. The verb "to teach" is *didaskō*, and "teacher," not "master," is a better translation of *didaskalos*.

6. Again, the KJV obscures this by translating the word *rabbi* as "master."

7. Chapter 11.

Part 3

# THE GOSPEL OF LUKE

# CHAPTER THIRTEEN

# What Is Different About Luke?

In chapter 1 we decided that the themes in the material unique to Matthew provided the best indication of the interests of the writer and his community. In other words, these themes provided the most direct route to Matthew's perspective on Jesus. The same is true of Luke's Gospel. More than anything else, the material unique to Luke shows the particular viewpoint of the Gospel. So, in this chapter we will examine this unique material to discover its themes. Later chapters will take up these themes and explore them in more detail.

## PROMINENT THEMES IN LUKE'S INTRODUCTION OF JESUS THAT ARE DEVELOPED LATER IN THE GOSPEL OF LUKE AND IN THE BOOK OF ACTS

The beginning of any written work shapes the readers' expectations of what is to follow. The care with which Luke has chosen the material in his introductory chapters shows in fact that nothing in the first two chapters finds a parallel in the other Gospels. One would expect, therefore, that these two chapters would introduce many of the distinctive themes to be taken up later in the Gospel, and such is the case.

*First, it is noteworthy that the main participants in the incidents de-*

*scribed in Luke 1 and 2 are relatively humble people.* Zechariah and Elizabeth (Luke 1:5), the parents of John the Baptist, are but a poor country
priest and his wife. Further, the coming Messiah is announced to shepherds working in the fields (Luke 2:8-20). These shepherds form a contrast to the Magi who come seeking Jesus in the first chapters of Matthew's
Gospel. The Magi come from a distant country seeking the One who is
to be king of the Jews (Matt. 2:1, 2). Their easy access to the court of
King Herod (Matt. 2:1-12) reveals their social status. The social status of
shepherds, featured by Luke, is much different. Not only did they have
no access to the court of the king, they were regarded with some suspi-
cion by even humble town-dwellers.

The other people in Luke 1, 2 are also of humble origins. Simon is
described as a righteous and devout man who lived in Jerusalem, but he
does not appear to have had any real status in the temple (Luke 2:25).
Likewise, the prophetess, Anna, an eighty-four-year-old widow, had little
status (Luke 2:36-38). In all these cases, Luke places the infant Jesus among
the common people, the kind He will associate with in His ministry.

The genealogy of Luke 3:23-38 further emphasizes this point. This
genealogy shows unexpected differences from that given by Matthew,
especially in the generations listed in Luke 3:28-30. The parallel section
of the genealogy, given in Matthew 1:7-11, traces Jesus' line through the
royal house of Judah. By and large, the ancestors listed in Matthew 1:7-
11 are kings. By way of contrast, Luke 3:28-30 lists ancestors who are
commoners.

Jesus' interest in the poor and outcast of society is a theme that permeates the rest of Luke's Gospel and shows up in the material unique to
Luke after chapter 2. No one could represent outcasts more clearly than
the ten lepers that Jesus healed (17:11-19). And while he was not poor,
the tax collector, Zacchaeus, was certainly despised (19:1-10). Even the
instructions Jesus gave in Luke 14:7-14 when He was invited to a feast
has a bearing on the Christian's relationship to the poor and outcast. The
poor should be invited to feasts, rather than those who can afford to
invite their hosts in return (vv. 12-14). The various women who are featured in six of the incidents unique to Luke likewise represent those who

are powerless, which leads us to a second theme.

*This second theme, introduced in Luke 1, 2 and taken up in the rest of the Gospel, is the attitude of Jesus toward women and their place in early Christianity.* The attention given to the activities of women in Luke 1, 2 may not strike the modern reader with quite the force with which it would have struck the ancient reader. Ancient literature was generally written by men and dealt almost exclusively with the male concerns of the time—business contracts, war, history, politics, and philosophy. Yet, right at the beginning of Luke's Gospel, a great deal of space is devoted to a conversation between two women, Elizabeth and Mary. And moreover, it is a conversation reflecting these women's concerns and interests regarding God's actions on behalf of His people.

Although the other Gospels also reveal that Jesus' attitude toward women was atypical of the ancient world, this is clearly of special interest to Luke. The material unique to Luke contains no fewer that six major incidents involving women. In addition to the visit of Mary to Elizabeth (1:39-56), we have the raising of the widow's son (7:11-17), the sinful woman forgiven (7:36-50), the comment concerning the women that follow Jesus (8:1-3), the healing of the crippled woman on the Sabbath (13:10-19), and the description of the reaction of the women near the time of the crucifixion (23:27-31). Further attention will be given to these passages in the next chapter.

*A third theme of Luke 1, 2 that is taken up later in both the Gospel and in the book of Acts is the role of law in the Christian community.* The first two chapters of Luke mention matters relating to the observance of the law no less than seven times.[1] For example, Zechariah and Elizabeth are described as righteous because they walk in all the commandments and righteous requirements of the law (1:6). Both John the Baptist and Jesus are circumcised eight days after they are born, and the circumcision of Jesus is specifically said to be carried out according to the law of Moses (1:59; 2:21, 22). In the light of the later debate about circumcision recorded in Acts[2] (the companion volume to the Gospel of Luke), it is no doubt significant that only Luke records that Jesus and John were circumcised. Every male Jew was circumcised, of course, so this is not previously unknown information. Nevertheless, Luke stresses this fact and affirms that Jesus' parents offered the sacrifices as prescribed by the law (Luke 2:24).

The rest of Luke's Gospel portrays Jesus as One who both observed the law and encouraged others to do so. He customarily attended the synagogue on the Sabbath (Luke 4:16; cf. 4:31) and urged those He healed to seek purification as prescribed in the law (Luke 5:14). Furthermore, in the book of Acts, the relationship between Gentile Christians and the law emerges as a real issue in the development of the church.

*A fourth theme, an interest in the Holy Spirit, is also shared between the Gospel of Luke and the book of Acts.* The Spirit is mentioned in Luke 1:17, 47, 80; 2:27, 40. Although the number of references to the Spirit drops off in the rest of the Gospel, there are places the Spirit is mentioned in Luke but not in the parallel passage in the other Gospels (Luke 10:21; cf. Matt. 11:25). In the book of Acts, moreover, the Spirit is given great prominence. The activity of the church begins after the dramatic giving of the Spirit on the day of Pentecost (Acts 2), and thereafter the message of Christianity spreads throughout and beyond the Roman Empire under the direct guidance and intervention of the Spirit (Acts 8:39; 13:2; 19:21).

*A fifth theme, related to the interest in the Holy Spirit, is the presence of prophecy and the activity of prophets.* In Luke 1, 2 Mary (1:46-55), Zechariah (1:67-79), and Simon (2:29-35) all give extended prophecies. Likewise, prophets are active at several key places in the book of Acts (Acts 11:27-30; 13:1; 21:9-11).

## THE PARABLES UNIQUE TO LUKE

Aside from Luke 1, 2 and the book of Acts, the bulk of the material unique to Luke consists of parables. These include the parable of the good Samaritan (10:25-37) and the parables of the lost coin (15:8-11) and the lost son (15:11-32), which stress the love of God for sinners and our obligation to them. Three of the unique parables deal with prayer: the parable of the friend at midnight (11:5-8), the parable of the widow and the judge (18:1-8), and the parable of the Pharisee and the tax collector (18:9-14). Another parable, the parable of the rich fool (12:13-21), deals with the proper use in this life of God's blessings. The parable of the dishonest steward (16:1-13) may have a similar theme, although the meaning of this parable is still debated by commentators. Finally, the parable of the rich man and Lazarus (16:19-31) deals with the role of miracles as a basis for belief and practice.

## THE HISTORY

The book of Acts is actually the second part of Luke's Gospel, although in English Bibles it is separated from the Gospel of Luke by the fourth Gospel. The opening verses of both Luke and Acts show that the two books are related. Both are addressed to Theophilus (cf. Luke 1:3 and Acts 1:1). Thus Luke and Acts actually form two volumes of one work, even though each would have been written on a separate scroll.[3]

Luke is unique as the only Gospel to include a history of the early church. It is Luke's Gospel that gives us an awareness of the continuation of Jesus' work and some knowledge of the growth and struggles of the earliest Christian groups. For Luke, the church continues the work of Jesus and is the sphere of God's activity on earth. One might even say that the Gospel of Luke is a record of the earthly Jesus, while the book of Acts is the record of the risen Jesus working through His followers on earth, guiding them by means of the Holy Spirit.

Acts traces the crucial transition of the early Christian community as it develops from a Jewish sect into a universal religion. This transition was initiated by the Holy Spirit and is attributable to such missionaries as Paul, who receives most attention in the last half of Acts.

The pattern of Acts, in which the gospel is first preached to the Jews, rejected, and then preached to the Gentiles (13:45, 46; 17:1-5; 18:5, 6), finds its roots in Luke's Gospel. The Gospel portrays Jesus as the Messiah of the Jews, who came to His people but was rejected by them. In the first chapter of the Gospel, the pregnant Mary's exultant comments speak of God helping "his servant Israel . . . according to the promise he made to our ancestors, to Abraham and to his descendants forever" (1:54, 55). The prophecy of Zechariah (1:67-79) clearly places Jesus within God's relationship to

*Jews.* It speaks in terms of both the house of David (v. 69) and the oath God swore to Abraham (v. 73). The stress on the observance of the law by Elizabeth and Zechariah, John the Baptist, and Jesus Himself dramatically portrays the Jewish roots of Jesus and His movement. As does Matthew 10:5-15, Luke 9:1-6 shows Jesus sending out His twelve disciples to preach concerning the kingdom of God, although Luke does not include the instruction of Matthew 10:5, 6, restricting the disciples to Jews and excluding even Samaritans.

But unique to Luke is the sending out of the seventy-two disciples, in Luke 10:1-12, 17-20. Between their being sent and their return, Jesus pronounces curses on the Jewish towns of Chorazin and Capernaum. Many commentators see in the extension of the number of those sent out from twelve to seventy-two as the beginning of the universalism of the Gospel, especially since several ancient sources identify seventy-two nations in the world. Luke 13:1-9 is probably also linked to this theme. The landowner had come to a fig tree three years in succession seeking fruit. If it proved still to be barren after one more year, it was to be cut down. So the favored nation of the Jews would be given one more year of grace, before being cut off. The crucifixion was the ultimate rejection of Jesus by the leaders of the nation. Even so, Acts shows that the message of salvation was taken first to the Jews and only offered to the Gentiles after the Jews rejected it.

In sum, Luke has a theology of history to share that is unique to his Gospel.

## LUKE 9:51-56 AND THE STRUCTURE OF LUKE

Luke 9:51-56 marks a turning point in the Gospel. This passage, unique to Luke, says that Jesus "set his face to go to Jerusalem" (v. 51). From this point in the Gospel, Jesus is portrayed as continuously moving in the direction of Jerusalem to meet His fate there. This has the effect of making all of Luke 9:51–21:38 part of the passion narrative as well as the last few chapters of the Gospel. As with both Matthew and Mark, the Cross is the central focus of Luke's whole Gospel, and the way that events are structured after 9:51 make this even more prominent in Luke. In other words, for Luke, as for Mark and Matthew, Jesus can be understood only in the light of His death and resurrection. This perspective dominates the whole Gospel.

### IMPLICATIONS FOR FUTURE CHAPTERS

The themes that have emerged from the material unique to Luke show a distinctive profile. So in our pursuit of Luke's perspective of Jesus, we should investigate these themes further. Thus, future chapters will deal with such things as Luke's portrayal of Jesus' relationship to women, the parables relating to prayer, and the parables portraying the love of God for sinners and the outcast. The last two chapters will consider the Last Supper and the Crucifixion as portrayed by Luke. These events are prominent in both Matthew and Mark as well, but we have not yet examined them in detail—and the passion narrative of Luke contains some interesting features. It will be instructive also to compare Luke's portrayal of Jesus' passion with that of John, which we will do in part 5.

---

1. Luke 1:6, 59; 2:21, 22, 23, 24, 41, 42.
2. Acts 15.
3. Matthew, Luke, John, Acts, and Romans are all approximately the same length, and there is a good reason for this. They are of a length suitable for writing on a standard-sized scroll.

CHAPTER FOURTEEN

# Women in Luke

## THE STATUS OF WOMEN IN FIRST-CENTURY PALESTINE

It becomes apparent just how atypical Jesus' attitude toward women was when that attitude is compared with what is known about first-century Jewish society. First-century Palestine was predominantly rural. Jesus grew up and spent most of His public ministry in the small towns of Galilee. These villages consisted of stone structures built around inter-locking courtyards, bisected by narrow roads. Typically, an extended family occupied the structures around one courtyard. In such households, tra-ditional family structures predominated, which, in fact, made good sense in most ways. The considerable work involved in purchasing, preparing, and cooking food; caring for children; clothing the family; and engaging in the other activities necessary to running a household dominated the time and energies of the women in the house. Men were occupied in working the fields or gaining a livelihood from a trade such as carpentry or an occupation such as fishing. The two roles—that of men and women—complemented each other well, and both were essential to the continued survival of the family. As far as it is possible to tell, few women questioned the way they spent their lives, even though some aspects of that society strike modern readers as oppressive toward women.

One would have to describe first-century Jewish society as male dominated. Women were excluded from the priesthood and from government leadership. By custom, they moved from the authority of their father to the authority of their husband when they married. Most women were married when very young, even prepubescent, although men were recommended to marry between eighteen and twenty.[1] Only the husband had the right of divorce, and control of a woman's dowry passed into the hands of her husband upon marriage. Married women wore a veil. The only adult women who did not wear veils were those who were not under the authority of a man, in other words, widows or prostitutes!

It is not to be expected, however, that women adopted a subservient role or that they did not have well-defined rights. For example, though the husband had the right to divorce, he was required to return his ex-wife's dowry if he did so. At marriage the two families exchanged expensive gifts, which were normally listed in the marriage contract. Gifts to the family of the bride from the family of the husband, called the bride price, were not returnable on divorce, except under exceptional circumstances. But the dowry was. Because these gifts were as lavish as each family could afford, it was common for much of the worth of the household to be tied up in the woman's dowry. Since it would impoverish most husbands to have to return their wife's dowry, this is one factor that made divorce very uncommon. Furthermore, women were able to find ways to communicate their attitudes and needs on a variety of matters to their husbands, despite the *theory* that they should be subservient to their wills. Marriage then, as now, was based around a relationship—a two-way affair. Genuine love and respect in marriage is not uncommon today, nor was it unknown in the days of arranged marriages.

Two aspects of first-century expectations regarding women are of particular importance to the stories of the New Testament. First, public interaction between men and women was not encouraged, though it did take place. In particular, so far as possible, unmarried women were kept from interacting with men.[2] This meant that women ate meals only with their immediate family and would normally be absent throughout a meal that involved guests. Of course, completely secluding a married woman from contact with others was possible only for the very wealthy who had servants to go to the market and care for the variety of tasks necessary for running a household. Such was not the case in the villages where Jesus grew up and spent most of His ministry. The way the houses were built and the great variety of tasks that needed to be done ensured that women were closely integrated into everything that happened in the village. But even in these villages, women of good repute would be very reticent in their dealings with males not of their household.

Second, while sons were expected to learn Torah (the law), there was no parallel requirement to educate daughters. In practice, this meant that most women were uneducated. Indeed, if the later rabbinic writings are any guide to attitudes in the first century, there was some antagonism to the idea that daughters should be educated. The first-century Rabbi Eliezer reportedly said, "If any man teach his daughter Torah it is as though he taught her lechery."[3] Generally speaking, it would have taken a strong personality to overcome this kind of resistance to teaching women the law, but there are a few examples of such individuals in the rabbinic literature. In particular, the opinions of Beruria, a woman, are cited at times, and on occasion her opinion prevails against her male counterparts. Little is known of this woman, except that she was the daughter of a rabbi and no doubt took part in the discussions between her father and his disciples as she grew to womanhood.

Such is the picture of the status of women in the first-century Palestine Jesus knew. In other parts of the Roman Empire, the role of women was different. Roman matrons had the right to initiate divorce on their own behalf, and those who had been left wealthy by deceased husbands or fathers had considerable freedom of action in business. They also attended theaters, races, circuses, and participated in meals where other guests were present. Scenes of meals, painted on walls and carved into funerary statues from the earliest period of the Roman Empire, portray women at feasts seated on stools, but by the first century they also reclined at tables like the men.

The role of women in Greek society was generally less open. The women of Sparta had been more active in their society, but later Greek culture was influenced by Athens, where women were kept away from public activities such as meals with guests. These restrictions broke down somewhat over time, but the basic attitudes remained.

Because Palestine was under Roman control, wealthy families in the major cities were probably more influenced by Roman customs than Greek. But Jesus' life and ministry did not take place in such circles. The background against which we should compare His attitudes is that of semirural Galilean peasant culture. In the rest of the chapter we will consider those passages unique to Luke that focus on Jesus' relationship to women, and we will discover that, by the standards of His time, Jesus was remarkable in His attitudes.

### JESUS: THE TEACHER OF WOMEN (LUKE 10:38-42)

Several aspects of Jesus' visit to the home of Mary and Martha (Luke 10:38-42) would have seemed unusual in first-century Palestine and reveal aspects of its culture not commonly seen in other sources. First, the meal is spent with two women, who appear to have initiated the invitation. Apart from Jesus, no men are mentioned in the entire incident.[4] That wealthy women would be in a position to assist Jesus is no surprise, even in that culture. Indeed, one passage unique to Luke specifically mentions the names of several women who provided for Jesus and His disciples out of their resources (8:1-3). This meal with Mary and Martha was, no doubt, an example of the kind of assistance that could be offered. So while the women's hospitality is unusual, it was not extraordinary.

But what is extraordinary is the role taken by Mary. She sits at the feet of Jesus with the disciples. In other words, she is taking the part of a disciple. More than that, Jesus gives her specific commendation for joining what was normally an exclusively male occasion. He defends her against her sister, saying that in abandoning the typical female role of meal preparation, Mary had actually chosen the better course (v. 42). What she desired should not be taken from her. In other words, Jesus was not only prepared to teach women in the same way He taught men, He actively encouraged their participation. Considering the culture of the time, this was indeed remarkable.

# The Four Faces of Jesus

### JESUS AS A CHAMPION OF WOMEN WITH A BAD REPUTATION (LUKE 7:36-50)

By any standard, the action of the "sinful" woman described in Luke 7:36-50 is remarkable, particularly considering the setting. Jesus had been invited to the house of a "certain Pharisee" (v. 36). This is all we are told about the host of the feast—he was a Pharisee. But just knowing that much reveals quite a bit about him. The Pharisees were very scrupulous about the law, especially the laws regarding cleanness and uncleanness. Even today, many Orthodox Jews do not allow an unknown woman to touch them, because they would not know if she was in a state of cleanness or uncleanness. In particular, this woman's "sinfulness" would make her unclean. So, from his perspective, the Pharisee was quite right to question why Jesus allowed Himself to be touched by such a woman (v. 39).

In normal circumstances, the only women who would be present at a meal involving male guests would be women of ill repute. The woman in Luke 7:36-50 is described as a "sinner" and no doubt fit the description of "a woman of ill repute." The likelihood of such a woman being invited to the house of a Pharisee is near zero. Her presence was a clear break with social convention, and so was her subsequent behavior. She stood weeping copiously over Jesus' feet and wiped them with her hair. Letting her hair down in public was yet another scandalous breach of social convention. A woman's hair was regarded as a significant aspect of her sexual attractiveness, which was one of the reasons that married women were to wear a veil in public. Any first-century Palestinian reader would be sensitive to the erotic aspects of this situation. The weeping woman then went on to anoint Jesus' feet with perfume. Not only would her presence be painfully obvious because of her weeping, but the odor of the perfume would impose its presence on all those eating. Again, from his perspective, it is no wonder that the Pharisee criticized Jesus' acceptance of the woman's ministry.

Jesus, though, strongly defended the woman. He began by telling the host a parable of two debtors who owe money to a money-lender, one 500 denarii, one 50 denarii. Neither could afford to pay, both were "forgiven."⁵ "Which one," Jesus then asked, "will love the more?"

The Pharisee replied, "The one who was forgiven more" (Luke 7:42, 43). Jesus told His host that because the woman had been forgiven much she therefore loved much. This was obvious in her behavior when compared with the Pharisee's behavior as a host: "When I came into your house you did not give me water for my feet, but she has wet my feet with her tears and wiped them with her hair. You did not kiss me, but she has not stopped kissing my feet from the moment she arrived" (vv. 44, 45). It was customary for a host to provide water to wash the feet of a guest,⁶ and the greeting of the Pharisee had clearly been quite distant. Jesus suggested that the contrast between the actions of the sinful woman and the self-righteous Pharisee revealed that the woman had been forgiven much, while the Pharisee had been forgiven little. The unstated implication was that the Pharisee might not have been forgiven at all!

Jesus finished by telling the woman that she was forgiven because of her faith. Those who heard Him began to debate among themselves the implications of Jesus' taking upon Himself the right to forgive sins. The strong message in this passage is that Jesus accepts even those who, like this particular woman, are clearly identified as sinners.

## JESUS' EMPATHY WITH WOMEN

Several of the accounts in the material unique to Luke show Jesus' empathy with women in unfortunate circumstances. These include the two healings found in Luke 7:11-17 and 13:10-19. In the first occasion, Jesus meets a funeral procession just leaving the small village of Nain. In the coffin is the only son of a widow. These bare details spell out a great personal tragedy. Not only has the woman had to survive the loss of status and emotional trauma of earlier losing her husband, she now has lost her only son, her best hope of future economic support. It was not for nothing that widows and orphans were portrayed so often by the Old Testament prophets as the most vulnerable members of society. The lot of this widow was indeed unfortunate. As described in Luke 7:13, when Jesus saw the funeral procession, He was deeply moved with compassion. He stopped the procession, raised the dead boy to life, and restored him to his mother.

The second healing involved a woman who was continuously bent over because she could not stand fully upright. Now, these are not the only times Jesus healed women (see Mark 1:30; 5:21-43, which are paralleled by Luke 4:38, 39; 8:40-56). But these two cases increase the percentage of women among those Luke reports as healed by Jesus. In these two cases, both of the women were particularly disadvantaged, and both cases show Jesus' compassion toward their plight.

A further example of Jesus' compassion to women in unfortunate circumstances is found in Luke 23:27-31. Like most of the passages we are considering in this chapter, these verses are unique to Luke's Gospel. They describe a scene from the last hours of Jesus' life as He was making His way toward the place where He would be crucified. Weakened from His beating, he could not carry the crossbeam of His cross by Himself. Simon of Cyrene carried it for Him, walking behind Jesus. We cannot know what Jesus was thinking at that time, but most of the time His thoughts must have been concentrated on the coming ordeal. Suddenly He stopped to speak to some women who were in the crowd. They were weeping for Jesus, and He urged them to weep, not for Him but rather for themselves, because of the terrible times that awaited them in the future.

This showed a remarkable empathy on the part of Jesus. He Himself was in the midst of a terribly painful execution. Yet at that time He had sufficient compassion to give attention to the future plight of those weeping for Him in His time of need. These very women, Jesus said, would be faced with terrible ordeals in the future. Indeed, this came true within the lifetime of many of them, when Jerusalem experienced all the horrors of a long siege as the Romans came to retake the city in A.D. 70. Jesus linked His suffering and the future suffering to be visited on the city. But He did not express feelings of pleasure at the prospect of future revenge, only real sympathy for the future fate of the women in the city.

### JESUS' ATTITUDE TO WOMEN AS PORTRAYED BY LUKE

The incidents discussed in this chapter, together with the visit of Mary to Elizabeth (Luke 1:39-56), which we examined in the previous chapter, comprise the occasions involving women in the material unique to Luke. They show Jesus' attitude to women to have been remarkable when compared to the background of His times. He accepted invitations to their houses. He allowed sinful women to approach and touch Him. He was moved with sympathy for women's plight when left bereaved or facing an uncertain future. He even accepted women as part of His inner circle of disciples. Some of these attitudes transferred themselves to the early church, where we find women taking prominent leadership roles. For example, Phoebe, the deacon of the church at Cenchreae, near Corinth (Rom. 16:1). Women took part in worship services, although there does seem to have been some abuse of this freedom (1 Cor. 11:2-16). There were women prophets among the early Christian prophets (Acts 21:9). It was even possible to contemplate the extraordinarily revolutionary concept that in Christ there was neither Jew or Greek, slave or free, *male or female* (Gal 3:28). Alas, this insight was quickly lost to the church and is being regained only in recent times. The consequences are still being worked out in the experiences of the different denominations. Many of these are in deep debate as to whether or not to allow women to become ministers or priests, and all denominations struggle with the issue of the roles women should take in the church. Perhaps the message of Luke finds particular relevance to these discussions. Jesus was at the forefront of transforming the role of women in His society. He reached out to include women in His innermost circle of disciples and defended their right to belong there. Modern Christians cannot but be challenged by His example.

---

1. *Aboth*, 5:21; *Kidd*, 29b. Several references to married women assume they are prepubescent: *Nidd*, 1.4; 5.4; 10.1, 76b; *Ket*, 6a-b. One of the requirements Josephus notes of the Essenes was that sexual activity commence only after the new wife has had at least three menstrual periods, to show she is capable of childbearing [*War*, 2.161 (13)].
2. A very famous passage in *Ecclesiasticus* reads: "Keep a close watch over a headstrong daughter, or she may give your enemies cause to gloat, making you the talk of the town and a byword among the people, and shaming you in the eyes of the world. Do not let her display her beauty to any man, or gossip in the women's

quarters" (42:11, 12, NEB).

3. *Sotah,* 3, 4.

4. No reference to Lazarus, brother of Mary and Martha mentioned in John 11:1, is found anywhere in Luke.

5. The Greek word *aphiēmi,* often translated as "forgive," can be used in a technical sense to mean "forgive" a debt. The word is used consistently through this passage, first in connection with "forgiving" the debt and then in connection with "forgiving" sins. This parallel is lost somewhat in the translation into English.

6. This is evident from John 13:1-11. In this incident each disciple is reluctant to take the role of a servant and wash the feet of the others but clearly expected that such should take place.

CHAPTER FIFTEEN

# Parables About Prayer

**MY FIRSTHAND EXPERIENCE OF EVERY PREACHER'S NIGHTMARE, OR HOW I LEARNED THAT JESUS WAS A GREAT TEACHER**

My first real experience as featured speaker brought with it both the thrill of holding a difficult audience spellbound and every preacher's nightmare—all in one weekend. It happened like this.

The things I had been doing in my local church when I was about eighteen or nineteen years of age must have caught the eye of one of the leaders of the Senior Pathfinders Adventure Club (SPAC). SPAC was composed of young people between fifteen and twenty who went out doing things such as snow-skiing, white-water canoeing, camping, and hiking. On this particular occasion the group had planned a long weekend devoted to white-water canoeing and wanted me to be the featured speaker. I would be responsible for taking two or three evening worships and the sermon in an informal church service.

Now this was very different from the kind of events I had been involved in up to this time. But with the supreme arrogance of the inexperienced, I was rather pleased to be asked and sat down to prepare a series of top-quality worships. I planned the series around topics that appealed to me but gave a bit of extra thought to the topic of the church service.

## The Four Faces of Jesus

For that meeting, I decided to talk on what must be at the heart of every Christian's experience—prayer.

Well, among the first things I experienced that weekend was white-water canoeing, and I had a great day learning to stay in the boat! The rain, which had started early in the day, stopped, and we all began to dry out toward the end of the day. There was a big fire, and the evening worship time was scheduled after the meal. We were all feeling nicely relaxed after a day of vigorous activity, and the mood around the fire was mellow as I stood up to take the evening worship. With youth groups there is no doubt about whether or not you have succeeded in holding the listeners' attention, and the worship that night was particularly well received. Because of this, I felt good about how the sermon would go the next day. Lack of self-confidence was not the cause of what later happened!

The next morning, we found a nice grassy slope that formed a natural amphitheater facing a quieter section of the river on which we had been canoeing the previous day. All the conditions were just right. The sun was shining in a blue sky, and the mild warmth was pleasant after the cold of the previous day. Insects were buzzing, the sounds of the river flowing past were muted, and everybody was prepared to listen as I stood up to speak.

I had thought about prayer quite a bit as I prepared my talk, and I had built the sermon around the issues that concern anyone who tries to pursue an active prayer life: Why pray when God knows all about us anyway? What do we do if we don't feel our prayers are going any farther than the roof? How do we find a suitable time to pray in a busy schedule? How can we keep prayer from becoming an empty ritual in which we recite the same words every day? I thought these were interesting issues and was happily working through them.

Because I was a very inexperienced public speaker at that time, it took me awhile to pick up what was happening with my listeners. But eventually it began to seep into my subconscious as I continued through my sermon. A few of those listening, mainly the older adults who had come along, were interested in what I was talking about, but most of the senior youth were frankly bored! Looking at them with growing alarm, I could see that their minds were busy elsewhere. Some were looking at the river; others were making patterns with bits of grass; others had laid back and were clearly dozing! Further experience has taught me to be glad that such a group wasn't actively talking while I preached, but at the time I was horrified. There can be few things worse for a beginning preacher than to realize that the carefully prepared sermon isn't working. It's acutely embarrassing. But just as a train locomotive starts at one end of a set of tracks and continues right to their end, once beginning preachers have started at the commencement of the sermon, they have to keep going till they have finished it. So here I was, in the middle of a boring sermon, desperate to bring it to an end. There are few worse feelings than knowing that what you are doing is just not working, but having to continue anyway! It may not the be the preacher's *worst* nightmare, but it has to come close.

Subsequent meetings that weekend went well, but obviously I had the wrong approach to my sermon on prayer. On later occasions, different approaches to this topic didn't seem to work either. It was only when I started working through what Jesus said about prayer that I was able to hold the attention of an audience. There is something interesting, something downright intriguing, about Jesus' approach to the topic of prayer. Luke's unique material contains no less than three parables in which Jesus addresses the topic—the friend at midnight, the widow and the judge, and the tax collector and the Pharisee. So let's turn to these parables and Jesus' teaching on the subject of prayer.

### THE FRIEND AT MIDNIGHT (LUKE 11:1-13)

The parable of the friend at midnight recounts the story of a single traveler who arrives at a house in a village in the middle of the night. His host is under strong social obligation to feed him, but he is out of bread, so he goes to borrow some from a friend. What happens at this second house gives us a fascinating glimpse into the day-to-day village life of the time. With what has already been said about the layout of such villages,[1] our imagination can re-create this scene for us.

The village is composed of interlocking households, each centered

143

on a small courtyard surrounded by small rooms. The walls separating the rooms and the houses are made of rough stones; their structure, together with their proximity and the population density, means that every household is constantly aware of the sounds emanating from their neighbor's house.

As evening fell on this particular day, the village had settled down for the night in its customary manner. The meals were eaten, the animals gathered inside the courtyard, and the outside gate was barred. With the passing of time, the sounds of the day became quieter. The children slowly drifted off to sleep. Finally, even the adult conversation became sluggish, and stillness took over the whole village. By the middle of the night, nothing was heard but the sounds of people and animals stirring in their sleep.

Suddenly there was the sound of somebody tapping on a closed shutter. A sleepy voice hissed from inside the room, "Who's there?"

"It's me," was the reply, "let me in. A friend has arrived, and I need three loaves of bread."

The reply in Luke 11:7 is very revealing. "Don't bother me. The door is already shut, and my children are with me in bed. It is not possible for me to help you."

Typically, all the family members would share the one bed. One can sympathize with the householder. If he succeeds in getting out of bed without arousing even one of the children, it's quite likely he will step on a chicken while getting to the outside gate. Everybody will awaken, and the noise will rouse the neighbors, and soon there will be an uproar! No wonder he wants to stay in bed!

" 'I tell you,' " says Jesus, " 'that even if he will not get up to give him anything because he is his friend, because of his friend's importunity he will get up and give him whatever he needs. And I tell you, Ask and it will be given to you, seek and you will find, knock and it will be opened to you. For all who ask receive, and all who seek will find, and it will be opened to the one who knocks. Which of you fathers, if your son asks for a fish, will instead of a fish give him a snake? And if he asks for an egg will give him a scorpion? Therefore, if you who are evil know how to give good gifts to your children, how much more will your heavenly Father give the Holy Spirit to those who ask him?' " (Luke 11:8-13).

Now, this is pretty scary stuff. How could Jesus use such an easily misunderstood parable? Is God like the lazy friend, reluctant to get out of bed to do His duty? Do we have to pester God until He finally does what He should?

No. In fact, the parable is saying just the opposite. Jesus puts a good deal of trust in the ability of His hearers to work out the somewhat complicated message of this parable. It is a parable of the *contrast* between God and the lazy friend in bed. God is good and is actively wanting to become involved in helping those who seek Him. In contrast, the friend in bed is lazy and wishes to avoid the strong obligation he has to provide a meal for his friend's guest. But even the lazy friend will get out of bed to do what is right. The key words of the parable are " *'How much more'* " (v. 13). We, who are evil, know how to give good gifts to our children; *how much more* will our heavenly Father give us good gifts, especially the gift of the Spirit (note the special interest of Luke again in the Spirit revealing Himself). So, God is anxious to give us good things. All we have to do is ask. The parable of the widow and the unjust judge makes a similar point.

### THE WIDOW AND THE UNJUST JUDGE (LUKE 18:1-8)

The widow in this parable had nothing but the rightness of her cause to bring before the judge. She had no money and no influence, and the judge neither feared God nor respected man (vv. 2, 4). Having no money, she could not bribe the unjust judge. Having no influence made it difficult, as she was most likely petitioning for a judgment against one who belonged to the judge's circle of acquaintances. The judge himself did not appear to have any points on which she could appeal to him. If he had feared God, she could have appealed to his sense of duty in rendering God's judgments (Deut. 1:17; 16:18-20). If he had feared men, she could have pursued him through the marketplace, demanding justice, and he would have been quickly shamed into settling her case. No, she could not gain justice in any of these ways. She could only keep coming

145

back. The judge reasons thusly: " 'She will eventually wear me down by continually coming. It would be better to give judgment in her favor quickly, so it doesn't seem as though I've given in just because she is persistent' " (v. 5).

As with the parable of the friend at midnight, Jesus makes a considerable demand on the thought processes of His listeners. It would be all too easy to misunderstand the comparison between God and the unjust judge that is made by this parable. Does God's apparent slowness to deal with injustice mean that He is unjust like the judge? Is the way to overcome this apparent reluctance of God to be so persistent that He finally gives in and provides what we want?

In no way! Like the previous parable, this is a parable of the *contrast* between God and humans. Even an unjust judge will give the helpless widow justice if he is asked often enough. *How much more* will God, the just Judge, do so for those who cry to Him for justice!

This parable is no less than a promise of God's immediate activity in dealing with the world's injustice. God is concerned about injustice. If only we ask, He will do something about it, and readily. Perhaps this is the meaning of the gloomy statement at the end of the parable: " 'Nevertheless, when the Son of Man comes, will he find faith on the earth?' " (v. 8). Perhaps the reason God has not intervened to right injustice is that there has been insufficient faith. Have enough people been seeking Him to intervene?

Nor should we leave this parable before exploring the difference between the concept of judgment presented here (and elsewhere in the Bible) and a common Christian conception of God's judgment. Christians are often ambivalent about God's judgment. Sure, many times we long to see God deal decisively with sin and death. But how confident are we about our place in the judgment? Do we not fear that we will be judged and found wanting? In other words, we picture ourselves as the defendant in the dock.

The longing for judgment expressed in the Bible is different; it is the longing of the plaintiff who has suffered an injustice that will be set right if only the case can go before a fair judge. The widow cannot get her case heard. If justice were done, she would prevail. Likewise, the righteous cry to God that He act against the injustices in the world. If only He would act, then much of the sorrow and injustice would disappear. Jesus' parable tells us that God *will* act and that He will act soon. He is not like an unjust judge who needs to be persuaded. He wants to act, if only He can find faith in His professed followers.

## THE PHARISEE AND THE TAX COLLECTOR (LUKE 18:9-14)

The next parable, the parable of the Pharisee and the tax collector, is also about prayer, although it deals with a different aspect of prayer—its content.

Few tax collectors are popular in any country in the world, either now or in Jesus' day. In fact, any of the tax collection systems used in the Roman provinces was structured in such a way as to encourage its abuse. It appears that tax collectors, for example, were appointed by a bidding process. Candidates bid on how much they agree to raise from a particular area. The one who bid the highest amount would normally get the contract. Let's say that his bid was for twelve talents. If he raised only ten talents, then he would still have to remit twelve talents to the government. But if he raised fourteen talents, he would be able to keep two talents for himself. The system had a built-in reward for those who collected more tax than they should. The successful bidder could then either appoint agents to raise the necessary taxes in his area or hold auctions of his own.

In other cases, local Roman administrators appointed tax collectors and raised taxes with the help of the local soldiers. But here, too, any taxes above what was expected would then go into the pockets of those who collected them. To most people in first-century Palestine, an "honest tax collector" seemed a contradiction in terms. In fact, several times in Luke, Jesus' opponents link "tax collectors and sinners" together in a single phrase, almost as though the two were synonymous (Luke 5:30; 7:34).

The Pharisee in Jesus' parable clearly shared the common prejudice against tax collectors. In his prayer he contrasted himself from "this tax collector." " 'God, I thank you that I am not as the rest of men, robbers, unrighteous, adulterers, or like this tax collector. I fast twice a week, and give a tithe of all that I acquire' " (vv. 11, 12).

That there was merit in the Pharisee no one would deny. Expressed negatively, he had not extorted money or committed sexual indiscretions—not uncommon sins even today! On the positive side, he fasted twice a week and gave tithe, which, strictly speaking, he needn't have. The Old Testament tithe was based on agricultural increase. One-tenth of the increase was dedicated to the upkeep of the temple and the support of the poor (Deut. 12:6, 7, 11, 15-19; 26:12, 13). That the Pharisee paid tithe on all he acquired meant, at the very least, that he gave to the temple one-tenth of any produce he bought for his own food. He would do this because he could not know for sure whether the original farmer had paid tithe on it. If his prayer indicates that he also paid tithe on his earnings from trade, then he would have been truly exceptional in his time.

This parable of Jesus has made such prayers unpopular among Christians, although at times one hears public prayers that are perilously close. But how typical they were of first-century Pharisaism may be judged by the following rabbinic prayer from a slightly later time. Rabbi Nehunia ben Hakaneh used to pray daily on leaving the rabbinical school:

> I give thanks to Thee, O Lord my God, that Thou hast set my portion with those who sit in the Beth ha-Midrash [house of instruction], and Thou hast not set my portion with those who sit in [street] corners, for I rise early and they rise early, but I rise early for words of Torah and they rise early for frivolous talk; I labour and they labour, but I labour and receive a reward and they labor and do not receive a reward; I run and they run, but I run to the life of the future world and they run to the pit of destruction.[2]

The tax collector, on the other hand, prayed a much different prayer. Even though it was customary to look toward heaven when praying, the tax collector would not even raise his eyes from the ground. He prayed a very short, but completely sincere, prayer: " 'God, be merciful to me, a sinner' " (v. 13). Jesus says that the tax collector, rather than the Pharisee, went to his house justified.

What was it about this prayer that made it effective, especially in contrast to what the Pharisee prayed? The difference was that the tax collector had a better idea of his need for forgiveness. The Pharisee, tied up with his confidence in his own merits, had forgotten the essential fact of his own sinfulness. The tax collector came to God fully aware that he was in great need of forgiveness. It was the prayer for forgiveness that was answered. The Pharisee, it appears, prayed only "to himself" (v. 11).[3]

## WHAT MADE JESUS' TEACHING ON PRAYER SO EFFECTIVE?

These parables are, without exception, well received by classes, audiences, and congregations. Clearly, Jesus could make prayer really interesting. What did He do that I should have done?

First, Jesus used a strong story to illustrate what He meant. This does not mean that He ignored important questions. Part of the interest of these parables is the unexpected twist Jesus gives to the whole thing by making a contrast rather than a comparison. Furthermore, the issues that He deals with are very real. Why should we persist in prayer? Why indeed pray at all if God knows our needs? Does the apparent slowness of God's response to calls for justice mean that He does not care? All of these questions are raised by the parables. The point is, though, that they are couched in an extraordinarily interesting way. Jesus had the knack of taking the commonplace events of life and finding a spiritual meaning in them.

Second, Jesus does not give us prepackaged answers. He lets us work the answers out for ourselves. Third, Jesus' message was essentially positive. God's goodness means that He will respond positively to those who ask. He will quickly answer calls for justice. He responds warmly to the sincere repentance of even the worst kind of sinner.

The unpleasant things that happen to us in life can sometimes unexpectedly teach us a great deal. My experimentation with preaching about prayer has shown me the danger of taking an overly intellectual approach to this very practical matter and illustrated to me how effective Jesus really was as a teacher. I like to think that it has also helped me with my selection of sermon materials!

---

1. In chapter 3.
2. *Ber.* 28b. The translation is that of Maurice Simon in *The Babylonian Talmud*, ed. I. Epstein (n.p.: Rebecca Bennet, 1959), 172.
3. This expression no doubt means that the Pharisee prayed aloud. I have taken the liberty of perceiving a nice double entendre in the phrase. Only the prayer of the publican was heard by heaven, not the prayer of the Pharisee.

CHAPTER SIXTEEN

# Parables of the Love of God

## THE DEBT WE OWE TO THE GOSPEL OF LUKE

The good Samaritan and the prodigal son are probably Jesus' best-known parables. Yet without Luke, they would have been lost to us, for Luke is the only Gospel that records them. Together with the two shorter parables from chapter 15—the lost coin and the lost sheep—they provide further evidence of Luke's interest in Jesus' love for sinners and outcasts.

## THE GOOD SAMARITAN (LUKE 10:25-37)

Jesus told the parable of the good Samaritan as a response to a challenging question posed by an expert in the law. In Luke 10:25-29, the lawyer asks Jesus what he needs to do to inherit eternal life. Jesus replies, " 'What is written in the Law? How do you read it?' "

The lawyer's reply shows he has a sophisticated understanding of the law. Instead of replying with a list of things he should and shouldn't do, he answers in terms of motives—an answer, incidentally, that Jesus Himself gave at times (Mark 12:30, 31). According to both the lawyer and Jesus, the whole of the law is summed up in the double duty of loving God completely and one's neighbor as oneself. Jesus commended the

151

lawyer's answer, saying, " 'You have answered correctly. Do this and you will live' " (Luke 10:28).

Modern Christians strongly feel the irony of Jesus' answer. They have been informed by reading Paul's letters to the Romans and Galatians and realize that it is impossible to be saved by keeping the law (Rom. 3:20). One cannot even keep the letter of the law, let alone have the right motivation of love. Our salvation is entirely dependent on God's forgiveness. In response, we give God the obedience of love.

These kinds of insights have been further sharpened in both Protestant and Catholic circles by the debates that surrounded the Protestant and Catholic Reformations. The modern Christian is heir to all these insights and quickly realizes that Jesus' response shows the futility of trying to earn merit with God. How much of this was clear to the lawyer is not made explicit in the text of Luke 10, but he must have felt some dissatisfaction with his ability to act in a totally loving way, because he attempts to "justify" himself by asking, " 'and who is my neighbor?' " (v. 29).

The lawyer's question is indeed the key one. God requires of us that we should love our neighbor as ourselves. But who exactly is that neighbor? Clearly, a neighbor includes more than just those in our immediate family, but how many more? Does it include only our coreligionists? Might it include only all those of our own race? This last possibility is certainly contemplated in the laws of the Old Testament. Our "brother" could include those of the nations whom we have not even met (Deut. 22:1-4). It is unlikely, though, that any in Jesus' audience would have thought that the term *neighbor* included anyone from outside the Jewish nation.

In reply to the question " 'Who is my neighbor?' " Jesus tells a parable about someone who is assaulted by robbers, beaten, stripped of his clothes and possessions, and left for dead at the side of the road.

In most places today, it would be rare for robbery victims to lose the clothes that they wear. In first-century Palestine, though, clothes were a valuable commodity. Most people would not own more than one change of clothes, if that. The very poor would be dressed in rags. This meant that clothes were well worth stealing.

Most of the route between Jerusalem and Jericho passes through hills that are normally in a desert condition. In these kinds of hot and dry regions, the victim of the robbery would quickly become dehydrated and delirious. Without his clothes, the wounded man would be in double jeopardy. With no help, the victim of the robbery would surely die.

In the parable, a priest happens to be traveling on that road, and when he saw the victim, he passed by, going to the other side of the path to do so. The priest's actions would have occasioned censure, but not surprise, in Jesus' listeners. Just as most drivers won't pick up hitchhikers today (for many good reasons), so there would be any number of reasons for the priest not wanting to stop to help the victim. For example, a priest would be concerned about purity. Blood would make him unclean and unfit for temple duty. Even if he was not serving in the temple in the immediate future, contact with blood would be a great inconvenience; priests were required to be very concerned about purity, even in everyday activities. If he became unclean, he would have to go through a ritual of cleansing. Not only that, the victim himself showed that there was very real danger present at that very spot, so a smart traveler would not wish to delay and also become a victim. Furthermore, the priest may well have wanted to avoid becoming involved in what might be a feud. So, when he saw the victim, he passed by and did not stop to help.

The next traveler happens to be a Levite. Like the priest, he did not stop either—for most of the same reasons. Because his position also brought him into close contact with the temple, the Levite, too, would have been concerned about personal purity. Nevertheless, perhaps he would stop to help? No. In the parable, the Levite likewise passed by the wounded man without stopping.

It was a hated Samaritan who stopped to offer assistance. There is something about hatreds based on religion that gives them an added intensity. Two different groups in society may have good economic or social reasons to dislike each other, but when religion is added, the hatred seems to take on an extra depth of bitterness. This was the case with the long-standing tension between Samaritans and Jews in the first century. This animosity went back to the time of the Jews' return from Babylonian exile. The "pure Jews," as they styled themselves, found themselves in conflict with the "people of the land," of whom the Samaritans were one group. The Samaritans had as their holy book, the books of the law, which form the first five books of our Old Testament. But their overtures were rejected by the returning Jews, and as a consequence, the Samaritans built a rival temple near Shechem.[1] This temple was served by a priesthood offering sacrifices in the manner prescribed in Leviticus. The Samaritans likewise observed the set feasts such as Passover.

There was little love lost between Jews and Samaritans, yet it was the Samaritan who stopped to help the robbery victim. He applied the customary first aid treatment for wounds—wine and oil. The wine was both for cleansing the wound and as a protection against infection. First-century wine had a much lower alcohol content than modern wines, but it would have had enough for a mild antiseptic action. The oil was used to keep the wounds moist and prevent their drying out. Once the victim's wounds were attended to, he was loaded onto the pack animal and transported to a lodging house where he could recover his strength.

Such is the story of the parable. Jesus then asked the lawyer, " 'Which of these three do you consider was neighbor to the one who had fallen amongst thieves?' "

The only possible reply was that only the Samaritan acted as a neighbor should. This, then, was the answer to the lawyer's question, " 'Who is my neighbor?' " Our neighbor is the one who is in need, even if that person is our enemy. No wonder the answer silenced the law expert. No doubt he would have delighted in a lively discussion as to who was to be considered a neighbor, but Jesus' answer took this principle and applied it more personally. His answer means that our behavior toward others will be dramatically turned around. Against all our upbringing, against all prejudice, even against common sense, we will love and assist our enemies. Here again is the principle we have already discovered in Matthew 5:43-48. In becoming perfect as God is perfect, Christians are to love as God loves. God is good toward all humanity. He sent His Son to die for the salvation of even those who hate Him. He is good to all, without distinction. The Christian's love is characterized by the fact that the Christian loves all, even one who is an enemy.

This is not the first time the parable of the Good Samaritan has been featured in this book. Chapter 5 quoted at length an interpretation of this parable by Augustine as an example of how the parable should *not* be used. We saw there that the parable of the good Samaritan is not an allegory. In fact, one of the strongest arguments Adolf Jülicher used to convince the scholarly world that parables should not be interpreted allegorically was simply to record how this parable (and others) had been misused through the centuries.

It is all very well to criticize how others have misused this parable, but doing so makes it all the more important to make sure that we use the good principles of parable interpretation developed in chapter 4. These principles include:

- sensitivity to the type of parable
- interpretation of the parable in a way that is consistent with the whole of the parable
- consideration of the parable's biblical, historical, and social context
- caution in adding an interpretation not warranted by the text, and, finally,
- regard for the emotional impact the parable makes on the reader

Let us apply each of these principles of interpretation to the parable of the good Samaritan to see if what has been said about it so far fits within the range of good interpretation.

First, what kind of parable is it—proverb, metaphor, figurative saying, simile or similitude, story parable, or allegory? Some of these possibilities can be eliminated fairly quickly. For example, it is clearly not a proverb or figurative saying. Further, it has already been established that the parable of the good Samaritan is not an allegory. Again, because it has neither an explicit or implied comparison, it is not a simile or a similitude. In fact, like the parable in Luke 14:16-24, this is a story parable. It tells a story to illustrate a point—whom should a Christian consider to be a neighbor? One is almost tempted to say that this parable should be classified as an argument by analogy.

Does interpreting this parable from the perspective of an argument by analogy provide an interpretation that is consistent with the whole parable? Yes. Does it fit its biblical and historical context? Yes. Have we been cautious in not adding anything further to the text? Well, you, the reader, should be the judge of that. But there is an almost overwhelming temptation to add more to this parable than is there. I was halfway between amused and angry about one sermon I heard on this parable. The preacher was sensitive to how the parable should be interpreted. Several times he mentioned that it should not be interpreted as an allegory. He then went on to say that there were some parallels, though, that he could not avoid making—the good Samaritan could represent only Jesus, while the man beaten and robbed represented our lost condition in sin. Well! After saying that the parable should not be used as an allegory, he then went on to give it an allegorical interpretation!

Should we condemn this preacher? I'm not sure. On the one hand, he really was misusing the parable, and more than that, he knew he was! I would argue strongly that he was not interpreting the parable correctly. But, then, he didn't say he was. He said he was making an application. Anyway, I personally would be uncomfortable to add anything to the parable that wasn't intended. I will leave it up to you to decide how you use the parable.

Nor should we overlook the powerful impact this parable makes on our everyday life as Christians. Like the expert in the law, we are happier talking about the fine details of what we should and should not do than we are in showing acceptance and love toward those who hate us. It is at that point that Christianity ceases to be theoretical and begins to shape the way we live.

There is an interesting footnote to this parable in the Gospel of Luke. The dialogue between Jesus and the lawyer is immediately followed by the account of Jesus' visit to Mary and Martha. The parable provided an answer to the second question asked by the expert in the law—the question of whom we should consider to be a neighbor. But the lawyer had shown some discomfort with Jesus' answer to his earlier question about what he should *do* to enter into the kingdom of God. We share that discomfort to an even greater degree, given our knowledge of Paul's letters.

Sure, keeping the law by truly loving God and our neighbor will earn us the right to heaven. But as sinners we cannot achieve this goal. Possibly the real answer to the question regarding what we need to *do* to become eligible for God's kingdom is given by the story of Mary and Martha. Perhaps it is deliberately placed immediately after the parable of the good Samaritan for that very reason. Martha was busy *doing* things. Mary, on the other hand, simply sat at the feet of Jesus and learned of Him. What, then, do we need to do to inherit eternal life? Sit at the feet of Jesus and become His disciples. Perhaps this incident gives a practical example of what Paul meant to be "in Christ."

### THE PARABLES OF THE LOST SHEEP AND THE LOST COIN (LUKE 15:1-10)

Luke 15 begins with the Pharisees and scribes accusing Jesus of receiving sinners and eating with them. Even modern societies, despite their increased sophistication in many areas, still tend to judge individuals by the associations they keep. The implication is that if you are friends with somebody, you must share their opinions and approve of their actions. The Pharisees added the dimension of holiness to this basic human attitude. In their thinking, to be holy, you must separate yourself from sin. In attempting to do this, you would not willingly come in contact with anything unclean. By their very nature, sinners were unclean. Moreover, sinners would not take the appropriate precautions to ensure that what they ate was clean by the high standards of biblical law. Eating with them could only make you unclean as well!

Jesus defends his actions by three parables. In the first, he talks of the behavior of a shepherd. If a shepherd has one hundred sheep and one becomes lost, he will leave all ninety-nine in the wilderness and go looking for the lost one. In the second parable, Jesus cites the example of a woman who has ten coins yet who will frantically search for one of them that is lost.

Like the parable of the good Samaritan, these two parables appear to be arguments from analogy. There is something analogous between the behavior of Jesus in seeking sinners and the behavior of the shepherd and the woman. Something is lost. Risks are taken and effort is expended to recover that which is lost. So also, in His ministry, Jesus concentrates on finding those who are lost and in need. He is happy to receive sinners and pleased to eat with them. This argument is further developed by the parable of the lost son(s).

### THE PARABLE OF THE LOST SON(S) (LUKE 15:11-32)

The parable of the lost son(s) is the most fully developed of the three stories. As with the rest of Jesus' parables, it authentically represents conditions in first-century Palestine. It was not unusual for a younger son to be sent abroad to provide for himself. In a country where most of the population was rural, both the nature of the available land and the laws of inheritance created conditions that led to such emigration. Under the laws of inheritance, property was divided equally among the sons, with the elder son receiving double. Thus, if there were two sons, the elder would receive two-thirds of the property, while the younger would receive one-third. Daughters were not excluded from the sharing of the family's wealth, part of which they would receive as a dowry at marriage, rather than at the death of the father. Under such arrangements, a prosperous farm would all too easily be subdivided into uneconomic lots after several generations. This was clearly seen by those dependent on the land. Thus, while the elder would customarily work the land when the father grew too old, the younger sons would find other occupations. Many sought their fortunes in other countries. For this reason and others—such as the fortunes of war—more Jews actually lived outside Palestine in the first century than lived in Palestine. It was unusual, though, for the younger son to demand his share of the property before his father planned to give it to him.

Nor was it remarkable that the younger son squandered his money. Famines were common as well, and in the parable, a famine struck about the time the younger son's resources ran out. Out of desperation, he sought employment feeding pigs. Pigs were unclean animals, and thus religious Jews despised the job of keeping pigs. Whether this particular young man shared a revulsion for pigs is unclear. The parable doesn't make the details of his riotous living explicit, but it is more than likely that his lifestyle took him outside the boundaries set by his faith. In any event, the contrast between a son of the household who has had money to spend and a penniless keeper of pigs must have been great. Not only this, many of those who first heard the parable would be unable to think of a more degrading job than feeding pigs.

The parable says that the young man came to himself and decided that his father's servants were better treated than he was and that he would go back home. On his return he was given the best robe, a ring, and shoes. The ring was probably a signet ring. With it he would be able to place the family seal on contracts and the like. The robe and shoes, but most particularly the ring, meant that he was received back into full membership of the household at the status that belonged to him as one of the two heirs.

The older brother's reaction on hearing that his younger brother had been received home with open arms was somewhat churlish, but we can understand his feelings. His comment contrasting the fatted calf that was killed for his brother with the fact that he had never been given even a goat to enjoy with his friends carries an important implication easily overlooked in the days of refrigerators. Without refrigerators, the meat of slaughtered animals had to be eaten within a short period. This was reflected in the law that specified meat more than three days old should not be eaten (Lev. 7:18; 19:5-8). Thus, the size of the animal dictated how many would be eating. A chicken would feed the family; a goat, a group of friends. The fatted calf, on the other hand, would mean that the whole village would be invited to the feast. The elder son was complaining that he had not been granted a feast for his friends, but here was the younger son who had "devoured [his father's] living with harlots"

(v. 30), and a village-wide feast was arranged on his behalf! No wonder the older son was upset! No wonder his father had to urge him to come into the feast!

The dramatic impact of this parable can perhaps be best seen by comparing it with another version of it, rewritten to fit modern conditions:[2]

A certain businessman had two sons. The businessman was a self-made man and so was very hard on his sons because he wanted them to be able to survive in the cut-throat world of business. This rankled both sons, and finally the younger son decided he could no longer work for his father. He demanded venture capital to begin a business for himself. At some sacrifice, the father gave the younger son the millions of dollars he needed, and the son left to set up his business in another state.

Their family had not been in the habit of keeping in touch, and while the father heard news of the son's business ventures, they had minimal personal contact. Now the younger son seemed to have a genius for backing failing businesses. Trying to keep news of this from his father eventually resulted in the son dropping all contacts with his dad.

Finally the son gave up trying to find a profitable business and squandered the last of the money. He was destitute and in need. His reputation had become so bad that he couldn't even find anybody to give him a salaried position. After some time on the dole, he decided that he would be better off with any kind of job. He went to one of the factories that his father owned and persuaded somebody he knew there to give him a job. Because of his shame, he legally changed his name, and with the passage of years, he was sure that his father and older brother would not recognize him if they met.

By hard work and diligent application, he eventually mastered the skills necessary to make good in business and devoted most of his working life to furthering the good of his father's companies, rising to a high position of management by his own merits.

About this time, the father suddenly became ill and needed to retire from controlling the company. As expected, his older son took over from him. One of the managers requested a private interview with the father. It was the younger son. He revealed himself to his dad and showed him a balance sheet he had had prepared, demonstrating that the businesses that he had been managing had actually contributed to the company's profits exactly twice what his father had given to him as venture capital and what he had lost.

The old man was visibly moved. He explained to his son that he had been told the very day his son had begun to work for him again. That he had kept a close eye on him as he worked his way up through the ranks. Because he had finally made good, his father was proud of him and wanted him to know that he would like his son to change his name back to his old family name.

This story illustrates a religious principle quite different from that shown in the parable of the lost sons. In fact, it illustrates the principle by which the younger son in Jesus' parable was wishing to reestablish his relationship with his household. In the speech he had prepared for his father, he said that he was no longer worthy to be a son. Instead, he wished to work as one of the hired servants (v. 19). But his father didn't let him finish this speech. He welcomed his son back into his family without reservation. All the son needed to *do* was to come home.

The account of the acceptance of the wastrel son is moving, yet the parable does not end with his return. It ends with the reaction of the older brother. The older brother was not happy to see the wastrel return. His attitude neatly parallels that of the Pharisees and scribes who complained that Jesus was consorting with sinners (v. 2).

Furthermore, the parable is incomplete. We never know what the older brother finally decided. Did he storm off and disregard his father's love? Or did he finally come to join the party and embrace his younger brother? The parable does not say. Perhaps it is deliberately left unfinished so it can function as an invitation to the Pharisees and scribes to join the party. They, with Jesus, should rejoice that sinners were coming to repentance.

Neither does the parable say what happened to the younger son. He is freely forgiven and freely taken back into the bosom of his family. But had he reformed? Or would he remain selfish and a wastrel? We like to think that he will be warmed by the love of his father and that he will have learned from his mistakes. But cold, hard experience teaches us that the wastrel normally remains the wastrel. Change will be possible only if he himself changes as he accepts unconditionally the love that is lavished on him by his father.

The message of the parable of the lost sons is the same as the message of the other two parables in Luke 15. God's love is all-encompassing. It reaches out to all, especially sinners and outcasts. These are the ones with whom Jesus spends His time. There is nothing we can do to earn God's love; it is freely given. Mind you, unconditional love carries its own demand, as the parable of the Good Samaritan shows. The one who is unconditionally loved will, in turn, love unconditionally. What distinguishes Christians is not just the fact that they have accepted the full and free forgiveness of God but that they love and forgive even their enemies. Unconditional love changes the way we live.

---

1. This is reason for the question of the Samaritan woman in John 4:20, " 'Our Fathers worshiped on this mountain, but you say that Jerusalem is the place where worship should take place.' "
2. In one of the major non-Christian religions, there is a parable rather like the one that follows. I have rewritten it to better fit a contemporary environment.

CHAPTER SEVENTEEN

# The Last Supper

The Last Supper of Jesus has held great significance for Christians from the earliest beginnings of the church to this day. It forms the basis for what the different denominations variously call the "Lord's Supper," "eucharist," or "mass." Whatever it is called, the commemoration of the Lord's Supper constitutes one of the central celebrations of Christian worship. This alone makes the Gospel record of the Last Supper worthy of close study.

It is called the Last Supper because it was the last meal that Jesus ate before He died. In describing the occasion, the Gospel record emphasizes several aspects of its meaning—its continuity with the old covenant made with Israel, the expectation of the future kingdom, the significance of the body and the blood, and the establishment of a memorial to Jesus.

## CONTINUITY WITH THE OLD COVENANT MADE WITH ISRAEL

Luke 22:7-13 makes it clear that the Last Supper was actually a celebration of the Passover by Jesus and His disciples. There is a rich background to this feast that illuminates the meaning of the Last Supper for Christians.

In Judaism, Passover was one of the three important yearly feasts in which every male Jew was expected to participate in Jerusalem (Exod. 23:14, 15; Deut. 16:16). The large number of Jews living outside Palestine made this impractical by the first century A.D., but even so, many Jews returned to Jerusalem at these times.

Passover gained its importance from its link with the Exodus of Israel from Egypt. The sons of Jacob had grown into a small nation but had become slaves in Egypt. God intervened to rescue them and sent Moses to be their leader. He also sent plagues to show His superiority over the gods of Egypt. In the last of these plagues, the angel of death killed the firstborn of all the households of Egypt, except those with the blood of the Passover lamb daubed on their door posts and lintels. It is hard to overestimate the importance of the Exodus in the Old Testament. It belongs to the birth of the nation, the setting up of its covenant with God, and becomes a potent symbol of God's power to act in history to save His people.

Each year at the feast of Passover, some of the events surrounding the Exodus were reenacted. For a period of seven days before Passover no leavened bread was eaten.[1] The Passover lamb was chosen early and was slaughtered and eaten the night before the Passover. It was entirely consumed, and those participating had to eat it fully clothed, dressed in a manner that would enable them to flee for their lives (Exod. 12:8-11). Some of the blood of the Passover lamb was to be placed on the door posts and on the lintel of the houses where Passover was celebrated, reminiscent of the time when the blood of the Passover lamb was a sign to the angel of the tenth plague, who otherwise would have slaughtered the firstborn in that household.

In giving a new meaning to the Passover, Jesus did two things. First, He underlined the continuity of Christianity with what went before. It did not arise without a past. Christians were the direct inheritors of the traditions of the Jews. This is one of the reasons the holy writings of Judaism are included in the Christian Bible as the Old Testament. Christianity is linked with God's action in history when He saved His people from bondage.

Second, Jesus took the Passover and filled it with new meaning. It points not just to God's act of salvation in the past but also to His supreme act of salvation in giving His Son to die on the cross. Several aspects of this new meaning are made explicit in the way the Gospels describe the Last Supper.

### EXPECTATION OF THE FUTURE KINGDOM OF GOD

According to Luke 22, the first thing Jesus said, after saying that He fervently wanted to eat the Passover with His disciples, connected this meal with the kingdom. " 'I tell you,' " Jesus said, " 'I will not eat it until it is fulfilled in the kingdom of heaven' " (v. 16). He then took a cup of wine and after telling them all to drink from it, he said, " 'For I tell you that from now on I will not drink of the fruit of the vine until the kingdom of God comes' " (v. 18). In both instances, Jesus highlighted the coming of the kingdom of God. As a later verse points out, the disciples will eat the bread and drink the wine in remembrance of this solemn occasion, but Jesus Himself will not partake until He does so in the coming kingdom. This is a new dimension that Jesus added to the Passover; it not only points to God's saving actions in history—the Exodus and the Cross—it points forward to the time when God will intervene again in history to establish His kingdom.

In an earlier chapter,[2] it has been pointed out that Matthew's Gospel portrays the kingdom of God as both present and future. It is present in the activity of the body of Christ, the church, but its full development belongs to the future. A similar dual focus is found in Luke. The kingdom is portrayed as present in the life and ministry of Jesus. In Luke 10:9, 11, for example, Jesus' disciples are told to point out the connection between their healing the sick and the nearness of the kingdom. But perhaps the clearest statement of the presence of the kingdom is Luke 17:20, 21, where Jesus tells the Pharisees that the kingdom of God is in their midst. This is not to say that the kingdom is depicted as being already present only in the Gospel of Luke. Luke 13:28, 29 speaks of a future kingdom in terms taken from the familiar language of prophecy.

But to which aspect of the kingdom of God does the Last Supper point? Its present aspect or its future aspect?

It refers to a time when Jesus will meet with His disciples in the kingdom, a time after His second coming. In other words, it is a reference to the future kingdom.

In sum, Jesus has attached a promise of the Second Coming to the Christian celebration of the Last Supper. Each time Christians celebrate the reenactment of the Last Supper, they not only look back to the great acts of God's salvation in history, the Exodus and the Cross, but they look forward to the time in the future when Jesus has returned and God's kingdom is fully revealed. Their celebration is nothing less than a reminder of Jesus' promise to return to deal with sin and to set up His kingdom.

## THE SIGNIFICANCE OF THE BODY AND BLOOD

Jesus next did something astonishing. He took the loaf of unleavened bread, prayed over it, broke it, and gave it to the disciples, saying, " 'This is my body, which is given for you' " (v. 19). Then He took a glass of wine and said, " 'This cup that is poured out for you is the new covenant in my blood' " (v. 20).[3] This is a dramatic change from the celebration of the Passover. Why? Because Jesus is making Himself the new Passover lamb. His body and blood are represented by the bread and the wine. Christians do not sacrifice the Passover lamb, because Jesus is their sacrifice. In this way the dramatic imagery of the Exodus is taken over by the bread and the wine. Just as the first Passover lamb protected God's people from the avenging angel of death, so also the new Lamb of God will protect His people.

It is also worthy of note that Jesus uses the language of covenant. The concept of covenant is very important in the Old Testament. The covenant was the contract, or treaty, that God made with His people. Its terms and conditions are set out in several places in the Old Testament, and the prophets frequently warned Israel that the terms of the covenant contained curses as well as blessings. In the New Testament, the concept of covenant is less prominent, although it is mentioned in Romans, Galatians, and especially Hebrews. The Gospels have five references to the covenant, four of them to Jesus' saying at the Last Supper.[4]

By saying that the cup represents the blood of the new covenant, Jesus is taking the important Old Testament concept of covenant and reapplying it to His followers. They are participants in a new covenant between God and His people. Just as the old covenant was established with sacrifice and the application of blood (Gen. 15:7-19; Exod. 24:3-8), so also the new covenant is based on a sacrifice—the death of Jesus. On the cross His blood was "poured out for" all those who would receive Him. In some way the death of Jesus ratified the new covenant. Just as the sacrificial animal's death atoned for the sin of the worshiper, so also the death of Jesus atoned for the sins of all who would receive Him.

## REMEMBRANCE

Jesus also transformed the aspect of reenactment present in the feast of Passover. The Passover was celebrated as a reenactment of the events of the Exodus—the food was the same and eaten under the same conditions. Everybody was dressed ready to flee as they ate the Passover. For Christians, though, the reenactment they participate in is the reenactment of different events. When Jesus said " 'Do this in memory of me' " (v. 19), He was asking His disciples to reenact the Last Supper. It was such an important occasion that Christians were to continue going through the same actions the disciples did that last time Jesus ate with them before He died. Well, not exactly the same actions, because Jesus had replaced the sacrifice, using the bread and wine to represent the Cross, the new sacrifice that replaced the Passover lamb. But the disciples were to meet and reenact what had happened on that important occasion. They were to take the bread and the wine and think about the death of Jesus. Not just His death, though. The reenactment of the Last Supper was to remind Christians of their links to Judaism and God's past acts in redeeming His people from slavery. It was to bring to remembrance the centrality of Jesus' death for Christians. But more than this, the reenactment of the Last Supper was to remind Christians that Jesus had promised to meet with them again at a future time, to eat bread and drink wine with them. They were to meet in the kingdom of God. This points forward, past the resurrection and ascension of Jesus, to the time of His second coming. The Christian celebration of the Lord's Supper, then, is to link them with God's people, past, present, and future. It is a promise of His salvation, freely given.

---

1. Leaven is the rising agent put into bread. Modern bakers use yeast for this purpose. Bread without leaven is very flat.

2. See chapter 6.

3. Some early manuscripts omit verse 20. Some scholars are inclined to think that this verse is not in the original but on grounds other than those used by text critics. Text critics are those who are expert at sifting through the various differences that exist between ancient manuscripts to determine which is the most likely original reading. The results of their work are included in the textual apparatus at the bottom of each page of the Greek New Testament. The 1993 fourth revised edition of the United Bible Societies' *Greek New Testament* includes verse 20 in the main text of Luke 22 and gives it a status of a "B" reading. An "A" reading is one the editors are nearly certain should be in the text; a "B" reading is one they are confident about: a "C" reading is one they are inclined to think should be included; while a "D" reading is one that the evidence is so equally balanced that it is not possible to make a decision on it. Thus, because verse 20 is a "B" quality reading, it is more than likely original to Luke.

4. Luke 1:72 is the other reference.

CHAPTER EIGHTEEN

# The Crucifixion in Luke

## THE CENTRALITY OF THE CROSS IN THE GOSPEL OF LUKE

The Cross dominates Luke's Gospel. About 180 of its approximately 1,150 verses (some 15 percent) deal with the events surrounding Jesus' betrayal, crucifixion, and resurrection. These verses constitute the longest connected narrative in the Gospel. But, as has been pointed out in an earlier chapter,[1] these events are given an even greater prominence in the Gospel by the note in Luke 9:51, where the reader is informed that Jesus "set his face to go to Jerusalem." From that point in the Gospel, Jesus is portrayed as moving toward Jerusalem to meet His fate. In other words, the Cross overshadows the last half of the Gospel.

The prominence given to the Cross by Luke and the other three Gospels is quite in keeping with the central message of Christianity. Christianity is about God becoming man, dying on the cross for our sins, being raised from the dead, and ascending to heaven (Phil. 2:5-11). In sum, the chapters of Luke under consideration here constitute the center of the Gospel.

In exploring these chapters we will draw on archaeological and historical information to illuminate aspects of the crucifixion that would have been well known to any first-century reader of Luke's Gospel. From there, we will draw out some of the meaning of the Cross as Luke would have us understand it. Finally, we will look anew at one of the participants in the drama and perhaps discover that the Cross has a more personal meaning.

## THE OBJECTIVITY OF THE REPORT

One of the striking things about the tone of the narratives describing the events surrounding the crucifixion in Luke and the other Gospels is their matter-of-fact language. They do not describe the agony of Jesus in anything but the barest detail, nor, interestingly enough, do they express any explicit anger at the injustice of the proceedings. It is almost as if they are giving only the bare report, while expecting the reader to think through the implications of the events. Mind you, public scourging and crucifixions were common enough that people living in the first century would witness them with some regularity, at least if they were living in the more important cities. There is no need for the Gospels to explain the intense pain of the victim, because those who heard the story would have already witnessed it for themselves. What, then, would those living in the first-century know firsthand about scourging and crucifixion?

## SCOURGING IN THE FIRST CENTURY

The reality of scourging became tangible to me in an unexpected manner. One of my interests is archaeology. This interest goes back to my teenage years, but it was as an undergraduate student that I stumbled across something related to scourging that made my blood run cold. I happened to be researching another topic, but it's always a temptation to become distracted by other interesting articles in the journals you are reading. On this particular day, I happened across some preliminary archaeological reports of a dig at Tel Hesban (biblical Heshbon). These were probably the first actual dig reports I had read. Most of my previous interest in archaeology had been from books and magazines that concentrated on the general picture. Now this general picture is very interesting, but I can't honestly say that the dig report I was looking at was exciting reading. It detailed the different squares in which the archaeologists had been digging and reported in fine detail the sequences of soil, rubble, pottery, and other finds associated with each square. From this mass of details it is possible to build up an overall picture of the whole site, but the actual details are rather prosaic. I was just about to give up and go back to the article I should have been reading, when I came across a picture of a lead ball with nails embedded in it. The caption explained that this appeared to be part of a Roman scourge.

I have since gone back and looked at that picture.[2] It is a small picture in a rather grainy black and white format. There is nothing remarkable about it, except for what my imagination quickly put together. A Roman scourge was made up of several of these lead balls. It was customary to melt the lead around nails or broken glass. The balls were then tied to leather straps, which were attached to a handle. The victim to be scourged would be stripped and tied to a post. Someone would then take the scourge and beat him on the back. The scourge was designed not only to strip away the skin but also to rip into the very muscles of the back. Care had to be taken that the rib cage wasn't breached and the lungs punctured, otherwise the victim died. Indeed, the wounds and loss of blood caused by such a punishment could often result in death, but death was not the goal. The goal was, rather, the infliction of the maximum amount of pain.

Figure 1: Picture of lead flogging head, found at Tel-Hesban (biblical Heshbon)

The Gospels recount that Pilate actually sought to release Jesus, and as an appeasement to the crowd's lust for blood, he offered to have Jesus scourged before His release (Luke 23:16). But nothing less than actual crucifixion would satisfy the crowd, so he handed Jesus over for crucifixion. Although Luke does not specifically mention it, Jesus would have been scourged as a matter of course, since this was customarily part of the events surrounding a crucifixion. Matthew 27:26 mentions that this was done in the case of Jesus.

All this I had known in a theoretical way, but just seeing that picture of a small component of a scourge made it real to me. Scourging, like crucifixion, was a horrific punishment, designed to inflict the maximum amount of pain. In fact, just as archaeology has revealed information about scourging, a remarkable find just north of Jerusalem also throws an interesting light on crucifixion.

## CRUCIFIXION IN THE FIRST CENTURY

The best archaeological evidence relating to first-century crucifixion was found in some tombs near Mount Scopus, north of Jerusalem. There archaeologists excavated four cave tombs. From pottery found in the tombs, they were able to determine that the skeletons there dated from between the second century B.C. and A.D. 70. There were bones from thirty-five individuals, and their manner of death reveals quite a bit about the violent conditions that prevailed in first-century Palestine. Three children appear to have died from starvation, and another child of four died after an arrow penetrated the occipital bone of his skull. A woman in her early twenties died in a fire. A young man of about seventeen likewise burned to death, but the pattern of charring on his bones suggest that he was deliberately burned to death on a rack. A woman of about sixty died from a massive wound to the head, of the type that would be inflicted by a mace. A woman in her early thirties died in childbirth. We know her death resulted from an unsuccessful attempt to give birth, because the skeleton of the unborn fetus was discovered in her pelvis. These deaths left evidence on the bones from which inferences could be drawn. The other bones were from individuals who died through illnesses that cannot be identified. Health was generally poor in those days. Political conditions were frequently unsettled. Wars were common. As a result, life expectancy was short, and the bones from these tombs reflect this fact.

For Christians, though, the most interesting bones are those of a young male, between twenty-four and twenty-eight years, called Jehohanan. Several of his bones show evidence of crucifixion, although it is the ankle bones that remove any doubt. Those that crucified him apparently had trouble removing the nail that had been driven through his ankles into the cross, because the nail is still in place, together with the knot in the wood in which it was embedded. They simply cut the feet from the body to make it easier to free the nail. Further, there is a groove in the lower third of Jehohanan's right radial bone, apparently caused by a nail put through the forearm to fix his arms to the cross beam of the cross.[3]

Contemporary written records show that it was customary to fix the upright post into the ground in preparation for the crucifixion. The victim was normally obliged to carry the crossbeam, although the Gospel record shows that Jesus was so weakened after His scourging that the soldiers compelled Simon from the crowd to carry the crossbeam for Him (Luke 23:26). When he arrived at the place of crucifixion, the victim's arms would be nailed or tied to the crossbeam, which was then fixed to the upright.

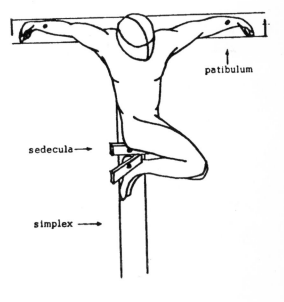

Last of all, the heels of the victim would be nailed to the upright. A piece of wood was normally provided on which the victim could sit to gain a little respite, though at the cost of pain and the risk of falling off. Wood was rare, so unnecessary height was avoided. Crosses were placed so that passersby could speak comfortably to the victim. Guards would ensure that nobody assisted the victim to die with any speed, but the mockers were often given the opportunity to torment the victim spread-eagled before them.

The evidence of the written records also suggests that there was more than one way the victim could be pinned. In fact, when there were several to be crucified, the soldiers would sometimes amuse themselves by placing them in different positions. There is some debate as to how to interpret the evidence of the remains of Jehohanan, and the different suggestions are reproduced in the figures accompanying these pages.[4] It was customary, though, to crucify the victim upright, as this prolonged the death agonies.

By the time the victim was finally mounted on the cross, he would have been considerably weakened by the pain and loss of blood occa-

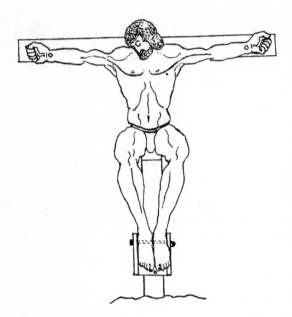

sioned by his scourging before crucifixion and by the violence associated with positioning him on the cross. The blood would attract flies to the naked body of the victim, and with pinned limbs it would be impossible to brush them away. Death, interestingly enough, was most frequently by asphyxiation. It is impossible to breathe properly while hanging from the arms, so the victim would have to push up with the feet to be able to breathe. The nails through the feet made this supremely painful. The victim would attempt to sit on the half seat but would slip off, painfully jarring his wounds. Then he would struggle to stand upright or sit on the half seat, and the process would continue on. Eventually, he would become so weakened that he could not push himself up and would die from lack of oxygen. This process could take some days if the victim was healthy. If, for some reason, it was wished to hasten death, the legs of the victim could be broken, so that being unable to struggle for breath, he would die fairly quickly.[5] The whole procedure was designed to provide the most horrifying death imaginable.

This, then, is background information most anybody living in the first century who heard the story of Jesus' crucifixion would already know. With this in mind, it is now possible to approach the Gospel accounts with greater understanding. What, then, do the four Gospel writers have to tell us about the events that culminated in the death and resurrection of Jesus?

### THE EVENTS SURROUNDING JESUS' DEATH

The four Gospels provide three independent versions of the crucifixion. The first of these are found in Matthew and Mark, which are very closely related. These two Gospels report the same events in exactly the same sequence, even to the details of what happened. The accounts in Luke and John show much greater variation and include some new information not known from Matthew and Mark. Even so, there is a remarkable consistency between the four accounts. They all agree in the basic outline of events.

Jesus and His disciples celebrated the Passover meal on Thursday evening (Luke 22:1, 7-14).[6] After the meal and having given a warning to Peter that he would betray Him (vv. 31-34), Jesus went from the upper room to the olive garden called Gethsemane, where He spent much of the night in anguished prayer. In His prayer, he petitioned His father to release Him from the task set before Him (His death), but eventually He submitted His will to that of God (vv. 39-42). Judas Iscariot, one of the twelve disciples, led an armed crowd to Jesus. As the crowd seized Jesus, some of the disciples attempted to resist with their swords. But Jesus prevented them and even healed an injury inflicted on one of the members of the hostile crowd (vv. 47-51). Jesus was thereupon led away, and Peter followed to see what would happen. While in the courtyard, Peter was challenged whether or not he was a friend of Jesus, but three times he denied it (vv. 54-62).

Jesus was then brought before the Jewish authorities, who found

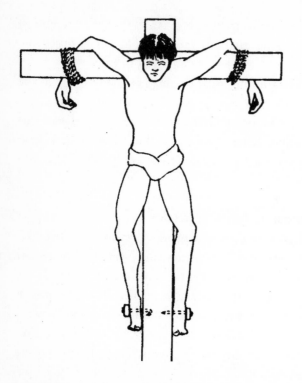

Him guilty of falsely claiming to be the Jewish Messiah (vv. 66-71). They then used this as the basis for the accusation they made to the Roman authorities that Jesus was advocating armed resistance against Rome (Luke 23:1, 2). The Roman official, Pilate, did not find an adequate basis for these charges and consequently sought to release Jesus. But the clamoring of the crowd prevailed, and Jesus was condemned to death by means of crucifixion (vv. 13-25). As He was taken out to the place of execution, a visitor, Simon of Cyrene, was compelled to carry the crossbar of Jesus' cross (v. 26).

Jesus was crucified with two others (vv. 39-44). He died quickly (vv. 44-46), was buried in a tomb (vv. 50-56), and then was seen alive by several different witnesses (Luke 24:1-43). He appeared to different groups of believers and then ascended to heaven, giving His disciples a commission to tell others of Him (vv. 44-53).

Such is the bare account of what happened, told in a tone similar to that adopted by the Gospels. The background knowledge concerning the details of crucifixion reveal the realities behind these bare facts. The times were harsh, and Jesus was overtaken by unreasoning violence and extraordinary brutality. He suffered as much pain as the best practitioners of the time could inflict on a human. But interestingly enough, neither the pain nor the injustice of an innocent man being condemned to die on a cross is the focus of any of the Gospel accounts. For them the meaning of the Cross lay elsewhere.

## THE MEANING OF THE CROSS

Although the Gospel of Luke does not provide editorial asides that provide explicit meaning for the Cross, much of the meaning the Gospel attaches to these events is revealed in its selection and placement of material.

First, much of *the significance of the Cross lay in who Jesus is*. He is not merely an unfortunate man who died an unpleasant death. Rather, He is One who bears a special relationship to God. The passion narrative of Luke reveals this fact in several ways. For example, when Jesus earnestly petitioned His Father to be released from the obligation to die (Luke 22:42), He addressed God directly. Now, Jesus had taught His disciples to pray to God as a Father, but there was a uniqueness in the closeness between Jesus and God. Further, at Jesus' trial, He identified Himself before the Jewish authorities as the Son of Man who would be seated at the right hand of the power of God at some time in the future (v. 69). When asked outright if He was the Son of God, He admitted as much (v. 70). He was accused of being the Messiah and king of the Jews (v. 67), and when Pilate asked Him whether this was true, He acknowledged it (Luke 23:3).[7] Thus, the cross of Jesus is significant, because of who it was that died—Jesus, the Messiah, the King of the Jews, the Son of God.

Second, *the Cross happened because it was God's will*. Luke's Gospel reveals this in several ways. For example, in Luke 22:42, Jesus seeks to be released from the necessity of His death, but God's will prevails. Furthermore, after the whole event, Jesus went to some trouble to show His disciples that the events of the crucifixion had been foretold by Scripture (Luke 24:44, 45). In the discussion with the disciples returning to Emmaus—an incident unique to Luke—He went so far as to establish from Scripture, *before* He revealed Himself to them, that it was necessary that the Messiah should suffer and then enter into glory (Luke 24:13-35, esp. vv. 25, 26). The whole sequence had been predicted in Scripture and, in fact, was *necessary,* which means that the Cross was not an unexpected tragedy. It was God's preordained will.

Third, *there is a link between the cross of Jesus and the Passover.* The Gospel of Luke introduces the events relating to the passion by placing them in relationship to the Passover (Luke 22:1). At the Last Supper, Jesus not only replaced the Passover sacrifice with His own body and blood, He urged His disciples to remember the occasion of His death on the cross in terms of the Passover sacrifice.[8] Jesus Himself is the Passover sacrifice. It is His blood that will bring salvation.

Fourth, there is a strong emphasis in Luke on *the innocence of Jesus.* He was cleared of all charges not only by Pilate, Procurator of Judea, but also by Herod, Tetrarch of Galilee. In other words, all the Roman officials involved in the trial were convinced of His innocence. Under Roman law, He had done nothing deserving of death. Further, while Herod acted unpleasantly to Jesus, Pilate showed himself to be Jesus' friend, attempting to obtain His release. The villains in the narrative are the Jewish leadership and the crowd under their control. It was they who demanded, and finally were granted, Jesus' death.

Fifth, there are several places in the final chapters of Luke where *the kingdom of God* becomes prominent. For example, the reenactment of the final supper that Jesus urged upon His disciples points forward to the coming kingdom (Luke 22:16, 18). After the meal, Jesus promised His disciples that they would sit on twelve thrones in the kingdom, judging the twelve tribes of Israel (v. 30). The kingdom is prominently mentioned twice in the narration of the crucifixion. Jesus was crucified because He was "king of the Jews" (Luke 23:38). One of the thieves asked to be remembered by Jesus when He came into His kingdom (v. 42).

Sixth, the Gospel of Luke emphasizes that *Jesus was resurrected with a real body.* When His disciples recoil from Him, fearing Him to be a ghost, He reassures them. He shows them the wounds on His body and asks them to touch Him. Finally, He asks for food and eats before them (Luke 24:36-43). This is no phantom. This is Jesus, raised from the dead with a real body. Indeed, without the Resurrection, the Cross would not have significance. Jesus' resurrection is the ultimate evidence that He is who

He claimed to be. That He does have the power to save His people.

Finally, *the events of the Cross and Resurrection lead to the missionary command given to the disciples*. They are to tell others what they know, beginning at Jerusalem. They are to wait there for the power that will be granted them from on high (Luke 24:48, 49). This theme is taken up in Acts. The disciples do wait at Jerusalem. They are given the power of the Holy Spirit. And from there they go to the ends of the known world with the message of Jesus.

These, then, are some of the things the Gospel of Luke emphasizes in its account of the crucifixion and resurrection of Jesus. What the modern reader would like, though, is a way to bridge the gap of nearly 2,000 years and find what the crucifixion means for us today. Perhaps the figure of Barabbas may be the appropriate vehicle to do this.

## BARABBAS

Barabbas appears in the account of the Crucifixion in Luke 23:18-25. He is introduced abruptly into the narrative, as Pilate attempts to obtain Jesus' release. Pilate offers the Jews a choice between Jesus and Barabbas.

Luke tells the reader that Barabbas was in prison because he had taken part in an insurrection in Jerusalem and because he was a murderer (vv. 19, 25). Now, the Jewish leaders had accused Jesus of claiming to be king of the Jews. This charge implied that He was advocating revolt against Rome. The penalty for such activity was death. Barabbas, on the other hand, was known to have actually taken part in a revolt. Thus the two prisoners were accused of the same offense. The difference was that Barabbas *was* guilty as charged. Further, he was a murderer, and the crowd knew it! By way of contrast, Jesus was anything but a murderer. He had not advocated revolt against Rome. Furthermore, the crowd knew this as well!

There is one other possible link between Jesus and Barabbas. A well-attested textual variant to Matthew 27:16, 17 gives Barabbas's name as Jesus Barabbas (Jesus, Son of Abba).[9] It is impossible to be sure that this was indeed his name, but this information does give rise to the following plausible scenario. Jesus was crucified with two others described by the Greek adjective *lestes*. This adjective means either "robber" or "insurrectionist." Crucifixion would be the near automatic fate of an "insurrectionist," and thus it appears quite likely that a crucifixion of three men on the charge of insurrection was already planned for the day that Jesus was brought before Pilate. The upright posts of the three crosses were already in place and the crossbeams prepared. One of these accused men happened to have the same first name as Jesus of Nazareth. Pilate thought the parallel too good not to try it out on the crowd. He presented them with two men, one of whom would be crucified—both called Jesus, both accused of the same crime. But one of them was guilty, the other innocent. Surely, the crowd would demand the release of Jesus of Nazareth rather than Jesus Barabbas. Pilate was wrong. Incredibly, the crowd chose Barabbas the murderer instead of Jesus the healer. The ironic thing, then, is that the cross on which Jesus died was prepared for somebody else. He died on the cross on which Barabbas should have died.

A little imagination will flesh out these sparse details. It is remarkable that the authorities even managed to capture Barabbas alive. There would have been no doubt in Barabbas's mind that if they took him alive he would be crucified. To take him alive several burly soldiers would have had to risk their lives to subdue him. He would have fought to the last. But subdue him they did.

What would go through the mind of a man thrown into prison knowing that he would be crucified? He would hope against hope that it was all a mistake, but this hope would be quickly dispelled by the judgment given against him by the Roman authorities. There would be only fear left. Fear and despair. There might even be a wish that the thing be over and done with as fast as possible.

The morning of crucifixion would inevitably arrive. A number of soldiers would come for him. He would struggle and be subdued with blows. They would drag him out before a crowd, and he would expect to be tied to a post in preparation for scourging. But no, he is taken to stand beside Jesus of Nazareth. It gradually dawns on Barabbas that there is a faint possibility of escape. But no sooner have his hopes been raised than they are immediately dashed again. The crowd has to choose between him and Jesus of Nazareth. There is no choice; why should they choose him over One who has gone about healing people? Why should they choose him instead of the

One who goes about preaching love and the goodness of God? But, amazingly, he is released, and Jesus is condemned!

We know nothing more of Barabbas and what he did. Did he run from the city as fast as he could? Or was he so fascinated that he stayed to watch what should have been his fate? As Jesus was tied to the post and the blood and skin and flesh began to spatter the soldier who did the scourging, did Barabbas think, "That should have been my back"? As Jesus was put up on the cross, did Barabbas think, "That man is dying on my cross"? Did this change his life? Did he repent and join with the disciples of Jesus after the resurrection?

We are not told. In fact, there is every reason to think that he did not. But Barabbas was one who more than any other should have understood what the early Christians were saying about the Cross of Jesus. They said that we have all sinned against God and therefore deserve to die. But Jesus took our place and died for us. As a result, Christians feel great love and gratitude to Jesus for His sacrifice in their place. They devote their lives to His service.

Barabbas knew that what he had done deserved nothing less than crucifixion. There was no doubt in his mind that he was guilty and that Jesus was innocent. But Jesus took his place on his cross.

There is an old Negro spiritual that runs like this:

Were you there when they crucified my Lord?
Were you there when they crucified my Lord?
Oh, Oh, Oh, Oh.
Sometimes, it causes me to tremble, tremble, tremble.
Were you there when they crucified my Lord?

Were you there? Was I there? Yes, we were there. We were Barabbas!

---

1. See chapter 15.
2. *Andrews University Seminary Studies* 14 (1976), plate XVI, reproduced on this page.
3. The details of the thirty-five sets of bones are conveniently gathered by J. H. Charlesworth, in his article, "Jesus and Jehohanan: An Archaeological Note on

Crucifixion," *Expository Times* 84 (1972-73): 147, 148.

4. The three diagrams are taken from the following sources: Charlesworth, "Jesus and Jehohanan," 149; Vilhelm Mller-Christensen, "Skeletal Remains from Giv`at ha-Mivtar," *Israel Exploration Journal* 26 (1976): 36; and Joseph Zias and Eliezer Sekeles, "The Crucified Man From Giv`at ha-Mivtar: A Reappraisal," *Israel Exploration Journal* 35 (1985): 27.

5. The medical cause of death is explored in the article, by William D. Edwards, Wesley J. Gabel, and Floyd E. Hosmer, "On the Physical Death of Jesus Christ," *Journal of American Medical Association* 255 (1986): 1455-1463.

6. The Gospel of John emphasizes the close link between the death of Jesus on the cross and the Passover sacrifice by identifying the day of the crucifixion as the day of preparation for the Passover (John 19:14). According to John's chronology, then, Jesus would have died about the time the Passover lamb was sacrificed. The Synoptic Gospels all place the Passover meal on the day *before* Jesus died (Matt. 26:17-20; Mark 14:12-17; Luke 22:1, 2, 7-14). This difference in dating has fascinated scholars for some time, and many explanations have been advanced as to why it came about. Some have said, for example, that either John or the disciples of Jesus may have belonged to a group of Jews who celebrated the Passover on a different day than did "official" temple Judaism. Others have explored the possibility that the "sabbath" mentioned in all of the Gospels was not the weekly sabbath but was the sabbath of the Passover feast. It must be admitted, though, that no really satisfactory explanation of this difference has yet been found.

7. Jesus' answer, " 'You have said so,' " is somewhat ambiguous. The Jewish authorities certainly took it to mean "yes" (Luke 22:71). Whether Pilate understood it to mean "no" is a moot point. Pilate asked Jesus, " 'Are you king of the Jews,' " to which Jesus replied, " 'You have said so' " (Luke 23:3). Pilate thereupon tells the Jewish authorities that Jesus was not guilty of the charges they had laid against Him (pretending to be Messiah, a king), which implies that Pilate thought Jesus had answered "no" to his question. Mind you, though, in the end the official charge did read that Jesus was crucified because He claimed to be king of the Jews (Luke 23:38). This point is ironic in the extreme. For Luke, Jesus was the Messiah, the true King of the Jews. It is just that His messiahship and kingship are different from what the others involved in the trial understood by the terms.

8. The evidence of this has been laid out in the previous chapter.

9. The 4th edition United Bible Societies' *Greek New Testament* gives this textual variant a "C" rating. In other words, the evidence is not strong enough to make a definite decision either way, although the editors are inclined to think that the reading "Barabbas" is to be preferred over "Jesus Barabbas."

Part 4

# THE PROBLEM OF SYNOPTIC RELATIONSHIPS

# CHAPTER NINETEEN

# Synoptic Relationships: The Raw Data

We have now looked at the Gospels of Matthew, Mark, and Luke. These three Gospels are linked together, and these links deserve our careful attention because they have important implications for how the Gospels should be studied, as well as for our understanding of how inspiration works.

It is a near certainty that Matthew, Mark, and Luke are related in some way. Exactly *how* they are related has fascinated several generations of scholars for more than one hundred years. The problem has all the hallmarks of a good mystery—lots of details, many competing theories (all of which have their vigorous champions who think everybody else is wrong), and the final word is not yet in. Some readers of this book will find the problem equally fascinating. Others will not. If you are one of the latter, you can probably get all the information you need by just glancing through this chapter and the following one, as important as the whole topic is. You can always come back to look at it again if you find that you need to pay more attention to it. I think, though, that you will definitely be interested in the chapter that deals with the implications of all this.

## THE THREE SYNOPTIC GOSPELS

When we start looking at the relationships between the four Gospels, one thing immediately stands out—John is different from the others. For example, of the material in John 1–17, only the stories concerning John the Baptist, the cleansing of the temple, the feeding of the five thousand, the triumphal entry, and the prophecy concerning Peter are in any way parallel to what is found in the other Gospels.[1] This may sound like quite a lot of overlap, but actually it forms quite a small proportion of these chapters, approximately 12 percent, in fact.[2] All the rest of the material in John 1–17 is found *only* in the Gospel of John. Mark, in comparison, has 609 verses, of which only 30 (or approximately 5 percent) have no parallel in the other Gospels. In other words, 95 percent of Mark's material is found in the other Gospels, compared to only 12 percent of John 1–17. The figure is slightly lower for Matthew and Luke than for Mark but still dramatically higher than that for John.

Once John begins reporting on the arrest and crucifixion of Jesus, there is more overlap with the other Gospels, but again, both what he chooses to report and the language he uses to report it are quite different from the other three Gospels. Because of the closer relationship that exists between Matthew, Mark, and Luke, these three Gospels are normally grouped together and called the "Synoptic Gospels."

### EXAMPLES OF THE DIFFERENT KINDS OF PARALLELS

Some things can best be understood by experiencing them, and this is true of the problem of synoptic relationships among Matthew, Mark, and Luke. There is just no substitute for taking two parallel accounts from the Gospels and underlining the words they have in common. While this would best be done using the original Greek text, the good news is that the result obtained from underlining a relatively literal translation (such as the RSV used below) is not that different from the result of underlining parallel Greek passages (if you would like to see how similar they are, the Greek of these parallel passages has been underlined and is available on the internet at www.avondale.edu.au under the name of the author in the list of theology faculty members).

You will find below some examples of the different types of relationships that exist between the three Gospels. Sometimes parallel accounts follow each other almost word for word. At other times, even when you would expect them to be word for word, there is very little in common between the two accounts. I have provided some examples of both of these extremes and some representatives of parallels that fit somewhere between them.

I suggest you take a highlighter or a pencil and underline the words in the examples below that are *exactly* the same in both passages (unless this is a library copy; you could use photocopies in that case.) In my underlining, I use an unbroken line for words that are exactly the same and in exactly the same order. If they are the same word but in a different tense, I indicate that by underlining only part of the word. If the words occur out of order, then I leave a gap between the words I underline. I normally do not underline synonyms, for a reason that will be explained later.

I have begun the first example for you so you can see how I go about it. You will find that you will have to make decisions as to which words to underline and how. But that is part of the fun and the big reason for you to do this exercise for yourself. It will give you a better idea of how subjective, or otherwise, the whole process is.

First, let's start with Matthew 24:15-28 and Mark 13:14-23, which come from the same part of two parallel accounts of Jesus' teaching on

## MATT. 24:15-28

<sup>15</sup>" 'So when you see the desolating sacrilege spoken of by the prophet Daniel, standing in the holy place (let the reader understand), <sup>16</sup>then let those who are in Judea flee to the mountains; <sup>17</sup>let him who is on the housetop not go down to take what is in his house; <sup>18</sup>and let him who is in the field not turn back to take his mantle. <sup>19</sup>And alas for those who are with child and for those who give suck in those days! <sup>20</sup>Pray that

## MARK 13:14-23

<sup>14</sup>" 'But when you see the desolating sacrilege set up where it ought not to be (let the reader understand), then let those who are in Judea flee to the mountains; <sup>15</sup>let him who is on the housetop not go down, nor enter his house, to take anything away; <sup>16</sup>and let him who is in the field not turn back to take his mantle. <sup>17</sup>And alas for those who are with child and for those who give suck in those days! <sup>18</sup>Pray that it may not

your flight may not be in winter or on a sabbath. [21]For then there will be great tribulation, such as has not been from the beginning of the world until now, no, and never will be. [22]And if those days had not been shortened, no human being would be saved; but for the sake of the elect those days will be shortened. [23]Then if any one says to you, "Lo, here is the Christ!" or "There he is!" do not believe it. [24]For false Christs and false prophets will arise and show great signs and wonders, so as to lead astray, if possible, even the elect. [25]Lo, I have told you beforehand. [26]So, if they say to you, "Lo, he is in the wilderness," do not go out; if they say, "Lo, he is in the inner rooms," do not believe it. [27]For as the lightning comes from the east and shines as far as the west, so will be the coming of the Son of man. [28]Wherever the body is, there the eagles will be gathered together.' "

happen in winter.' " [You can continue to underline if you so desire; your "answers" can be checked against the underlined text below.] [19] " 'For in those days there will be such tribulation as has not been from the beginning of the creation which God created until now, and never will be. [20]And if the Lord had not shortened the days, no human being would be saved; but for the sake of the elect, whom he chose, he shortened the days. [21]And then if any one says to you, "Look, here is the Christ!" or "Look, there he is!" do not believe it. [22]False Christs and false prophets will arise and show signs and wonders, to lead astray, if possible, the elect. [23]But take heed; I have told you all things beforehand.' "

the signs of the end of the age. These are remarkable for the closeness of the parallels:

My problem is that I wish to include "answers" so the patterns are obvious to a casual reader but to do so in a way that still gives you reason to actually do the underling for yourself (if you stop after this first example, you will have received a misleading impression of the relationship between the Gospels). Although it is perhaps not entirely satisfactory, I have chosen to reduce the size of the type till the text is barely readable. That way you can see the pattern (and check to see if yours is similar) without being too distracted by the text.

## MATT. 24:15-28

<sup>15</sup>"So <u>when you see the desolating sacrilege</u> spoken of by the prophet Daniel, standing in the holy place (<u>let the reader understand</u>), <sup>16</sup><u>then let those who are in Judea flee to the mountains;</u> <sup>17</sup><u>let him who is on the housetop not go down</u> <u>to take</u> what is in his <u>house;</u> <sup>18</sup><u>and let him who is in the field not turn back to take his mantle.</u> <sup>19</sup><u>And alas for those who are with child and for those who give suck in those days!</u> <sup>20</sup><u>Pray that your flight may not be in winter</u> or on a sabbath. <sup>21</sup><u>For</u> then <u>there will be</u> great <u>tribulation, such as has not been from the beginning of the</u> world <u>until now</u>, no, <u>and never will be</u>. <sup>22</sup>And if those <u>days</u> had <u>not</u> been <u>shortened, no human being would be saved; but for the sake of the elect</u> those <u>days</u> will be <u>shortened.</u> <sup>23</sup><u>Then if any one says to you,</u> 'Lo, <u>here is the Christ!'</u> or <u>'There he is!' do not believe it.</u> <sup>24</sup>For <u>false Christs and false prophets will arise and show great signs and wonders</u>, so as <u>to lead astray, if possible</u>, even <u>the elect</u>. <sup>25</sup>Lo, <u>I have told you</u> beforehand. <sup>26</sup>So, if they say to you, 'Lo, he is in the wilderness,' do not go out; if they say, 'Lo, he is in the inner rooms,' do not believe it. <sup>27</sup>For as the lightning comes from the east and shines as far as the west, so will be the coming of the Son of man. <sup>28</sup>Wherever the body is, there the eagles will be gathered together."

## MARK 13:14-23

<sup>14</sup>"But <u>when you see the desolating sacrilege</u> set up where it ought not to be (<u>let the reader understand), then let those who are in Judea flee to the mountains;</u> <sup>15</sup><u>let him who is on the housetop not go down</u>, nor enter his <u>house, to take</u> anything away; <sup>16</sup><u>and let him who is in the field not turn back to take his mantle.</u> <sup>17</sup><u>And alas for those who are with child and for those who give suck in those days!</u> <sup>18</sup>Pray that it may not happen in winter." [etc.—you can continue to underline if you so desire; your "answers" can be checked against the underlined text below] <sup>19</sup>"<u>For</u> in those days <u>there will be</u> such <u>tribulation as has not been from the</u> beginning of the creation which God created <u>until now</u>, and never will be. <sup>20</sup>And if the Lord had <u>not shortened</u> the <u>days, no human being would be saved; but for the sake of the elect</u>, whom he chose, he <u>shortened the days.</u> <sup>21</sup>And <u>then if any one says to you,</u> 'Look, <u>here is the Christ!'</u> or 'Look, <u>there he is!' do not believe it.</u> <sup>22</sup><u>False Christs and false prophets will arise and show signs and wonders, to lead astray, if possible, the elect</u>. <sup>23</sup>But take heed; <u>I have told you</u> all things <u>beforehand.</u>"

While these kinds of parallels are not that common, there are a number of them. For example, compare Matthew 4:18-22 with Mark 1:16-20 or Matthew 20:20-28 with Mark 10:35-45. Most of the examples that are this close come from parallels between Matthew and Mark, although there are a few examples of very close parallels between Matthew and Luke (Matt. 6:25-34 and Luke 12:22-31). All these examples have more than 60 percent common vocabulary. I know this, because when I wrote my Ph.D. dissertation, I discovered something interesting while doing this kind of comparison. To make my point, I had to gather statistics of all the parallels to the Gospel of Matthew. In the end, that meant that I had to count manually all the words I had underlined. From there on, though, I was able to use my computer to generate many of the statistics I needed. The whole process was instructive and interesting in its own way but not something I would have chosen to do for fun!

There is another group of parallels that have quite a number of words and phrases in common but not quite as many as in the examples above. For example, compare Matthew 9:1-7; Mark 2:1-12:

## MATT. 9:1-7

[1]"And getting into a boat he crossed over and came to his own city. [2]And behold, they brought to him a paralytic, lying on his bed; and when Jesus saw their faith he said to the paralytic, 'Take heart, my son; your sins are forgiven.' [3]And behold, some of the scribes said to themselves, 'This man is blaspheming.' [4]But Jesus, knowing their thoughts, said, 'Why do you think evil in your hearts? [5]For which is easier, to say, 'Your sins are forgiven,' or to say, 'Rise and walk'? [6]But that you may know that the Son of man has authority on earth to forgive sins'—he then said to the paralytic—'Rise, take up your bed and go home.' [7]And he rose and went home.'"

## MARK 2:1-12

[1]"And when he returned to Capernaum after some days, it was reported that he was at home. [2]And many were gathered together, so that there was no longer room for them, not even about the door; and he was preaching the word to them. [3]And they came, bringing to him a paralytic carried by four men. [4]And when they could not get near him because of the crowd, they removed the roof above him; and when they had made an opening, they let down the pallet on which the paralytic lay. [5]And when Jesus saw their faith, he said to the paralytic, 'My son, your sins are forgiven.' [6]Now some of the scribes were sitting there, questioning in their hearts, [7]'Why does this man speak thus? It is blasphemy! Who can forgive sins but God alone?' [8]And immediately Jesus, perceiving in his spirit that they thus questioned within themselves, said to them, 'Why do you question thus in your hearts? [9]Which is easier, to say to the paralytic, 'Your sins are forgiven,' or to say, 'Rise, take up your pallet and walk'? [10]But that you may know that

the Son of man has authority on earth to forgive sins'—he said to the paralytic—[11]'I say to you, rise, take up your pallet and go home.' [12]And he rose, and immediately took up the pallet and went out before them all; so that they were all amazed and glorified God, saying, 'We never saw anything like this!' "

## MATT. 9:1-7

[1]"And getting into a boat he crossed over and came to his own city. [2]And behold, they brought to him a paralytic, lying on his bed; and when Jesus saw their faith he said to the paralytic, 'Take heart, my son; your sins are forgiven.' [3]And behold, some of the scribes said to themselves, 'This man is blaspheming.' [4]But Jesus, knowing their thoughts, said, 'Why do you think evil in your hearts? [5]For which is easier, to say, 'Your sins are forgiven,' or to say, 'Rise and walk'? [6]But that you may know that the Son of man has authority on earth to forgive sins'—he then said to the paralytic—'Rise, take up your bed and go home.' [7]And he rose and went home.' "

## MARK 2:1-12

[1]"And when he returned to Capernaum after some days, it was reported that he was at home. [2]And many were gathered together, so that there was no longer room for them, not even about the door; and he was preaching the word to them. [3]And they came, bringing to him a paralytic carried by four men. [4]And when they could not get near him because of the crowd, they removed the roof above him; and when they had made an opening, they let down the pallet on which the paralytic lay. [5]And when Jesus saw their faith, he said to the paralytic, 'My son, your sins are forgiven.' [6]Now some of the scribes were sitting there, questioning in their hearts, [7]'Why does this man speak thus? It is blasphemy! Who can forgive sins but God alone?' [8]And immediately Jesus, perceiving in his spirit that they thus questioned within themselves, said to them, 'Why do you question thus in your hearts? [9]Which is easier, to say to the paralytic, 'Your sins are forgiven,' or to say, 'Rise, take up your pallet and walk'? [10]But that you may know that the Son of man has authority on earth to forgive sins'—he said to the paralytic—[11]'I say to you, rise, take up your pallet and go home.' [12]And he rose, and immediately took up the pallet and went out before them all; so that they were all amazed and glorified God, saying, 'We never saw anything like this!' "

There are further examples which, although obvious parallels, have even less in common than those examined so far:

# The Four Faces of Jesus

## MATT. 12:9-14

⁹"And he went on from there, and entered their synagogue. ¹⁰And behold, there was a man with a withered hand. And they asked him, 'Is it lawful to heal on the sabbath?' so that they might accuse him. ¹¹He said to them, 'What man of you, if he has one sheep and it falls into a pit on the sabbath, will not lay hold of it and lift it out? ¹²Of how much more value is a man than a sheep! So it is lawful to do good on the sabbath.' ¹³Then he said to the man, 'Stretch out your hand.' And the man stretched it out, and it was restored, whole like the other. ¹⁴But the Pharisees went out and took counsel against him, how to destroy him."

## LUKE 6:6-11

⁶"On another sabbath, when he entered the synagogue and taught, a man was there whose right hand was withered. ⁷And the scribes and the Pharisees watched him, to see whether he would heal on the sabbath, so that they might find an accusation against him. ⁸But he knew their thoughts, and he said to the man who had the withered hand, 'Come and stand here.' And he rose and stood there. ⁹And Jesus said to them, 'I ask you, is it lawful on the sabbath to do good or to do harm, to save life or to destroy it?' ¹⁰And he looked around on them all, and said to him, 'Stretch out your hand.' And he did so, and his hand was restored. ¹¹But they were filled with fury and discussed with one another what they might do to Jesus."

## MATT. 12:9-14

⁹"And he went on from there, and entered their synagogue. ¹⁰And behold, there was a man with a withered hand. And they asked him, 'Is it lawful to heal on the sabbath?' so that they might accuse him. ¹¹He said to them, 'What man of you, if he has one sheep and it falls into a pit on the sabbath, will not lay hold of it and lift it out? ¹²Of how much more value is a man than a sheep! So it is lawful to do good on the sabbath.' ¹³Then he said to the man, 'Stretch out your hand.' And the man stretched it out, and it was restored, whole like the other. ¹⁴But the Pharisees went out and took counsel against him, how to destroy him."

## LUKE 6:6-11

⁶"On another sabbath, when he entered the synagogue and taught, a man was there whose right hand was withered. ⁷And the scribes and the Pharisees watched him, to see whether he would heal on the sabbath, so that they might find an accusation against him. ⁸But he knew their thoughts, and he said to the man who had the withered hand, 'Come and stand here.' And he rose and stood there. ⁹And Jesus said to them, 'I ask you, is it lawful on the sabbath to do good or to do harm, to save life or to destroy it?' ¹⁰And he looked around on them all, and said to him, 'Stretch out your hand.' And he did so, and his hand was restored. ¹¹But they were filled with fury and discussed with one another what they might do to Jesus."

192

Finally, there are some examples of parallels that are quite different from each other. Sometimes these occur where you would expect a great deal of common vocabulary. Take, for example, the account of the crucifixion of Jesus. As it is recorded in Luke 23:26-38, there is a total of 209 words. The parallel passage in Matthew 27:32-44 has 169 words. Both these passages clearly describe the same event, but they only have twenty-three words in common in the underlying Greek text. These words are: "Cyrene," "Simon," "the cross," "place," "skull," "divided his garments casting lots," "the king of the Jews," "on [the] right," "on [the] left," and "others he saved himself." One would be hard pressed to describe the crucifixion without using these words. In fact, one would be hard pressed to describe the crucifixion with less than twenty-five words in common with either Matthew or Luke. In the passage immediately preceding this example, the statistics are likewise startling. Matthew 27:15-26 has 192 words, while Luke 23:13-25 has 163. Only nine of these words are common between the two accounts.[3] The example I have chosen for you to look at is Matthew 26:26-30, which parallels Luke 22:14-23. This describes the Last Supper, the basis for the Christian eucharist, which we would expect to be remembered accurately because it was often reenacted by the early Christians. But the two accounts are quite different:

## MATT. 26:26-30

26"Now as they were eating, Jesus took bread, and blessed, and broke it, and gave it to the disciples and said, 'Take, eat; this is my body.' 27And he took a cup, and when he had given thanks he gave it to them, saying, 'Drink of it, all of you; 28for this is my blood of the covenant, which is poured out for many for the forgiveness of sins. 29I tell you I shall not drink again of this fruit of the vine until that day when I drink it new with you in my Father's kingdom.' 30And when they had sung a

## LUKE 22:14-23

14"And when the hour came, he sat at table, and the apostles with him. 15And he said to them, 'I have earnestly desired to eat this passover with you before I suffer; 16for I tell you I shall not eat it until it is fulfilled in the kingdom of God.' 17And he took a cup, and when he had given thanks he said, 'Take this, and divide it among yourselves; 18for I tell you that from now on I shall not drink of the fruit of the vine until the kingdom of God comes.' 19And he took bread, and when he had given thanks he broke it and gave it to

The Four Faces of Jesus

hymn, they went out to the Mount of Olives."

them, saying, 'This is my body which is given for you. Do this in remembrance of me.' [20]And likewise the cup after supper, saying, 'This cup which is poured out for you is the new covenant in my blood. [21]But behold the hand of him who betrays me is with me on the table. [22]For the Son of man goes as it has been determined; but woe to that man by whom he is betrayed!' [23]And they began to question one another, which of them it was that would do this."

## Matt. 26:26–30

[26]"Now as they were eating, Jesus took bread, and blessed, and broke it, and gave it to the disciples and said, 'Take, eat; this is my body.' [27]And he took a cup, and when he had given thanks he gave it to them, saying, 'Drink of it, all of you; [28]for this is my blood of the covenant, which is poured out for many for the forgiveness of sins. [29]I tell you I shall not drink again of this fruit of the vine until that day when I drink it new with you in my Father's kingdom.' [30]And when they had sung a hymn, they went out to the Mount of Olives."

## Luke 22:14-23

[14]"And when the hour came, he sat at table, and the apostles with him. [15]And he said to them, 'I have earnestly desired to eat this passover with you before I suffer; [16]for I tell you I shall not eat it until it is fulfilled in the kingdom of God.' [17]And he took a cup, and when he had given thanks he said, 'Take this, and divide it among yourselves; [18]for I tell you that from now on I shall not drink of the fruit of the vine until the kingdom of God comes.' [19]And he took bread, and when he had given thanks he broke it and gave it to them, saying, 'This is my body which is given for you. Do this in remembrance of me.' [20]And likewise the cup after supper, saying, 'This cup which is poured out for you is the new covenant in my blood. [21]But behold the hand of him who betrays me is with me on the table. [22]For the Son of man goes as it has been determined; but woe to that man by whom he is betrayed!' [23]And they began to question one another, which of them it was that would do this."

In fact, this kind of variation between Luke and the other two Gospels is very common from Luke 22:14 to the end of Luke's Gospel.

The final example illustrates something different. Some parallels, almost all of those between Matthew and Luke, show a combination of passages that are quite different, interspersed with passages that are ex-

194

actly the same. The example given below is the report of John the Baptist's preaching in Matthew 3:1-12 and Luke 3:1-11:

## MATT. 3:1-12

[1]"In those days came John the Baptist, preaching in the wilderness of Judea, [2]'Repent, for the kingdom of heaven is at hand.' [3]For this is he who was spoken of by the prophet Isaiah when he said, 'The voice of one crying in the wilderness: Prepare the way of the Lord, make his paths straight.' [4]Now John wore a garment of camel's hair, and a leather girdle around his waist; and his food was locusts and wild honey. [5]Then went out to him Jerusalem and all Judea and all the region about the Jordan, [6]and they were baptized by him in the river Jordan, confessing their sins. [7]But when he saw many of the Pharisees and Sadducees coming for baptism, he said to them, 'You brood of vipers! Who warned you to flee from the wrath to come? [8]Bear fruit that befits repentance, [9]and do not presume to say to yourselves, 'We have Abraham as our father;' for I tell you, God is able from these stones to raise up children to Abraham. [10]Even now the axe is laid to the root of the trees; every tree therefore that does not bear good fruit is cut down and thrown into the fire. [11]I baptize you with water for repentance, but he who is coming after me is mightier than I, whose sandals I am not worthy to carry; he will baptize you with the

## LUKE 3:1-11

[1]"In the fifteenth year of the reign of Tiberius Caesar, Pontius Pilate being governor of Judea, and Herod being tetrarch of Galilee, and his brother Philip tetrarch of the region of Ituraea and Trachonitis, and Lysanias tetrarch of Abilene, [2]in the high-priesthood of Annas and Caiaphas, the word of God came to John the son of Zechariah in the wilderness; [3]and he went into all the region about the Jordan, preaching a baptism of repentance for the forgiveness of sins. [4]As it is written in the book of the words of Isaiah the prophet, 'The voice of one crying in the wilderness: Prepare the way of the Lord, make his paths straight. [5]Every valley shall be filled, and every mountain and hill shall be brought low, and the crooked shall be made straight, and the rough ways shall be made smooth; [6]and all flesh shall see the salvation of God.' [7]He said therefore to the multitudes that came out to be baptized by him, 'You brood of vipers! Who warned you to flee from the wrath to come? [8]Bear fruits that befit repentance, and do not begin to say to yourselves, 'We have Abraham as our father;' for I tell you, God is able from these stones to raise up children to Abraham. [9]Even now the axe is laid to the root of the trees;

Holy Spirit and with fire. [12]His winnowing fork is in his hand, and he will clear his threshing floor and gather his wheat into the granary, but the chaff he will burn with unquenchable fire.' "

every tree therefore that does not bear good fruit is cut down and thrown into the fire.' [10]And the multitudes asked him, 'What then shall we do?' [11]And he answered them, 'He who has two coats, let him share with him who has none; and he who has food, let him do likewise.' "

## MATT. 3:1-12

[1]"In those days came <u>John</u> the Baptist, <u>preaching in the wilderness</u> of Judea, [2]"<u>Repent</u>, for the kingdom of heaven is at hand.' [3]For this is he who was spoken of by <u>the prophet Isaiah</u> when he said, '<u>The voice of one crying in the wilderness: Prepare the way of the Lord, make his paths straight</u>.' [4]Now John wore a garment of camel's hair, and a leather girdle around his waist; and his food was locusts and wild honey. [5]Then went out to him Jerusalem and all Judea and all the region about the Jordan, [6]and they were baptized by him in the river Jordan, confessing their sins. [7]But when he saw many of the Pharisees and Sadducees coming for baptism, <u>he said to</u> them, '<u>You brood of vipers! Who warned you to flee from the wrath to come?</u> [8]<u>Bear fruit that befits repentance,</u> [9]<u>and do not</u> presume <u>to say to yourselves, 'We have Abraham as our father;' for I tell you, God is able from these stones to raise up children to Abraham. [10]Even now the axe is laid to the root of the trees; every tree therefore that does not bear good fruit is cut down and thrown into the fire</u>. [11]I baptize you with water for repentance, but he who is coming after me is mightier than I, whose sandals I am not worthy to carry; he will baptize you with the Holy Spirit and with fire. [12]His winnowing fork is in his hand, and he will clear his threshing floor and gather his wheat into the granary, but the chaff he will burn with unquenchable fire.' "

## LUKE 3:1-11

[1]"In the fifteenth year of the reign of Tiberius Caesar, Pontius Pilate being governor of Judea, and Herod being tetrarch of Galilee, and his brother Philip tetrarch of the region of Ituraea and Trachonitis, and Lysanias tetrarch of Abilene, [2]in the highpriesthood of Annas and Caiaphas, the word of God came to <u>John</u> the son of Zechariah <u>in the wilderness</u>; [3]and he went into all the region about the Jordan, <u>preaching</u> a baptism of <u>repent</u>ance for the forgiveness of sins. [4]As it is written in the book of the words of <u>Isaiah the prophet</u>, '<u>The voice of one crying in the wilderness: Prepare the way of the Lord, make his paths straight</u>. [5]Every valley shall be filled, and every mountain and hill shall be brought low, and the crooked shall be made straight, and the rough ways shall be made smooth; [6]and all flesh shall see the salvation of God.' [7]<u>He said</u> therefore to the multitudes that came out to be baptized by him, '<u>You brood of vipers! Who warned you to flee from the wrath to come? [8]Bear fruits that befit repentance, and do not</u> begin <u>to say to yourselves, 'We have Abraham as our father;' for I tell you, God is able from these stones to raise up children to Abraham. [9]Even now the axe is laid to the root of the trees; every tree therefore that does not bear good fruit is cut down and thrown into the fire</u>.' [10]And the multitudes asked him, 'What then shall we do?' [11]And he answered them, 'He who has two coats, let him share with him who has none; and he who has food, let him do likewise.' "

# Synoptic Relationships: The Raw Data

## SOME BRUTE FACTS THAT NEED EXPLAINING

The above examples will have given you a little glimpse of how complex the problem is. In the Synoptic Gospels, you can find an example of just about every kind of relationship—everything from parallel passages in which the words are almost exactly the same to parallel passages that are quite different and all kinds of variations in between. As you might expect, there has been no end of suggestions as to how these kinds of relationships might be explained. We will look at some of these in the next chapter. But for now, let us put down the "brute facts" that any theory will need to explain.

*First, there does appear to be a relationship of some sort between the three Synoptic Gospels—Matthew, Mark, and Luke—while John appears to be quite distinct.*

*Second, there is often very close agreement between the Gospels in the accounts of the same event/saying/incident, even down to exact wording.* Furthermore, these come in all possible permutations:

A. There are some where all three Synoptic Gospels are in very close parallel. For example, the beginning of the account of Jesus cleansing the temple, in Matthew 21:23-27; Mark 11:27-33; and Luke 20:1-8. Or the parable of the fig tree, in Matthew 24:32-35; Mark 13:28-32; and Luke 21:29-32.

B. There are examples where two of the three Synoptic Gospels are very closely parallel. We have already seen the parallel accounts of Jesus' saying about the great tribulation, in Matthew 24:15-28 and Mark 13:12-23. From the same section of Matthew comes the parable of the faithful and the unfaithful servants. Matthew 24:15-51 is very closely parallel to Luke 12:42-46, but Mark does not have this parable.

C. There are some examples where two Gospels are in broad agreement, but the third is somewhat different. Take, for example, the saying in Matthew 20:25-28, comparing how the rulers of the Gentiles show their greatness to how the disciples should comport themselves. This is *very* closely paralleled in Mark 10:42-45, but although Luke 22:24-27 represents the same saying, Luke expresses it quite differently. On the other hand, Mark 12:38-40 is very closely paralleled by Luke 20:46-47, while the version in Matthew 23:6-13 is quite different.

D. There is another category of sayings that one would expect to have accounts that are very closely parallel but that are not. We have already seen this above in the parallel accounts of the Last Supper, in Matthew 26:26-30 and Luke 22:14-23. One might also think of the genealogies recorded in Matthew 1:1-17 and Luke 3:23-38. Not only do they differ in terms of which end of the genealogy they begin with and in how far back they go, but several of the actual names in the genealogy are different, especially between Matthew 1:7-11 and Luke 3:28-30.

*Third, the parallels between the Gospels are based on the Greek, not on any underlying Aramaic or Hebrew.* There is still debate on which language Jesus used. As near as we can tell, Palestine was multilingual in Jesus' day. Different population groups spoke one or more of four languages. The Roman soldiers and governing elite spoke Latin and often Greek, as well. Greek was the language of those cities most influenced by Greeks, such as the ten cities of the Decapolis. Aramaic was the language of the villagers and farmers, while Hebrew was kept alive as the language of the Holy Scriptures. Inscriptions in all four of these languages have been found in Palestine dating from the time of Jesus. But which of them did Jesus speak?

Jesus spent most of His time in the small villages in Galilee, where most people would speak Aramaic. Not only this, there are several quotations in Mark in Aramaic (Mark 5:41), and when Jesus cried out in agony on the cross, He cried out in Aramaic (Mark 15:34). At the very least, this shows that Jesus *spoke* in Aramaic. Indeed, He likely preached to the crowds in Aramaic and taught His disciples in that language as well. Hebrew is close to Aramaic, and Jesus would have heard the Scriptures read in Hebrew. So Jesus probably could get by in Hebrew if He had to. Whether He spoke Greek is uncertain. Had He been a trader in a larger city, He would have needed it, but how often He would have needed to use Greek in Galilee is debated. Some say Galilee was strongly influenced by Greek ideas and language, while others deny this. The point, though, is that although Jesus most likely taught in Aramaic, the close literary relationships between the Gospel accounts took place *after*

Jesus' teachings had been translated into Greek.

*Fourth, almost everything recorded in Mark has parallels in the other Gospels.* Indeed, as has already been mentioned, only thirty of the 609 verses of Mark do not have parallels in either of Matthew or Luke. These include:

The accounts of one parable and two healings:

1. Mark 4:26-29—The parable of the seed growing of itself
2. Mark 7:31-37—The healing of the deaf/mute by Jesus placing a finger in his ear
3. Mark 8:22-26—The healing (in two stages) of the blind man at Bethsaida

And three short texts:

4. Mark 3:20—Jesus' relatives think Him crazy
5. Mark 9:49—Salt with fire
6. Mark 14:51—The fleeing young man

If we discard these thirty verses, Mark has 10,650 words. Of these, 8,189 appear either in Matthew or Luke (7,678 in Matthew; 7,040 in Luke).[4] So not only is nearly all the content of Mark found in either Matthew or Luke, so are most of the actual words of Mark's Gospel.

*Fifth, where Matthew and Luke have common material that is also in Mark, they preserve it in the same order.* There are only two exceptions to this general rule in Matthew and four in Luke. Otherwise, there is a remarkable consistency in the pattern, especially when compared to material Matthew and Luke have in common that is *not* in Mark. In these cases, the material frequently appears in a different order.

*Sixth, after Luke 22:13, the parallels between Luke and the other two Synoptic Gospels change in quality.* In this latter part of the Gospel of Luke, the percentage of vocabulary common to the other Gospels drops dramatically, and although the Gospel is describing events surrounding the crucifixion in a way consistent with the other Gospels, it also does so in a way that is quite distinct from Matthew and Mark—and from John, for that matter.

*Finally, Luke 1:1-3 makes references to sources from which he gained material to write his Gospel.* Despite the efforts of some to assert otherwise, the language used in these verses is consistent with the use of either oral or written sources. They do reflect the fact that at least one Gospel writer worked from sources.

Any hypothesis that is put forward to explain the relationships between the three Synoptic Gospels has to provide satisfactory explanations of these "brute" facts. In the next chapter we will look at three of the most widely regarded explanations.

---

1. John 1:19-28; 2:13-22; 4:43-54; 6:1-15, 16-21; 12:1-8; 13:21-30, 36-38. A case could be made for considering John 11:45-57 to be part of this group, but a comparison with Matthew 26:1-6; Mark 14:1, 2; and Luke 22:1, 2 will show that there is almost no connection between them.
2. The passages concerned have a total of 87 verses, while there are some 741 verses in John 1–17.
3. The common words are: "Barabbas," "[to] crucify," "for what evil has he done?" "Jesus," and "[he] delivered."
4. Werner Georg Kümmel, *Introduction to the New Testament*, rev. ed. (London: SCM, 1957), 57.

# CHAPTER TWENTY

# Synoptic Relationships: The Theories

## THE OLD CERTAINTY: THE TWO-DOCUMENT HYPOTHESIS

The problem of synoptic relationship was first discussed in Germany and then taken up in England during the first part of this century. The appearance of the book, *The Four Gospels: A Study in Origins,*[1] by Burnett H. Streeter, took advantage of all this previous work and appeared to announce the definitive solution to the issue—a solution that satisfied most of the English-speaking scholarly community for the next two decades. During this time period, commentaries on the Gospels were able to dismiss the issue of the relationships between the Synoptic Gospels in one or two sentences, with a footnote to Streeter's book. In fact, in some writings, the two-document hypothesis was described as one of the "assured results of criticism [scholarship[2]]."

What, then, is the two-document hypothesis? According to this hypothesis, the Gospel of Mark was written first. Matthew and Luke both had access to Mark and used it to write their Gospels. They did this independently of each other.

How, then, should the material, which is common to Matthew and Luke, be explained? Matthew and Mark both used another written source, now lost, labeled by scholars as "Q."[3] Diagrammatically, this hypothesis would look like this:

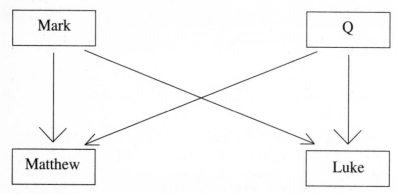

Actually, Streeter's theory was a bit more complicated than this. He thought there were two more written sources, called "M" and "L," that contained the materials unique to Matthew and Luke respectively. Later writers didn't stress these two additional sources much. Neither did they give too much credence to Streeter's suggestion that Luke came out in two editions.

The strength of any hypothesis lies in its ability to account for the raw data. How well does the two-document hypothesis account for the data outlined in the previous chapter?

First, it explains well the parallels in which combinations of the three Gospels have a high percentage of common vocabulary. This is accounted for because, according to the two-document hypothesis, Matthew and Luke were independently copying from Mark, or "Q." The common vocabulary comes from the fact that one was the source of the other, or that Matthew and Luke used a common source. The variations in the amount of common vocabulary is considered to be attributable to the different amounts of care used in the copying.

The two-document hypothesis also satisfactorily explains the fact that the parallels are based on the Greek text, not on the original Aramaic speech of Jesus, because Mark, the source of the other two Gospels, was written in Greek. It also explains why we find parallels to almost all of Mark in the other two Gospels—Matthew and Luke used Mark as a source. Indeed, if one follows this hypothesis, one can explain why most of the things unique to Mark might have been left out by Matthew and Luke. Since the healing of the blind man at Bethsaida, in Mark 8:22-26, took place in two stages, it might give the impression that Jesus was not able to do the job right the first time. Thus Matthew and Luke might have omitted this story from their Gospels for this reason. In Mark 7:31-37, Jesus heals the deaf-mute by the unusual method of putting His finger in the man's ear. The parable of the seed growing by itself (Mark 4:26-29) is paralleled by the more elaborate parable of the weeds, in Matthew 13:24-30. Matthew may have wanted to use the parable of the weeds and decided the other parable was too much like it. It is not surprising that Matthew and Luke didn't record that Jesus' relatives thought He was crazy (Mark 3:20), and the saying of salt mingled with fire (Mark 9:49) could have been left out because it is a bit hard to understand. This leaves only Mark 14:51, 52, the mention of the young man in Gethsemane escaping by leaving his linen cloth in the hand of his attackers and fleeing naked into the darkness. Some commentators suggest that this might be an autobiographical reference to Mark himself. In any event, it has not proven difficult to explain why the other Gospel writers might not wish to use the thirty verses of Mark that find no parallel in Matthew or Luke.

The two-document hypothesis likewise gives a good reason why Matthew and Luke follow the same order of events as Mark when they are using material found in Mark's Gospel but follow a different order when they have material in common that is not in Mark. On this hypothesis, they both had Mark in front of them and used it as the basis of their chronology of events.

In fact, the only data that is not convincingly explained by means of the two-document hypothesis are the so-called "minor" occurrences when Matthew and Luke agree against Mark. For example, sometimes the wording of Matthew and Luke is the same, and the wording of Mark is different. Now, the two-document hypothesis could account well for Matthew and Mark agreeing against Luke or for Mark and Luke agreeing against Matthew. In these cases, the explanation would be that either Matthew or Luke was following the text of Mark more closely than was the other. But how can the two-document theory explain those instances when Matthew and Luke agree, but Mark is different?

Streeter devoted a chapter to this issue in his book, and since that time, other major efforts have been put forward to explain these situations. Some of the "minor agreements" are explained as fairly obvious corrections to Mark's poor grammar. Indeed, Mark's use of Greek often falls short of the higher standards shown by Matthew, and especially Luke. So it is conceivable that both would have independently corrected Mark's grammar in the same way. Other "minor agreements" could be explained by the process of transmission of the text. As a scribe copied one Gospel, say Luke, he might be unconsciously influenced by the language of Matthew. Thus, in their copying of manuscripts, scribes would inadvertently tend to smooth out the differences between the three Gospels. If the two-documentary hypothesis reflects what really happened, then some such process must be the explanation. But these "minor agreements" helped convince some scholars that the search for a better solution to the problem should commence.

## AN OLDER HYPOTHESIS REVIVED: THE GRIESBACH HYPOTHESIS

Although there were the occasional earlier academic rumblings, it was the work of William R. Farmer that effectively reopened debate on the issue of synoptic relations. Farmer's book, *The Synoptic Problem: A Critical Analysis,*[4] appeared in 1976, two decades after Streeter's work. Mind you, Streeter's book did little more than set out what had been the common understanding among scholars since the late nineteenth century. This makes Farmer's contribution all the more significant.

Farmer insisted that the best way to explain the data regarding synoptic relationships is that Matthew was written first, that Luke was acquainted with Matthew's Gospel, and that Mark was written last, using both Matthew and Luke. Diagrammatically, Farmer's theory might look something like this:

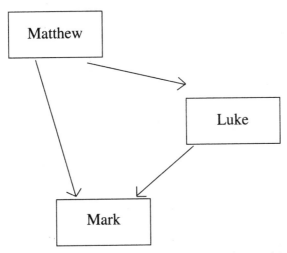

In fact, this same suggestion had been put forward in the late eighteenth century by the German scholar Johann Jakob Griesbach, who had been actively studying this issue. Hence, it is commonly referred to as the Griesbach hypothesis, although it is sometimes also known as the two-Gospel hypothesis.

Farmer and other enthusiastic proponents of this view point out its relative simplicity. It explains the data on the basis of the documents we already have; the hypothesis does not require the existence of a source ("Q") lost to us. Furthermore, proponents argue that this theory better fits the tradition of the early church, which says that Matthew was the first to write down the words of Jesus in Aramaic. They give less attention to how the words of Jesus in Aramaic ended up in a Gospel written in Greek, but one would presume it was accomplished by a process that included translation of some portions of the original.

How well does the Griesbach hypothesis account for the known facts? Like the two-document hypothesis, it accounts for the fact that there is a close relationship between some parallels and not others by pointing to the varying processes of copying from one document to another. The parallels are based on Greek, because all the copying was done from Greek originals to Greek texts. Mark has so much in common with the others because they form the principal sources of his information.

# The Four Faces of Jesus

In the initial debates, the two-document hypothesis triumphed over the Griesbach hypothesis, due largely to the phenomenon of the *sequence* of common materials in the Gospels. As we saw in the previous chapter, when the parallels between Matthew and Luke are also found in Mark, they almost always are recorded in the same order. But when the parallels between Matthew and Luke are absent from Mark, the order in which they appear varies considerably between the two Gospels. The two-document hypothesis provided what appeared to be a good explanation for this—when Matthew and Luke used Mark, they used his chronology of events; when they used "Q," which in any event was composed mostly of sayings and parables, they felt free to rearrange the order. Earlier scholars advocating the Griesbach hypothesis did not provide a really satisfactory explanation of this phenomenon of sequence. It was Farmer's alternative explanation of the phenomenon of sequence that did more than anything else to revive the Griesbach hypothesis.

Farmer explained the phenomenon in this way. Matthew, the first Gospel to be written, reflected the perspective of the Jewish Christians. Luke, written next, was composed from a Gentile perspective, a perspective influenced by Paul's mission to the Gentiles. At Rome, tension periodically arose between these two different communities of Christians, each of which used one or the other of the two different Gospels to bolster its perspective of things. Mark wrote his Gospel in an attempt to harmonize the positions of the Jewish Christians and the Gentile Christians. He did this by taking the Jewish-Christian Gospel of Matthew and the Gentile-Christian Gospel of Luke and choosing from them mainly those passages they had in common, although if the two Gospels recorded events in a different order, Mark did not use that event. This explanation also provides a reason why most of the Gospel of Mark is found in either Matthew or Luke. It is because Mark derived nearly all his information from both of those Gospels.

## OR SHOULD THE EXPLANATION BE IN TERMS OF ORAL TRANSMISSION?

For nearly two centuries, most attempts to resolve the problem of synoptic relationships have been in terms of literary explanations. In other words, the relationship was explained in terms of one writer copying from a preexisting Gospel. But throughout that time there has always been a minority viewpoint that relies on oral tradition. Two Scandinavian scholars, Harald Riesenfeld and Birger Gerhardsson, and, more recently, the German scholar Rainer Riesner, are among the best-known advocates of an oral-transmission view, although they are by no means alone in this.[5] Both Riesenfeld and Gerhardsson rely strongly on first-century Jewish background. Jesus was called a rabbi, so the argument goes, and like all good rabbis, He would have taught His disciples to memorize His teachings. In their turn, disciples taught others by having them memorize the teachings of Jesus. The Gospels were constructed from this common pool of memorized materials.

How well does a hypothesis of oral transmission explain the data from the previous chapter? Carefully transmitted oral tradition would exhibit many of the characteristic features of the Gospel parallels, including those places in which the parallels are very close. The Gospels would all be dependent on a Greek version of the common oral tradition. The common order of events shared by Mark with Matthew and Luke would likewise belong to the common oral tradition. Finally, this theory accounts well not only for the minor agreements of Matthew and Luke against Mark but also for the other types of minor agreements that any two of the three Synoptic Gospels show against the third.

## WHAT DOES ROBERT THINK?

When I am lecturing on this subject, it is about at this point that the class begins to show a little restlessness. We have three competing explanations, all of which have strengths and weaknesses. The class often wonders aloud why don't I just tell them which is the "right" solution, rather than getting bogged down in all this fine detail? Then they will go away and learn about the correct theory! Well, as was said earlier, the final winner has yet to be declared. Most everybody involved in the dialogue is convinced that they have the answer and that the other theories are wrong. For some years now I have been busily debating the pros and cons of the different positions and have always found it both baffling and fascinating that two intelligent people can take the same data and get quite different results. Each position is clearly articulated and gives a sophisticated explanation of the data. No clear winner in the debate has emerged.

But which of the three solutions predominates in the scholarly environment? It is hard to say, but the two-document hypothesis still appears to be the majority opinion. Mind you, those advocating the Griesbach hypothesis publish a great deal and are making significant inroads in some quarters. There is also the occasional voice raised in defense of the possibility that oral traditional transmission best accounts for the data.

But where do I stand? Or, as my students sometimes ask, "What does Robert think?" I am an example of the kind of chaos that exists in the study of synoptic relationships these days. In this chapter, I have only summarized the three *major* viewpoints. There are a great many different variations on these, and I follow one of them. Let me explain how I came to the position that I now hold.

I did my first underlining of parallel accounts in the Gospels as an M.A. student writing on the passion narrative in the Gospel of Luke. I had been taught the two-document hypothesis and became convinced at that time that although Luke used Mark and "Q," he used independent tradition for the passion narrative. It was important to an argument I was advancing in my paper, although the amount of effort involved in cutting and pasting and then underlining the parallel accounts to establish the point seemed inordinate. But if nothing else, it gave me a feel for the kind of phenomena that existed in the Gospels.

For my Ph.D. dissertation, I chose the topic of the Matthean Community. I was trying to work out as much as I could about it, and my earlier work on Luke had alerted me to the fact that there was interesting data to be gained by comparing the parallels between the Gospels. In particular, I thought that many of the conclusions being drawn from comparisons between Matthew and Luke were made on the basis of parallels that were not close enough to support the kind of things that were being said about them. In a preliminary guided research project, I worked through some of the issues in the problem of synoptic relationships. I happened to be working under the supervision of an enthusiastic supporter of the Griesbach hypothesis. Now, at that time I still subscribed to the two-document hypothesis, so he and I had a very interesting debate regarding the merits of both positions. In the end, neither of us convinced the other, although we did agree to remain friends!

Not until I was sorting out my detailed analysis to the parallels between Matthew and the other Gospels did I notice something that, to my knowledge, has not yet appeared in the scholarly literature. There is a difference between the kind of parallels that exist between Matthew and Mark and those that exist between Matthew and Luke. The exercise taken from Matthew 3:1-12 and Luke 3:1-11 in the previous chapter is an example of the type of phenomena that struck me—long passages of words in exactly the same sequence, embedded within unrelated material. There are several examples of this kind of phenomena in the parallels between Matthew and Luke,[6] but they do not exist in parallels between Matthew and Mark. The parallels between Matthew and Mark show greater percentages of common vocabulary, but not these long sequences of words in exactly the same order.

In the process of underlining the common vocabulary in the parallels between the Gospels, I had been convinced gradually that the relationship between the Gospels was probably not based on one Gospel writer copying from an earlier Gospel but on both of them being familiar with a carefully controlled oral tradition. Now, this kind of subjective judgment is possible only to those who have actually done the work of analyzing the parallels meticulously. How could I convince others? They were unlikely to just take my word for it. Then I saw how the difference I have just described might assist me in demonstrating my theory, because the long sequences of words in exactly the same order is the kind of thing one would get if one writer was copying from another. When one is relying on memory, one remembers the basic gist of things and uses much of the same vocabulary but often uses synonyms and changes the tense, etc. This is exactly the kind of phenomena we observe in the parallels between Matthew and Mark. Thus, while I follow a form of the oral-tradition hypothesis, I also believe there was a document rather like "Q" that formed the common link between Matthew and Luke for those passages where they appear to have copied from a common document.

This puts me in a minority as far as explanations of the Synoptic Gospels are concerned, so I have tried to report on the viewpoint of the three major positions to make you better informed regarding what others are thinking. My students normally express uneasiness in discussing questions that have not yet received good answers, but I assure them that this is the very thing that makes this issue so interesting. We are working together figuring it out! But if the answers aren't clear yet, why study it at all? The issue is important for two reasons. One relates to how to study the Synoptic Gospels, the other relates to our doctrine of inspiration. Both of these are vital issues and are important enough to warrant a chapter of their own.

---

1. Burtett H. Streeter, *The Four Gospels: A Study in Origins*, London: MacMillan, 1956.
2. William R. Farmer, *The Synoptic Problem* (Macon, Ga: Mercer University Press, 1976). At first, the term *criticism* as a shorthand for *scholarship* seems a trifle odd. Originally, it had been planned to include an appendix on "The Academic Study of the Gospels in the Twentieth Century," but considerations of length made this impossible. It is available under the author's name in the list of theology faculty at the following internet address: www.avondale.edu.au and explains the curious usuage of the word *critical* for serious scholarship.
3. The German word for source is *Quelle,* and the Germans who first worked on this hypothesis used the letter Q as shorthand for this source, a practice taken over by English-speaking scholars who used the work of the Germans as their starting point.
4. Macon, Ga: Mercer University Press, 1976
5. Birger Gerhardsson, *The Gospel Tradition* (Malmö, Sweden: CWK Gleerup, 1986); and Harald Riesenfeld, *The Gospel Tradition and its Beginnings: A Study in the Limits of "Formgeschichte"* (London: Mowbray, 1957); also published as an article in *Studia Evangelica,* ed. Kurt Aland, et al. (Berlin: Akademie, 1959), 43-65; Rainer Riesner, "Jesus as Preacher and Teacher" in *Jesus in the Oral Tradition,* ed. Henry Wansbrough; JSNTSup 64 (Sheffield: JSOT, 1991), 185-188.
6. Matt. 3:1-12 and Luke 3:1-20; Matt. 8:5-10, 13 and Luke 7:1-10; Matt. 12:38-42 and Luke 11:29-32; and Matt. 24:45-51 and Luke 17:42-46, especially in the wider context of Matthew 24 and Luke 17. Perhaps Matthew 8:18-22 and Luke 9:57-62; Matthew 11:25-27 and Luke 10:21, 22 should be added to this list. The only possible example of such phenomena from parallels between Matthew and Mark is Matthew 10:16-22 and Mark 13:3-13.

CHAPTER TWENTY-ONE

# Synoptic Relations: The Implications

## IMPLICATIONS FOR THE STUDY OF THE GOSPELS

While the problem of the synoptic relationships may not be *the* issue dominating the study of the Synoptic Gospels, it is fundamental to any serious study of the topic. Hence it is hard to overestimate its importance.

In earlier decades, one of the "assured results of modern criticism" was that Mark was written first and that both Matthew and Luke had Mark and "Q" before them as they wrote. This gave scholars a very powerful tool for studying Matthew and Luke. They could take Mark's Gospel as one of the sources behind Matthew and Luke and examine in what ways the two later Gospels had changed Mark. If they could find a consistent pattern in these changes, it should reveal something of the interests and theology of that particular writer and his community. For example, when Mark refers to "the kingdom of God," Matthew nearly always omits the phrase or substitutes "kingdom of heaven." A first-century Jew would be reluctant to say the title "God." This was but one of a pattern of differences between Matthew and Mark that convinced many scholars that Matthew had a Jewish Christian background. Learned and lengthy commentaries were written on the assumption that Matthew and Luke used Mark as a source. These commentaries gave importance to even slight changes of grammar and wording.

But what is the situation today? Have scholars abandoned this kind of study of the Gospels? No. But because there is now no unanimity among scholars as to the solution of the problem of synoptic relationships, there is a growing disunity in the methodology used to study the Synoptic Gospels. This was brought home forcefully to me a few years ago at the conference of the Society of Biblical Literature, important professional meetings that are held annually in the United States. I attended one set of meetings in which William Farmer was a prominent participant. Not everybody involved agreed with Farmer on how the Synoptic Gospels were formed, but all in that room were sensitive to the fact that there was no longer only one view of how the synoptics were related. At the same set of meetings, I attended a session devoted to "Q" research. There, I was in a room full of scholars who were basing their entire research efforts not only on the assumption that "Q" exists but also on the belief that it is possible to be fairly confident of what is in it. It was as though the debate on the legitimacy of the two-document hypothesis had never taken place. The two different groups I observed that year were working from irreconcilable assumptions. Thus, one of the results of the renewed debate about synoptic relationships is that scholarship on the Synoptic Gospels is now less unified than was the case some decades ago.

Another consequence of this reopening of debate on the issue of synoptic relationships is that one has to be more careful in the assumptions that are made about methodology. Nobody doubts that there is a relationship of some kind between the three Synoptic Gospels and that this relationship can be very helpful in their study. But more care needs to be given to differentiating between conclusions that rely on the assumption of one Gospel being used as a source of another and conclusions that are based on the more general assumption that there is some kind of relationship between the Synoptic Gospels without necessarily defining exactly what that relationship is. In this book, for example, we have already looked at the Gospel of Matthew to try to ascertain what is distinctive about it. In doing so, no assumptions were made about any sources that Matthew used. It would have been much easier to arrive at the conclusions we did by assuming that Matthew made changes to Mark and "Q." But it was not necessary to do so. As long as there was *some* relationship between the Gospels, it was still possible to make the kind of conclusions we did.

This is true of all study of the Synoptic Gospels. Some of the old certainties have gone, and scholarship is no longer as united in its methodology as it once was. But this should not detract from the powerful tool provided to serious students by the simple acknowledgment that there is a relationship between the three Synoptic Gospels. The three Synoptic Gospels are related, and the patterns of their similarities and differences reveal a great deal of the distinctive interests of their respective writers and the communities they represent. These relationships enable us to discern the perspective each Gospel takes of the events in the life, death, and resurrection of Jesus. Each of these different perspectives acts like an independent witness to the matters essential to Christianity.

These, then, are some of the consequences that the problem of synoptic relationships has for the study of the Gospels. Another important set of consequences relates to the doctrine of inspiration.

### IMPLICATIONS FOR THE DOCTRINE OF INSPIRATION

The Bible is authoritative for Christians. True, different denominations—and even different groups within a given denomination—allow various degrees of authority to the Bible. Some Christian groups see the Bible as their sole authority in matters of belief and practice. Others want to balance this authority with a component derived from human reason. But almost all Christians concede some authoritative role to the Bible. This is often expressed under the concept of inspiration.

When they say that the Bible is inspired, Christians are stating that the Bible derives from God in some way. Indeed, this is the very basis of the Bible's authority. Inasmuch as the Bible derives from God, what it says has God's authority. But if the Bible derives from purely human processes and ideas, then it has no more authority than any other human writing. This is the reason for the violent debate over the issue of biblical inspiration that broke out in America toward the end of last century and continued through the first third of this century. At this time, ideas developed in Europe, particularly in Germany, that began to be debated in American universities. In their extreme form, these ideas included doubts concerning the possibility of such miracles as the virgin birth and the Resurrection. The Bible, it was said, should be studied "scientifically," just like any other book.[1] These "liberal" ideas came to be described as "liberalism," and gradually the theology faculties in the universities became more and more liberal.

Liberal ideas were vigorously opposed by some leading "conservative" scholars, who defended such "fundamental beliefs" as the virgin birth, the bodily resurrection of Jesus, and the inspiration of Scripture. This impassioned defense of orthodoxy caught the imagination of many sincere Christians who were becoming progressively uncomfortable with the "liberal" ideas coming out of the universities. They felt strongly that no concessions should be made to these new ideas, and thus Christian Fundamentalism took root in the United States. Christian Fundamentalism has had a fascinating and complex history, as indeed have the more "liberal" churches. Debate concerning inspiration has been vigorous and sustained; mainly, one suspects, because of the underlying issue of authority. Does God speak through the Bible or not? For the same reason, debate over inspiration is not restricted to Fundamentalism. All Christian communities grapple with this issue as they try to make sense of the biblical data and integrate it into their theology and worldview.

The relationships that exist between the Synoptic Gospels is of real significance to this particular aspect of the debate, because every model of inspiration has to take account of the data discovered from research into the problem of synoptic relationships. For example, one of the crucial issues in inspiration is: What role does the human writer play? The Synoptic Gospels provide us with a clear model of how the Gospel writers were functioning. In particular, Luke 1:1-3 gives vital clues as to how the Gospel of Luke was composed and, indeed, gives a significant role to the human writer. This is evidence that needs to be considered, along with what is said elsewhere in the Bible, when forming any concept of how inspiration works. In fact, it is instructive to compare what the prophets say about *their* processes of writing with what Luke 1:1-3 says, and perhaps we should begin with that prophetic model.

This is the way Jeremiah describes the writing of the prophetic book attributed to him:

> In the fourth year of Jehoiakim the son of Josiah, king of Judah, this word came to Jeremiah from the Lord: "Take a scroll and write on it all the words that I have spoken to you against Israel and Judah and all the nations, from the day I spoke to you, from the days of Josiah until today". . . . Then Jeremiah called Baruch the son of Neriah, and Baruch wrote upon a scroll at the dictation of Jeremiah all the words of the Lord which he had spoken to him (Jer. 36:1-4).

According to what is said here, the derivation of Jeremiah's message is clear—God had spoken directly to Jeremiah. So what Jeremiah dictated to Baruch was nothing less than the very words of God. Therefore reading them was like directly hearing God speak. That this particular version of Jeremiah's prophecies was destroyed when the king burned it (Jer. 36:23) does not change this basic pattern revealed in Jeremiah 36:1-4, because Jeremiah was told to write it out again (Jer. 36:28).

According to the account given in Jeremiah 36:1-4, there was an almost overwhelmingly divine component in his prophecy. But what was the role of the human messenger? Did Jeremiah and Baruch play no role other than writing words at the dictation of God? From the evidence available to us, this seems unlikely. Many of the words in the prophecy are Jeremiah's description of events that had happened. These are distinct from the oracles in which he describes what God has told him. Furthermore, one needs ask to what extent Baruch, the scribe, was involved in gathering all these different materials together. This question is all the more urgent because there are differences between the Masoretic (Hebrew) text of Jeremiah and the Septuagint (Greek) text. The Masoretic text of Jeremiah is the Hebrew text on which most English translations are based. The Septuagint (usually abbreviated LXX) is the Greek version of the Old Testament. The LXX should not be dismissed too quickly; it is based on a translation of now-lost Hebrew originals that were several centuries earlier than the time the Masoretic text of the Old Testament was standardized. The Masoretic text of Jeremiah has about 2,700 words more than the Hebrew text from which the LXX was translated. Several of these are single words, but some are longer passages.[2] Furthermore, there are differences in order between them, particularly in the oracles of the nations.[3] Just how these differences came about and whether any of them should be traced back to the scribal activity of Baruch has no satisfactory explanation at this time. But they do highlight that there is a significant human element even in this prophetic book of the Old Testament, saturated as it is with direct communication from God.

The model of inspiration revealed in Luke 1:1-4 is quite different. The Gospel writer says,

> Since many have undertaken to set down an orderly account of the events that have been fulfilled among us, just as they were handed on to us by those who from the beginning were eyewitnesses and servants of the word, I too decided, after investigating everything carefully from the very first, to write an orderly account for you, most excellent Theophilus, so that you may know the truth concerning the things about which you have been instructed (Luke 1:1-4).

Luke does not count himself among the eyewitnesses. Like others, he has derived his information from eyewitnesses and has carefully investigated whether what they told him was true. There was no command from God to write. The evangelist himself "decided" to write an orderly account.

One might describe this as a "research" model of inspiration. All the writer's human resources were called upon; the evidence was carefully weighed. He evidently discarded some stories about Jesus because he thought they were incorrect. The writer's mind was exercised in how best to begin the Gospel and what should follow thereafter. All this highlights the human component of the whole process. But does this mean that the Gospel of Luke should be discarded as a merely human document? Certainly not. The Gospel itself claims to be only a reliable witness of the events surrounding the life of Jesus and the growth of the early Christian communities, but there is something more here. This Gospel has the qualities necessary for incorporating into Scripture. In some way it was suitable for the early Christian church to use in worship, just as was the Old Testament—indeed, just like Jeremiah. Nor has the church repented of this practice. The Gospel of Luke is regarded as Scripture just like the prophecies of Jeremiah. While there is a strong human component in Luke's Gospel, there is also a distinctive element of the divine.

Perhaps the best model of inspiration is a model drawn from a comparison with Jesus Himself. According to orthodox Christian doctrine, Jesus is both fully human and fully divine.[4] The Bible is like this too. It is a document that derives from God; it is inspired. But it is also a document that derives from humans. It is written in human language by human authors with their human limitations. But the human aspects of the Bible should not blind us to its divine origins. On the other hand, neither should its divine origins blind us to its human aspects.

What has all this got to do with the problem of synoptic relationships? Quite a bit. If we are comfortable with Luke's revelation that his Gospel is the product of his own research and decision to write, then the relationships we have observed between the Synoptic Gospels do no more than confirm what Luke 1:1-4 says. We see the human aspect of the Gospels' composition in a clear light. We can investigate the meanings of words, the cultural and political background of the time, and the way the Gospels differ from each other without feeling that we are doing a disservice to holy things—because these matters relate to the human aspect of Scripture. Mind you, we must always be careful not to lose sight of the divine origins of Scripture as we study its human components. The Bible is inspired; it retains its authority for Christians. The

Gospels form part of the heart of Scripture, because of their witness to Christ. What we know about synoptic relationships only helps us better understand this crucial witness.

## IMPLICATIONS FOR THE HISTORICITY OF THE GOSPEL ACCOUNTS

Looking at the similarities and differences between the Synoptic Gospels raises the issue of their historical reliability. Some differences in detail occur in the Gospels that, indeed, appear to be irreconcilable. For example, Matthew 8:28 reports that *two* demoniacs came out of the tombs in the region of the *Gadarenes*. These demons called themselves legion and were subsequently allowed to transfer themselves to a herd of pigs, which destroyed themselves by running into the Sea of Galilee. On the other hand, both Mark 5:1 and Luke 8:26, 27 report that *one* demoniac came out of the tombs in the region of the *Gerasenes*, to met Jesus. Mark and Luke agree with Matthew in almost every other detail of this account. Now it is possible to reconcile the difference between Gadarenes and Gerasenes by suggesting that they are two variations on the same name, but it is not possible to reconcile *two* demoniacs with *one* demoniac. There was either one or two; it could not be both! This is but one example of a more general phenomena discussed in the chapter that dealt with the raw data of synoptic relationships.[5] Sometimes two Gospels agree against a third. Even where there are only two accounts of one incident, differences often occur. Do such differences mean that the Gospel accounts are historically unreliable?

Let's look at this question in terms of two groups of professionals who frequently have occasion to test the likelihood of events—police and historians.

When trying to reconstruct the events surrounding a crime, the police face great difficulties, especially with witnesses. The probability is that some witnesses will not be telling the truth, and these are not confined just to those guilty of the crime. Some witnesses, in their desire to be helpful, report events that did not actually happen. Others might wish to conceal some events because they fear they will incriminate somebody they love. Establishing the facts of the matter can have great importance, so a great deal of attention has been given to the characteristics of reliable and unreliable testimony.

Interestingly enough, when two or three witnesses agree in exactly every detail, it is evidence of *un*reliable testimony. Why? Because two witnesses of the same event will normally remember different aspects of that event. In the nature of things, they will often disagree on minor details. The broad features of the event will be the same but not all the details. Two people who agree in every detail give evidence that they have rehearsed their answers, and their motives for doing so are normally somewhat suspect.

Historians find the same thing to be true. In reliable accounts there are differences in detail and perception. Furthermore, even eyewitnesses of great historical events can be mistaken about what happened. Each individual can see only part of a battlefield, for example. Perhaps the top officers have some idea of what is happening, but usually even they do not have as much information as they need to form a full picture of events. Historians have to use these partial, and sometimes conflicting, reports to reconstruct what happened.

How does all this relate to the Synoptic Gospels?

If the Synoptic Gospels agreed in every detail, then it would probably be evidence of their unreliability, rather than evidence of their historical reliability. In fact, in many ways, the Synoptic Gospels show the characteristics of reliable eyewitness testimony. There is broad agreement on what happened, yet the different accounts vary somewhat in the details they report. This does not take away from the overall reliability of the report but rather adds to the probability that in the three Synoptic Gospels we have three useful witnesses to the events of Jesus' life.

There are further considerations that make it likely that the events recorded in the Gospels are historically reliable. For a start, it is easy to underestimate the notoriety Jesus would have had in His lifetime. This notoriety would arise in part because of the small size of Galilee and Judea and, in part, because of the small population of those regions. For example, Jerusalem, the largest city in either state, had a population of less than 80,000 at the time of Jesus.[6] Furthermore, Capernaum, the center of Jesus' public ministry, had a population of perhaps 1,500 people at any time in its history, and was much smaller during the first century.[7]

Jesus was notorious; everybody knew Him. This was inevitable, anyway, in such places as the villages of Galilee, because there everybody knew everybody else. They had grown up together. They worked together. They attended each other's feasts, weddings, and funerals. In other words, Jesus was well known by a great number of people, and it would not be possible to say things about Him that were clearly incorrect. Too many people would know the truth was otherwise. The enemies of Christianity would have little trouble in discrediting the whole thing if gross errors of fact were to be found in the Gospels.

Another feature of the Gospels indicating their historical reliability is their candor regarding the faults of the disciples, a candor remarkable in the ancient world. These were the men who became the early leaders of the Christian communities, yet their failings are clearly laid out for all to read. The ancients, as well as the moderns, very rarely reported embarrassing things about their leaders, at least not when they were in power or when they were revered. Neither was there anything like the modern free press to report on various happenings. But in the Gospel accounts, we have a "warts and all" view of the disciples. This might be something that the enemies of Christianity could have made up but is hardly something the early church would have invented.

All in all, there is no reason to suppose that the data brought out by a careful investigation of the synoptic problem provides any basis for doubting the basic historicity of the events reported by the Gospels. In fact, it probably does quite the opposite. Rather, it is evidence of their reliability.

---

1. See further "The Academic Study of the Gospels in the Twentieth Century" available under the author's name in the list of theology faculty members at the following internet address: www.avondale.edu.au.
2. Jer. 33:14-26; 39:4-13; 51:44b-49a; 52:27b-30 are all missing from the LXX.
3. In the Massoretic text they are at the end of the book; in the LXX they are inserted after 25:13 and are in a different order.
4. For a fuller description of this, see the chapter entitled "The Gospel's Witness to

Jesus," in part 6.

5. See chapter 19.

6. Magen Broshi, "Estimating the Population of Ancient Jerusalem," *Biblical Archaeology Review* 4 (June 1978), 10-15.

7. So Stanislao Loffreda, *Recovering Capharnaum* (Gerusalemme: Edizioni Custodia Terra Santa, 1986), 18. Loffreda is one of the archaeologists who has excavated Capharnaum.

Part 5

# THE GOSPEL OF JOHN

CHAPTER TWENTY-TWO

# Key Elements in the Thought-World of the Beloved Disciple (John 3 and 6)

## THE GOSPEL OF JOHN IS DIFFERENT FROM THE OTHERS

In many ways, moving from the Gospels of Matthew, Mark, or Luke to the Gospel of John is like moving into another world. Most of the familiar accounts of Jesus' activities and His teachings, found in the Synoptic Gospels, are missing,[1] and in their place John gives a small number of representative miracles or signs, interspersed with extended discourses. These signs and discourses largely revolve around a few simple ideas. John introduces these ideas in his first chapters and then gradually develops them throughout the rest of the Gospel, eventually combining them to form a distinctive symbolic universe. In other words, the beloved disciple[2] uses these ideas to build up a coherent and total understanding of Jesus. John's Gospel is both very simple and very profound—simple because the basic ideas it uses are simple; profound because the total picture is very sophisticated.

What, then, are these simple ideas John develops through his Gospel? In this chapter, we will explore two of them at some length—one concept that is related to spatial orientation (above/below) and one that is related to time. The chapter will begin by examining these two ideas in general terms, after which it will explain how they are like a key that unlocks the meaning of John 3 and 6. In a later chapter, we will explore how John develops some of his other ideas in his Gospel, particularly those associated with the different titles of Jesus.[3] But now, let's consider the concept of above/below as used in the fourth Gospel.

## ABOVE/BELOW

It would be hard to find more simple concepts than "above" and "below," yet John's Gospel uses them to make one of the most profound statements concerning Jesus. It does so by associating different pairs of terms, or images, with either the realm above or the realm below. For example, heaven by its very nature is the realm above, while the earth is the realm below. God is in heaven. The devil is found on earth, and he works here. Life is associated with the realm above; death is related to the world below. The spirit belongs above; the flesh belongs below. Light and truth belong above; darkness and lying belong below. Together, God, heaven, life, light, truth, and spirit form a linked cluster, all belonging to the realm above. Conversely, the devil, death, darkness, flesh, and earth belong to the realm below. The contrasts may be presented like this:

| ABOVE: | God | heaven | life | light | truth | spirit |
|---|---|---|---|---|---|---|
| BELOW: | devil | earth | death | darkness | lying | flesh |

These contrasting pairs form a series of underlying themes running throughout John's whole Gospel. In particular, it portrays Jesus as the One who has come from the realm above, down into the world, the realm of darkness, sin, and death. He has come to tell us that He is from the realm above and will return there. This theme runs as a thread through several of the key discourses in John. It also forms the basis of much of the misunderstanding of Jesus shown by Nicodemus, His disciples, and the crowd. One of the crucial themes of the whole Gospel is that Jesus comes from, and has returned to, the realm above.

# Key Elements in the Thought-World of the Beloved Disciple

## THE FUTURE INTO THE PRESENT

While the contrast between the world above and the world below has to do with spatial orientation, the Gospel also places importance on ideas associated with time. In particular, many of the things that in traditional thinking belong in the future are said to have come into the present.

Take, for example, the last judgment. Both the Old and New Testaments place the last judgment[4] at the end of the age. At the end of the age the wicked nations gather against the people of God. God intervenes on behalf of His people. Both wicked and righteous are gathered before him and are judged. Those who are worthy receive eternal life, and those who are judged unworthy are destroyed (Zech. 14; Joel 3:9-21; Rev. 20:7–22:25, etc.). Eternal life belongs to the age to come. In that age humankind will not die, sin will be taken away, and peace will reign. The imagery used to describe this varies—the prophets portray the nations beating their swords into plowshares, their spears into pruning hooks, and point to a time when every man will sit under his own fig tree (Isa. 2:4; Mic. 4:3, 4). The New Testament, on the other hand, paints a picture of a golden city where there is no night, where God has wiped away all tears and banished sin and death (Rev. 21:10-15). But the essential idea in both sets of images is the same—in the age to come, when God has intervened directly in the events of world history to establish His own kingdom, there will be a time when sin and death are no more. It will be the time when each person may truly have eternal life. As a diagram, this traditional view of the end of the age would look something like this:

|  | Judgment | |
|---|---|---|
| This Age | ‖ | Age to Come |
| Sin | ‖ | Resurrection |
| Death | ‖ | Eternal life |

The fourth Gospel shares this view of the future resurrection and judgment (John 5:25). But alongside this more traditional view, there is a marked tendency to bring into the present many of those events and blessings that were traditionally considered to belong exclusively to the

227

future. For example, in the person and ministry of Jesus the judgment has arrived. In fact, the believer has passed through the judgment and even now has eternal life (John 3:18, 19). For this Gospel, the diagram has to be changed to look something like this:

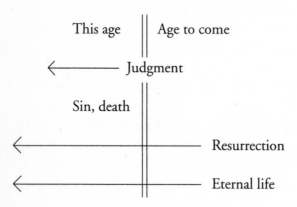

This, then, is the second fundamental idea developed by John's Gospel that we will investigate in this chapter—that the future has come into the present. In the rest of the chapter we will look at John 3 and 6 and see how this idea, and the theme of above and below, are the keys to understanding these well-known dialogues.

## ABOVE AND BELOW IN THE DIALOGUE WITH NICODEMUS (JOHN 3:1-15)

In John 3, the role of Nicodemus is ambiguous. He is introduced as a ruler of the Jews who comes to Jesus at night. Now, because the visit takes place at night and because the Jews are so often the enemies of Jesus in the Gospel (John 5:16, 18; 7:1, etc.), we initially expect that Nicodemus belongs to the realm below. But if this is so, how is it that in the very first words that Nicodemus addresses to Jesus he says, " 'We know that you are a teacher who has come from God' " (John 3:2)? This is the fundamental truth about Jesus championed by the Gospel—that Jesus has come from God, from the realm above. Does not this insight mark Nicodemus as one who understands Jesus aright? Not really, as the subsequent dialogue shows. Even though he got the words right, at this point Nicodemus does not properly understand what he has just said.

"Jesus answered and said to him, 'Truly, truly I tell you, no one is able to see the kingdom of God unless they are born *anōthen*' " (John 3:3). I have left the Greek word *anōthen* purposely untranslated. In a few places in the New Testament (and in only a few) it is just not possible to find a translation of a Greek word that fits its context, and this is one of them. The reason is this: The Greek word *anōthen* has two possible meanings, and you need to know both to understand what is going on in the text.

The most common meaning of *anōthen* is "from above," although it may also mean "again." Jesus clearly means that one must be born "from above" to see the kingdom of God. Nicodemus, though, misunderstands because he chooses the wrong meaning of *anōthen*. He has not fully understood that Jesus comes "from above." Therefore, he asks Jesus how it is possible to be born "again," the other possible meaning of the word. After all, you cannot go back into your mother's womb and come out a second time (John 3:4). This is certainly true and should have prompted Nicodemus to think of other possible meanings for the word Jesus used, but at this stage he is thinking only in terms of the realm below. In the horizons of thought confined to this world, what Jesus says does not make sense.

Jesus goes on to make His meaning clear. " 'No one can enter the kingdom of God without being born of water and the spirit' " (John 3:5). The reference to the spirit is an unmistakable indication of how the previous saying should have been understood. The spirit belongs to the realm above. Thus Jesus had not said to Nicodemus he must be born "again," but he must be born "from above." Like the wind,[5] the spirit cannot be seen directly, but its effects can be seen (John 3:8).

Even though Jesus has made His meaning clear, Nicodemus still doesn't understand and admits it (John 3:9). Jesus tells him, "If I speak of earthly things and you do not understand, how will you understand if I speak to you of heavenly things?" (John 3:12). Nicodemus had misunderstood because coming from the perspective of a teacher of Israel, he was taking into account only earthly things. Heavenly realities were not open to him.

The verses immediately following introduce themes that subsequent chapters of John's Gospel will take up again and again: " 'Truly truly I say to you that we tell what we know, and bear witness to what we have seen, and you do not receive our witness. . . . Nobody has gone up into heaven except the one who has come down from heaven, the Son of Man. And just as Moses lifted up the serpent in the desert, so also it is necessary that the Son of Man be lifted up, in order that all who believe in him might have eternal life' " (John 3:11, 13-15). The realm of the above, heaven, is known only to one—Jesus—because He is the only One who has come down from heaven. He bears witness to what He knows and has seen. Nicodemus is unable to understand His witness because he does not properly comprehend that Jesus comes from the realm above.

Jesus has just said that He has come down from heaven; now He goes on to say that He is to be lifted up again into heaven. But His lifting up is like when Moses lifted up the serpent on a stake in the wilderness so that those who looked and believed were saved (John 3:14; cf. Num. 21:9). The ambiguity of this image is retained in the English. Jesus is lifted up on the cross. Paradoxically, this lifting up returns Him to the world of "the above." In John, the hour in which Jesus is glorified is also the hour in which He suffers on the cross (John 12:23; cf. v. 24), so His lifting up on the cross is also His exaltation to heaven.

In conclusion, it is by means of Jesus being lifted up on the cross and thereby being exalted to heaven that a believer might have eternal life (John 3:16). But note the time reference. In traditional thought, eternal life is something that belongs to the future kingdom of God, but here it is said to be something available in the present. This introduces the other major theme we are exploring in this chapter—that in Jesus the future has already arrived. The next few verses (John 3:16-21) expand on this theme.

## In Jesus the Future Judgment Has Arrived in the Present (John 3:16-21)

John 3:16-18 states: " 'For God so loved the world that he gave his only son, so that all who believe in him might not perish but might have eternal life. For God did not send his son into the world to judge/condemn[6] the world, but to save the world through him. The one who believes in him is not judged, and the one who does not believe has been judged already, because he has not believed in the name of the only begotten Son of God.' "

In this passage, the future has truly come into the present because the last judgment has arrived on earth in the person of Jesus. We are judged now by whether or not we believe in Him, and we receive eternal life now on the basis of that judgment. Indeed, if we believe, we no longer enter into judgment, because we have passed beyond the judgment and entered into eternal life already. Furthermore, those who believe have (present tense) eternal life (John 3:16). But those who do not believe have already been judged and condemned.

Is this a direct contradiction of John 5:29, which speaks of a future resurrection and judgment? In fact, in John 5:19-30 we find both future and present judgment almost side by side (cf. v. 24 and v. 25). Instead of contradicting what has been said about present judgment, John 5:19-30 explains further how present judgment works. By our belief in Jesus we can already know what the verdict of the last judgment is going to be—it will be a verdict of "not guilty." So that if we believe, we do not need to enter the judgment. If, however, we do not believe, then we also know already what the outcome of the last judgment will be—we will be condemned. Our deeds are evil. We know what God's judgment on sin is; it is destruction. As sinners who have turned our backs on Jesus, we will be destroyed. Thus our belief, or nonbelief, in Jesus is an anticipation of the last judgment. We have eternal life by virtue of the fact that we believe in Jesus now and now know what our verdict at the last judgment will be. In other words, our belief has taken us past the time of the last judgment and into the new age. We have been granted eternal life already. We have (present tense) eternal life if we believe in Jesus.[7]

## DRINKING THE BLOOD AND EATING THE FLESH: ABOVE AND BELOW IN JOHN 6:22-59

Jesus' miraculous multiplication of five bread rolls and two fish to feed more than five thousand people provides the occasion for a crucial confrontation between Jesus and the crowds. This confrontation begins with the crowds enthusiastically seeking Him, but Jesus deliberately provokes them with the question of His identity until they finally turn away from Him. At issue is Jesus' insistence that He has come from above and the crowd's refusal to view Him in anything but earthly terms. This tension is evident right from the moment the crowd finds Him.

Jesus accuses the crowd of a motivation belonging to the realm below—they seek Him because they had something to eat, not because they recognized that the miracle was a sign of something else (John 6:26). The crowd responds by asking for what they consider to be an appropriate sign: Moses fed manna to the children of Israel. He did this every day for forty years, so surely Jesus should feed them again (vv. 30, 31). Jesus replies that the true bread from heaven is the One who came down from heaven and gives life to the world (v. 33). The crowd responds that it would like to have this bread (v. 34), whereupon Jesus makes it explicit that He is the bread of life and that if they come to Him they will not hunger (v. 35).

The crowd grumbles at this because it knows both Jesus' father and mother. How then can Jesus say that He comes from heaven, if His origins are with earthly parents (vv. 41, 42)? Jesus responds by speaking of His Father who sent Him. Again, the source of confusion lies in the fact that the crowd is looking at Jesus from only an earthly perspective. His true Father is God, not Joseph. Jesus continues by speaking of the link between eating the true bread and belief in Him (vv. 47, 48). Just as earthly bread sustains earthly life, so also the true bread from heaven will sustain eternal life. In other words, in calling Himself the true bread from heaven, Jesus is using a rich image quite consistent with the sign of the multiplication of the loaves and fishes. But His hearers cannot understand the image because their thinking is confined to the earthly plane, thereby showing themselves to be creatures of the realm below. They become increasingly agitated with the idea of eating Jesus' flesh. Jesus gives them enough clues to understand that eating His flesh is equivalent to believing that He has come from above, but His hearers consistently overlook them. They want to be His disciples but only on their earthly terms, terms that Jesus refuses. He demands that they eat His flesh and drink His blood. In other words, He demands that they look beyond earthly things to see that He has come from the realm above. When they cannot, they grow angry and leave. "Therefore, when they heard these things, many of his disciples said, 'This is a hard saying, who is able to hear it?' . . . many of his disciples turned aside and no longer walked with him" (vv. 60, 66).

## To whom will we go? (John 6:60-71)

Every so often we read something in Scripture that strikes a very poignant and contemporary chord in us. For me, John 6:67, 68 is one such passage. Up to this moment Jesus has enjoyed enormous popularity. Crowds have flocked to Him. He has performed remarkable signs— turning water to wine, healing a man lame for thirty-eight years, and miraculously multiplying a few loaves and fish to feed more than five thousand individuals. But now all this is of no avail. The crowd refuses to understand Him and, as He further explains Himself, they turn away and walk no more with Him. He then turns to His inner circle of disciples and asks, " 'Perhaps you also wish to go?' " Simon Peter answered him, " 'Lord, to whom will we go?' " (John 6:67, 68). The disciples have also been deeply troubled by what Jesus had said. They, too, have found His sayings hard. But if they do not stay with Jesus, where else is there to go?

This question still strikes me today with great force. Where is there to go? What would be the consequences of my abandoning Christianity? Well, if what Jesus said about Himself was not true, if there is no God, it may well be that the existentialists would have it right when they say that life is essentially meaningless. Under such circumstances there would be no reason why one course of action is more commendable than another. Or why one should live one's life by the principle of unselfish love. Love is not to be rationally preferred to hate, which might have a higher survival quotient. Who knows, if Jesus was wrong, perhaps Nietzsche was right that one should prefer the strong and despise the weak. All in all, this is a very gloomy option but one that I personally would probably be forced to adopt if I abandoned my belief in God.

This rationale, though, is not the basis for my belief in God. If I believed in God because the alternatives were unthinkable, then I would have to do so at the cost of intellectual integrity. But every so often it is good to sit down and think of the alternatives to belief. Sometimes I find Jesus' words hard to understand. When brought up short by some of the grim facts of reality, particularly the certitude of death, one can sympathize with the first-century followers of Jesus who found it hard. But like Peter, I also have to confess that I do not know where else I would go if I left Jesus.

## SUMMING UP

The Gospel of John takes two relatively simple concepts—the spatial image of above/below and the temporal image of the future discovered in the present—and uses them in a profound way to develop the reader's understanding of Jesus. Jesus is the One who came "from above" to the world "below" to bring eternal life. Eternal life is given to those who believe that Jesus came "from above." Believers do not enter into judgment, because, if they believe in Jesus, they are already judged worthy of eternal life. In other words, they have passed beyond the judgment.

Those who belong to the realm below can think only in terms of the world below. They cannot understand that Jesus is "from above." The birth "from above" is misunderstood as a physical rebirth (an impossibility), and they cannot comprehend what it means to "eat the flesh and drink the blood" of Jesus, which will alone give nourishment that lasts eternally. But those born "from above" can understand, and because they believe Jesus came from above, they have eternal life now.

---

1. In part 4, chapter 19, we have already noted that the first seventeen chapters of John describe only five events that are found in the other Gospels—the preaching of John the Baptist, the cleansing of the temple, feeding the 5,000, the triumphal entry, and the prophecy concerning Peter. The rest of John 1–17 comprises material unique to John.

2. The author of the fourth Gospel identifies himself as the beloved disciple (John 21:24) but does not name himself. Stephen Smalley, *John: Evangelist and Interpreter* (Exeter: Paternoster, 1978), 68-82, carefully outlines the various suggestions that have been made about who this might be. From the evidence given in the Gospel, it appears most likely that the beloved disciple should be identified as John. If you wish to examine the reasons for saying this, Smalley may be consulted profitably.

3. See chapter 27, "The Disturbing Jesus of the Fourth Gospel."

4. It is called the last judgment to distinguish it from other judgments of God—judgments such as the those declared against Philistia, Moab, Ammon, Edom, Damascus, Hazor, Kedar, Elam, Babylon (Jer. 47–51), Tyre, Egypt (Ezek. 27–32; Isa. 19, 23), etc. In the view of the Old Testament, God has been active through history executing His judgments on the evil nations.

5. John 3:8 provides the translator with another impossible dilemma. The Greek word *pneuma* means both wind and spirit (as does the Hebrew word *ruach*, its Old Testament counterpart). The image in John 3:8 doesn't make sense without knowing this double meaning—but no single English word has both meanings, so the translator cannot render the entire meaning of the underlying Greek in this instance.

6. The Greek verb *krinō* is normally translated as "judge." In John 3:17 it means "to judge guilty," and therefore the translation "condemn" is most appropriate. This has, however, the unfortunate consequence that the linguistic link between "condemn" in verse 17 and "judge" in verse 18 is lost in most English translations.

7. The Gospel of John is not the only place in the New Testament where this concept is found. Although Paul uses different terms to describe it, his concept of justification by faith also relies on the concept of anticipated future judgment. The Greek term *dikaiosunē* (justification, righteousness) is a term associated with the law courts. It is what the judge would say when pronouncing a verdict of "not guilty." Thus justification is the result of judgment. Our faith (belief) in Jesus anticipates the verdict of the last judgment, hence the phraseology "justification by faith."

# CHAPTER TWENTY-THREE

# Jesus at the Feast of Tabernacles (John 7)

### MY EXASPERATING QUESTION

Looking back, I can understand why people found me exasperating when I was eighteen—the year I started to take religion seriously again. Because sermon after sermon had been telling me that the key to Christianity was to know Jesus Christ personally, I decided that I should get to know what Jesus was like. I already knew quite a lot about what He said and did and that He was the Son of God. But now I wanted to know something more than what could be said *about* Him. I wanted to know what He was like, really like.

The first thing I did was to start asking my Christian friends. When I asked, "What was Jesus like?" they would happily answer, "He was the Son of God" or "He was God who became man." These answers were all in terms of who He *was*, not what He was like. To me, these answers were too theoretical, because knowing that Jesus was the Son of God did not tell me what He was like. Others of my friends would answer in terms of what He had done: "Jesus healed the sick" or "Jesus was kind to children." I found this type of answer unsatisfactory also. I wanted to know what He was *like*, not what He did.

At about this point in these conversations, I stepped over the bounds of social convention and became exasperating to my friends. I would let people know that I thought their answers inadequate and kept repeating my question. When somebody answered, "Jesus was the friend of sinners," I would interrupt and demand, "Yes, but what was He like?" When somebody said, "He was kind to children," I would impatiently interrupt, "You're not answering the question. I want to know what He was like." Even quite patient friends soon began to show enough irritation at this kind of persistence to get me to drop the matter.

About this time, I arrived by mistake an hour early one afternoon for some meetings in which I was involved. I didn't have enough time to do anything useful, so I drove a little way down the road and parked the car in an area of land leveled for the construction of a new school. There was nothing in the car to read except a copy of the *Good News New Testament*. So I picked it up and idly began reading through the Gospel of John. When I got toward the end of chapter 7, something in the text electrified me. I got so excited I needed to walk around. I got out of the car and began pacing, shaking my head every so often, and saying "Wow!" I have since read John, chapter 7, many times, both in English and in Greek, but the excitement of that afternoon still stays with me. Let me see if I can recreate it for you, as we look at the background and text of that chapter.

## THE FEAST OF TABERNACLES

The events recorded in John, chapter 7, took place at one of the yearly Jewish festivals called the Feast of Tabernacles. The ancient sources give quite extensive background information about what took place in connection with this festival, information that illuminates John's account in a remarkable way.

The Feast of Tabernacles, or Feast of Booths, was one of the three times each year when all male Israelites were required to appear at Jerusalem (Deut. 16:16, 17). Associated with the harvest, the Feast of Tabernacles was sometimes called by the alternate name of Ingathering (Exod. 23:14; 34:21-24).

During the seven-day festival, both visitors and regular inhabitants of Jerusalem were expected to live outdoors. They were to construct temporary booths and live in them as a reminder of their days of living in tents during their wilderness wanderings on the way to the Promised Land (Lev. 23:39-43). One can only imagine the carnival atmosphere at such times. The harvest was in. Food was plentiful. Everybody was living outdoors. Visitors and old friends met and rejoiced together.

By late in the Old Testament era, the Feast of Booths had gained special status, as is shown by its appearance at a key place in the prophecies of Zechariah. Zechariah, chapter 14, describes the day of the Lord. The heathen nations surround Jerusalem and take it. At this point, God Himself intervenes and destroys most of the wicked. The land is convulsed. Only Jerusalem remains a mountain; the rest of the Promised Land becomes a plain. Two rivers flow from Jerusalem to water the whole land. In the similar prophecy of Ezekiel, chapter 47, the river is said to flow from the temple itself. As it is described in Zechariah, those who are left alive will come up to Jerusalem each year to worship the Lord of hosts and keep the Feast of Booths. Worshiping at the Feast of Booths will guarantee the water needed for crops. Those who do not come will not get the water (Zech. 14:16-19). Thus, within the Old Testament, the Feast of Booths is associated with the miraculous events of the end of time and with the divine gift of water.

Leviticus 23:40 gives the instruction, " 'On the first day you shall take the fruit of majestic trees, branches of palm trees, boughs of leafy trees, and willows of the brook; and you shall rejoice before the Lord your God for seven days.' " At the time of Jesus' ministry, a set form had developed.[1] On each of the seven days of the feast, the priests would lead a procession from the temple down to the Gihon spring. The crowd of onlookers would carry a lemon in their left hand and a bunch of myrtle and willow twigs tied with palm frond in their right. At the spring, the priest would fill a golden pitcher with water, while the choir sang "With joy you will draw water from the wells of salvation" (Isa. 12:3). Then, as the procession moved up the hill toward the temple, the choir would sing the hallel psalms (Pss. 113–118). The climax of the ceremony came when the water from the spring was poured over the altar of burnt offerings, together with wine from a drink offering. A slight elaboration of this ceremony marked the last day of the Feast of Booths as more important than the preceding days.

## WHO IS JESUS, AND WHERE IS HE FROM?—ABOVE AND BELOW IN JOHN 7

This, then, was the festival that was going on at Jerusalem as the events narrated in John 7 take place. According to the fourth Gospel, the question on everyone's mind at this particular Feast of Booths is: "Who is Jesus?" Although as the chapter unfolds, this question becomes "Where is He from?" As the people argue with each other, some say He is a good man, while others say He deludes the people (John 7:11, 12).

When Jesus finally appears in the middle of the festival, some in the crowd speculate that He might be the Messiah because here He is, teaching openly in the temple even though there are standing orders that He should be arrested on sight (vv. 25, 26). Others say that Jesus could not be the Messiah, because they know where He came from. When the Messiah comes, no one will know from where He has come (v. 27). This is particularly ironic, because it is clear to the careful reader that the crowd does not in fact know where Jesus has come from. Not only this, they do not know where He is going, as is shown in what He says to them after word gets back to the religious authorities and they send soldiers to arrest Jesus.

Jesus tells the crowd that He will be with them for a only a small amount of time. They will then seek Him and will not be able to find Him because they cannot follow where He goes (vv. 33, 34). Like Nicodemus in an earlier chapter, the crowd misunderstands what Jesus says because the people can think only in earthly terms. Jesus has come from the realm above and intimates that He will shortly return to it and that His listeners will not be able to follow Him there. His listeners, though, cannot conceive of this possibility and speculate that He intends to go to the Diaspora, the Jews living outside Palestine (v. 35).

The question regarding the Messiah's origins arises yet again after Jesus' speech on the last day of the feast. This occasions further debate among the crowd whether Jesus might be the Messiah. Some say He is, but others answer, " 'Does the Christ come from Galilee? Does not the scripture say that the Christ comes from the seed of David and from Bethlehem the village of David?' " (v. 42). At this point, the modern reader becomes frustrated with the Gospel. *We* know that Jesus is descended from David and that He was born in Bethlehem, David's hometown. But this information is recorded *nowhere* in the Gospel of John. The problem of Jesus' Galilean origins is left deliberately unanswered by John's Gospel. However, by the time we have read as far as John 7, although this unanswered question gives us pause, a moment of thought reveals why no explanation is given. For the fourth Gospel, Jesus does not come from either Galilee or Bethlehem. He comes from above. To ask whether He is from Bethlehem or Galilee fails to recognize this heavenly reality. While asking such a question might make sense in terms of the realm below, it reveals only that the questioners have not understood Jesus' real origins.

## THE LAST AND GREATEST DAY OF THE FEAST

On the last day of the feast, Jesus stands up and declares, " 'Let anyone who is thirsty come to me and let the one who believes in me drink. As the scripture said, rivers of living water will flow out of their belly' " (vv. 37, 38). Verse 39 explains that this saying refers to the future giving of the Holy Spirit.

It is easy to imagine the scene. Jerusalem is thronged with visitors, and the harvest celebration has been in full swing for seven days. Everybody has talked, eaten, slept, and rejoiced for the entire week. Every day, as the solemn procession makes its way down to the Gihon spring, crowds of well wishers gather. They shout; sing the psalms; and wave their myrtle, willow, and palm branches. The water is collected into the golden jug and is slowly brought up the slope. As it enters the temple courtyard, a great shout of exultation goes up.

Precisely at this moment Jesus stands up. He points to the group carrying the water and says, " 'If you are thirsty, come to me and drink' " (v. 37). By saying this, He is claiming nothing less than the fact that the whole ceremony points to Himself. He says, in effect, " 'You see that water? It points to what I will give you—a river that will never run dry. I am the One who will make this ceremony become real.' "

## "WOW, SO THAT'S WHAT HE IS LIKE!"

The narrative does not, at that dramatic moment, mention the guards who are sent to arrest Jesus. Nevertheless they are there, and they hear what Jesus says. We know what kind of men they are. Soldiers and guards needed to be tough, physically tough. In war they fought with short pieces of sharpened metal. Their job was to get close to another human and kill him by using their swords to give him a fatal wound, and all this while their enemy is trying to do the same to them. In other words, the best soldiers were good killers, and they did their killing face to face. Not only strong physically, they were normally also brutal. What happened to Jesus later at His arrest was merely typical of how soldiers entertained themselves. They thought it great fun to take a helpless human being and to torture him. It was this kind of brutal man that was chosen to be a soldier or a guard.

These were the men who go back to report to the religious authorities, who immediately demand, " 'Why have you not brought him?' " (v. 45). It was their answer that caused me to say "Wow!" that day I was parked at a construction site, casually reading my Bible to fill in the time. The soldiers replied to the authorities, " 'Nobody has ever spoken like this man' " (John 7:46). I had an immediate and vivid picture of Jesus standing up at the feast to make His dramatic claim. The soldiers leave their positions at the edge of the crowd and begin to shoulder their way toward Him. But as they move, they listen to what Jesus is saying. They are so struck by it they slow down and eventually stop and just listen. Not one of them goes forward to arrest Jesus.

I had been asking my Christian friends, "What is Jesus really like?" Here, then, was a partial answer: He is the kind of man who interrupts a solemn procession to tell the participants that He is the meaning of the ritual they are acting out. He is the kind of man who can capture the attention of the crowd, priests, and enemies. But more than this, He is the kind of man who makes such an impression on people that even brutal guards are stopped in their tracks to listen entranced. This is what Jesus is like!

## BUT WHAT ABOUT MY LOGICAL FALLACY?

I have used this incident from my own past several times in sermons and talks, but it was only as I was writing it out for this chapter that I realized my response had a logical inconsistency in it. I had been refusing to accept any answer to the question of what Jesus was like that was expressed in terms of what He did. But my own answer was also in terms of what He did!

Nobody ever challenged me on this point when they listened to me talk about it, but when I wrote it down, the logical inconsistency became clear. So perhaps I need to rethink my earlier rejection of all those answers from my friends. After all, how do we know our own friends and family except by what they do and say? Reflecting on this, I think the difference between my reading of John 7 and what others had been telling me was this—my reading of John 7 had given me an insight that was my own and not secondhand.

Indeed, as you have read what I have just written, you might be thinking that although the soldiers' reaction is interesting, it's not really as dramatic as I have made out. But that only illustrates my point. It was dramatic for *me*, because it was something I had gained from my own reading of the New Testament. Perhaps the real lesson to be learned from my experience is this: We cannot know Jesus secondhand. If we want to know what He is like, we each need to sit down and read the Gospels for ourselves. There we will find insights that belong to us alone, and it will be these that make Jesus real to us.

---

1. This is nicely summarized by Raymond E. Brown, *The Gospel of John* (Garden City, N.Y.: Doubleday, 1966), 1:327. See also the comments on the rabbinic theology surrounding the ceremony by J. Jeremias, in *Theological Dictionary of the New Testament*, ed. G. Kittel (Grand Rapids, Mich.: Eerdmans, 1967), 4:277, 278.

# CHAPTER TWENTY-FOUR

# Jesus Loved, So He Stayed Away (John 11)

Until quite recent times, death was for twentieth-century Western society what sex was for Victorian society—something everybody knew about and that almost everybody would experience, but something that was never talked about, especially in front of children. When Uncle Harry died, the children were normally told that he had gone on a long journey, and when their parents died, children were not permitted to go to the funeral as it might upset them. The grieving widow was given tranquilizers so she might get through the funeral without collapsing. The man was expected to do the manly thing and keep a stiff upper lip. Public tears were permissible to the womenfolk but were considered unmanly in a man.

Fortunately, these attitudes are found less and less frequently. It is now widely known that grief is a process by which the body heals itself after great loss. If this process is prevented, it may cause psychological and, sometimes, health problems. Most of us even know about the different stages the bereaved person goes through—denial, anger, despair, gradual adjustment, acceptance, etc. But knowing the process does not always help the individual concerned. The pain is very real, and knowing its purpose and its process does not change its intensity. Oftentimes the bereaved feel they are losing their grip on reality, and this is very disturbing, even though the bereaved knows that others also experience such feelings.

For those who have strong religious convictions, the death of a loved one can also be a time of considerable religious turmoil. If God could have saved your friend or lover, why didn't He? Why did God not step in to make the little change when that would have been all that was necessary to save his or her life? Where was God? Why did God not act? Does God know what it is like? How does God feel about death?

We do know what the Son of God felt like in the face of the death of somebody He loved. The account is found in John 11. This chapter has many of the answers concerning how Jesus dealt with death, how He approached the family of the dead man, what He felt, and what He did. It is a chapter full of paradoxes, pain, and hope.

When Jesus first learned that Lazarus was ill, His attitudes and actions must have seemed incomprehensible to Mary and Martha, Lazarus's sisters. John 11 begins by pointing out the close friendship between Jesus and the family of Mary, Martha, and Lazarus. Mary was the one who had anointed Jesus' feet and wiped them with her hair. When Lazarus became sick, the sisters immediately informed Jesus, who sent back the message, " 'This sickness is not for death, but for the glory of God' " (John 11:4). Then follows two of the most remarkable verses in John's Gospel: "Jesus loved Martha and her sister, and Lazarus, *therefore* when he heard that he was sick, he stayed where he was for two days" (John 11:5, 6, emphasis supplied). The strangeness of these verses was apparent to me almost from the first time I read them. The fact that Jesus loved Martha, Mary, and Lazarus meant that he stayed away to let Lazarus die! He loved, *therefore*[1] He stayed away. Was the fact that "Jesus loved . . ." the cause of His allowing the death of Lazarus? Why? Was the death of Lazarus something Jesus permitted because it was the loving thing to do? Why? We will return to these questions later in this chapter.

How Jesus understood death is perhaps best revealed in what He next said to His disciples. He told them that Lazarus was asleep. They were pleased at this, assuming that the fever had broken and that Lazarus's body was using sleep to heal itself. Jesus then plainly told them that Lazarus was dead. In comparing death to a sleep, Jesus was drawing upon a well-known Old Testament way of describing death (King "So-and-so" slept with his fathers; e.g., 1 Kings 14:31; 15:8, 24; etc.). It also conveys the experience of the dead person. Dying is like going to sleep. The sleeper will be awakened at the resurrection, and it will be like waking up after a full night's sleep.[2]

This is of great comfort. If death is like sleep, then we need be no more afraid of it than of sleep. There is sorrow at parting, but it is the sorrow of saying farewell to a friend whom you know you will meet again—even if not in this lifetime. It is not the desperate sorrow of those with no expectation of ever meeting again.

Jesus had left Judea because the Jewish leaders were plotting against His life. The disciples pointed this out when Jesus told them of His intention to return to Judea and visit Lazarus (John 11:8). But regardless of the risk, Jesus intended to go, and His disciples decided to accompany Him.

### JESUS, THE RESURRECTION AND THE LIFE

The meeting between Jesus and Martha is full of pathos and interest. Martha began immediately with what was uppermost in her mind: " 'Lord, if you had been here, my brother would not have died. But even now I know that whatever you ask of God he will give you' " (John 11:21, 22). At first sight, knowing as we do that Jesus will soon raise Lazarus to life, this sounds like a remarkable confession of faith in Jesus. It is a confession that is stronger than death itself. Jesus had sent a message back to the sisters that the illness of Lazarus was not to death, and here is evidence that Martha has believed what Jesus said and, despite her brother's death, still thinks that Jesus is able to ask God to restore Lazarus. The following conversation, though, soon makes clear that while Martha's statement is indeed a remarkable affirmation in the light of the fact that Jesus' message had proven false, she had no expectation that Jesus would be the one to raise Lazarus. In answer to Jesus' comment, " 'Your brother will rise,' " Martha replies: " 'I know that he will rise in the resurrection on the last day' " (John 11:23, 24). Thus Martha was confident that her brother would rise in the general resurrection at the end of time, but she had little or no expectations that Jesus would be able to do anything right then.

In His reply to Martha, Jesus articulates what is surely the main point of the whole story: " 'I am the resurrection and the life. Whoever believes in me, even though he dies, will live, and all who live and believe in me will never die. Do you believe this?' " (John 11:25, 26). Jesus challenges Martha to believe. Not just to believe, but to believe in the face of death itself, in the face of disappointment in Jesus. Jesus asks her to believe that the resurrection is tied up with believing in Himself. This is the belief that gives eternal life. This is the belief that is stronger than death itself and that will bring her brother to life.

By raising Lazarus, Jesus will demonstrate that He is the resurrection and the life. If He is able to raise even one dead person to life, then He is also able to raise all dead persons to life.

## WHAT DID JESUS FEEL?

Martha brings Mary to Jesus, and Jesus sees her and those around her weeping. John 11:33-35 gives His reaction: "Therefore, when Jesus saw her weeping and the Jews who accompanied her weeping, he was angry (*enebrimēsato*)[3] in spirit and troubled himself. And he said, 'Where have you placed him?' They answered, 'Lord, come and see.' Jesus wept." Here is Jesus' reaction to death. He is angry in its presence. It is an evil thing that He wishes to destroy. He is very troubled. He weeps with the afflicted.

Jesus is our mirror of God. As He later said to Thomas, " 'If you have seen me, you have seen the Father' " (John 14:9). If we want to know how God feels about death, then Jesus' reaction is a fair indication. God feels angry about death. He feels angry about sin that causes death. He is troubled. He weeps with those who weep.

## LAZARUS, COME OUT!

Jesus then asks for the stone to be removed. Martha (who still appears to be wavering between belief and doubt) objects strongly. After being dead four days, the body will be well on the way to decomposition. It will, as she says, "stink." Jesus says to her, " 'Did I not say to you that if you believe you will see the glory of God?' " (John 11:40). So Martha permits the stone to be removed.

The scene that follows is extraordinary. I am not sure how close everybody got to the tomb, but they would all be very interested to see what would happen. They would form a semicircle around the opening. Jesus and the two sisters would stand toward the front of the little crowd of well-wishers and disciples. Jesus prays audibly and then says loudly, " 'Lazarus, Come out!' " In response, a bandaged figure staggers out of the tomb. Wrapped up as he is, Lazarus can hardly move, but somehow he comes out. Jesus then tells the people to unwrap the bandages. The Gospel doesn't say, but you can imagine what must be going through the minds of those who go to unwrap Lazarus. What would they expect to find? Lazarus was dead and had been dead for four days in a hot climate. As they unwrap him, will they find a rotting body? Will there be some indescribable horror awaiting them—a rotting body that now moves? Slowly the bandages come off. With fear they unwrap the last layer, but the fear rapidly turns to excitement. There is a living body underneath those bandages! They hurriedly unwrap the last strands. Lazarus stands there alive and well and healthy! He and his two sisters embrace! Everybody is leaping for joy!

## ECONOMY OF MIRACLE

One of the interesting things about this whole episode is how ordinary Jesus chooses to make the miracle. It would have been much more impressive if He had caused the stone to disintegrate into a puff of dust. If He had miraculously drawn Lazarus out of the tomb and then caused his bandages to melt away. After all, these feats would pale into insignificance alongside raising a dead man to life. If Jesus could raise Lazarus to life, He could easily have done these other things. But He chose not to. He chose to involve those around the tomb, having them do what they could do—rolling away the stone, unwrapping the bandages. What humans could do, they should do. The application to illness and healing today is unmistakable. God cannot generally be expected to intervene and perform a miracle when the particular healing is within the capabilities of modern medical science. Humans should use the intelligence and resources they have before seeking divine aid. To do less would be presumption.

### WHAT WAS THE ATTITUDE OF THOSE WHO WITNESSED THE MIRACLE?

Among those who witnessed the miracle, there were two reactions. Many believed on Jesus, but others went to the Pharisees and told them what Jesus had done. The Pharisees did not doubt the truth of the story, but they still did not believe in Jesus. Instead, their reaction was fear. They feared that Jesus' actions would cause such an uproar that the Romans would come and destroy both the city and the temple.

This raises the fascinating problem of belief. What are adequate grounds for belief? Are miracles, even extraordinary miracles such as raising someone from the dead, adequate grounds for belief? Certainly, the evidence of this story shows that not everyone who witnessed the miracle believed. The response to the miraculous multiplying of the loaves and fishes (John 6) shows the same thing. All the crowd began following Jesus because of the miracle, but when the people were challenged to follow the consequences of their belief, they all turned aside and did not walk with Jesus anymore.

The parable of Lazarus and the rich man, recorded in Luke 16:19-31, also provides an interesting commentary on this point. Normally, the different actors of Jesus' parables are identified by generic characteristics, such as " 'A certain rich man . . . ,' " " 'The sower . . . ,' " " 'What shepherd amongst you . . . ,' " etc. But in the parable of the rich man and Lazarus, we are actually given the name of one of the characters in the parable. At the climax of the story, the rich man wishes Lazarus to go back from the dead to warn his brothers that they will be punished in the life to come for their evil deeds in this life. Abraham replies, " 'They have Moses and the prophets, let them hear them.' " The rich man pleads, " 'Father Abraham. If somebody went to them from the dead they would repent.' " The reply comes, " 'If they do not hear Moses and the prophets, neither will they believe if someone rises from the dead' " (Luke 16:29-31).

The parallels with the raising of Lazarus in the Gospel of John are very clear. The Pharisees are experts in Moses and the prophets, the written Scripture, yet they do not believe. Even when Lazarus was raised from the dead, they still did not believe!

What is the basis for our belief in Jesus today? Is it miracle, or is it Scripture? Miracles do not convince if Scripture does not convince. But more than this, miracles, no matter how dramatic, cannot give irresistible evidence that they are from God (they may be from the evil one). Indeed, if a sound nonsupernatural explanation is possible, miracles do not give irrefutable evidence that they originate from a transcendent God who is interested in our welfare.

Within some people there is belief. This belief is founded on Scripture. Within others, there is no belief. They have the same evidence, but they do not believe. This is one of the mysteries of religion.

### WAS THE LOVE OF JESUS THE REASON HE STAYED AWAY? WHY?

Perhaps the most difficult question yet remains to be answered. Why did Jesus' love for Mary, Martha, and Lazarus cause Him to stay away until He knew that Lazarus was dead? It would be too easy to give a trite answer here.

Jesus' words " 'What will come about will be for the glory of God' " provide a clue. Jesus had to take the long view. Jesus could see the outcome. Jesus knew that Lazarus would be raised to life and that this would be an extraordinary witness to the glory of God, providing remarkable comfort to the family and to His own disciples when the time of His death came. It would also show them that Jesus has the power over death itself and demonstrate once and for all that Jesus is indeed the resurrection and the life. It would show that if only they would believe in Jesus, then they, too, would be raised to life. Having lived through this experience, Mary and Martha would have a faith stronger than death. Their faith would carry them through death. They would look with certainty to the future resurrection, when Jesus will call all the dead out of the tomb—some to the resurrection of life, some to the resurrection of damnation (John 5:28, 29).

Jesus' love caused Him to share the sorrows of the grieving sisters. Not only this, He was angry at death. His ultimate goal was to defeat death completely, but the only way to do this was through His own death. Only by being lifted up on the cross could He draw all humanity to Himself. Only by Jesus being lifted up toward heaven could all humanity have life. To deal with sin and death, Jesus was not able to change the natural consequences of sin. Death still reigned. His death and resurrection would provide the power to ultimately overcome death, but between then and the time of His future return, there would be many deaths. Many would wonder why their Lord did not come when summoned. Many would wonder why He sent a message of comfort that there would be life, when all that followed was death. Many would say in anguish, " 'Lord, if only you had come, my brother need not have died.' "

How, then, does Jesus react to death? He gets angry. He plans to deal decisively with sin and death. He is troubled. He weeps with those who weep. But there are no easy answers. Death is still fearful. It is like sleep, but it is still a painful loss. It will ultimately be overcome but at great cost to God Himself. God gave His own Son to die, so that if we believe in Him, then we need not die His death—the fearful death of sin, the death of despair, destruction, and separation from God.

Jesus' reaction to death shows how God reacts to death. Where is God when a loved one dies? God is there. He is angry at the death. He is deeply troubled. He weeps. God can see the ultimate outcome. For Him, death is a sleep, but He also shares the sorrow of loss. He knows the horror of death because in His Son who suffered and died, He experienced death and bereavement. God really does know and understand. He knows our anger, He knows our pain, He knows our loss. God loves us so much that at whatever cost to Himself, He will rid the universe of sin. But God also loves us so much that He does not take shortcuts that do not work. God loves us so much that sometimes He must stay away for two days!

# Jesus Loved, So He Stayed Away (John 11)

1. The Greek word translated "therefore" is *oun*. In the Greek New Testament, this word almost always strongly conveys the idea of consequence, of "therefore." In John, it sometimes is used in a way that might be better translated "for" (in other words, as a conjunction used to move the story along), but the way it is used in this context shows that some idea of "therefore" is meant.

2. Oscar Cullmann shared with the nonacademic world something that had been well known for some time in academic circles when he wrote a short book called *Immortality of the Soul or Resurrection of the Dead* (London: Epworth, 1958). As he says, "No other publication of mine has provoked such enthusiasm or such violent hostility," and indeed, the work engendered a great deal of intense debate. The book points out that if a person believes in an immortal soul, then the doctrine of the resurrection of the dead makes no sense. The writers of the New Testament believed in the resurrection of the body, not the immortality of the soul. They may have used terms such as "soul" and "body," but in a way consistent with Hebrew ideas, not Greek ideas. The New Testament view is that the dead sleep until the resurrection (which is a resurrection of the total individual—body and soul together). For a technical presentation of these ideas, see Rudolf Bultmann, *Theology of the New Testament* (London: SCM, 1952), 1:190-246. A similar, and less technical exposition (which does not require a knowledge of Greek), may be found in George Eldon Ladd, *A Theology of the New Testament* (Grand Rapids, Mich.: Eerdmans, 1974), 457- 478.

3. The verb *embrimaomai*, used here, is an intensive form of *brimaomai*, meaning "to snort with anger, be wrathful, furious" *(A Lexicon Abridged from Liddel and Scott's Greek-English Lexicon* [Oxford: Clarendon, 1926], 135). The intensive form means to "be sore vexed, be indignant" (abridged Liddell and Scott, 217, 218). Elsewhere in the New Testament, this verb is used in the sense of "speak harshly to, criticize." To translate this as to "be deeply moved," as do most English translations, is to miss an important aspect of what Jesus is experiencing. He is angry in the face of his greatest enemy—death.

CHAPTER TWENTY-FIVE

# The Farewell Discourse
# (John 13–17)

## JOHN 13–17 IN THE OVERALL STRUCTURE OF THE GOSPEL

The Gospel of John appears to have a carefully designed structure. Chapter 1 begins by presenting the general concepts that will be advanced in the Gospel and then introduces several of the Gospel's principal protagonists. Chapters 2–12 follow a general pattern. This section of the Gospel is dominated by an interlocking series of miracles (called "signs"[1]), dialogues, and discourses. The discourses between Jesus and Nicodemus, Jesus and the Samaritan woman, and Jesus and the crowd provide opportunity for developing the key concepts by which the fourth Gospel seeks to help the reader understand Jesus. Some of these discourses have a clear relationship to foregoing signs. The first of these signs is identified as the occasion at which Jesus turned water into wine (John 2:11), while the healing of the official's son, in John 4:43-54, is identified as the second sign (v. 54). Other signs include the multiplication of the bread and fish to feed a crowd in excess of five thousand (John 6:1-14, identified as a sign in v. 14). This sign forms the occasion for the long discourses that climax in Jesus' demand that His hearers eat His body and drink His blood (John 6:22-71). The healing of a man blind from birth (John 9) follows the discourse in which Jesus identifies Himself as the Light of the world (John 8:12-20). The last miracle identified as a sign is the raising of Lazarus from the dead (John 11). This gives evidence of Jesus' claim that He is the resurrection and the life (v. 25) and is the event that finally provokes Jesus' enemies to plot His death (John 11:45-57; 12:9-11).

Chapter 13 marks a turning point in John's Gospel. After chapter 13, no miracle is identified as a sign. Instead, the rest of the Gospel divides naturally into three large sections—the events of the night before Jesus is betrayed (John 13–17), the events surrounding the crucifixion (John 18, 19), and the Resurrection appearances of Jesus (John 20, 21). Chapters 13–21 constitute one-third of the verses in John's Gospel,[2] showing yet again the emphasis on the Crucifixion, shared by all four Gospels. In this chapter, we will consider the section of John that records the events and conversations of the night before the Crucifixion. In the next chapter, we will look at John's portrayal of Jesus' death and resurrection.

## LEADERSHIP THROUGH SERVICE (JOHN 13:1-20, 31-35)

John 13 begins with these words, "Before the feast of the Passover, when Jesus knew that his hour had come to return from this world to his Father; having loved his own in the world, he loved them to the end. And when supper was ready, and the devil had already put it into the heart of Judas (son of Simon Iscariot) to betray him, Jesus, knowing that the Father had given all things into his hands and that he had come from God and would return to God, rose. . . ." These words introduce the Last Supper in the fourth Gospel. They highlight several themes—the coming Passover,[3] Jesus' supreme power, His status as the One come from heaven, and finally, His love for the disciples. This love is shown in His actions and highlighted in His remarks following the meal.

Jesus' comment in Luke 7:44, chiding His host for not providing water for His feet, shows that washing the feet of a guest at a meal was a courtesy but not a necessary obligation. From the earlier reference, it is not clear whether or not the host himself would perform the actual function of washing the feet. Most likely this would be a role delegated to servants. In any event, the fact that Jesus wanted to wash His disciples' feet filled them with some alarm. Peter tells Jesus that He would *never* wash his feet, not now or in the future (John 13:8). In the custom of the time, there was something highly improper about a master washing the feet of a disciple. John highlights the problem by his introduction, where he carefully states Jesus' actual status—He has been given all power; He has come from God and returns there. Even so, before Jesus and His disciples begin to eat their meal, He takes the bowl and the towel and washes the feet of all present at the table.

Jesus then says, " 'You call me teacher and lord, and rightly so, for I am. If I your lord and teacher have washed your feet, you should also wash one another's feet. For I have given you an example so that you should do to each other what I have done to you' " (John 13:13-15). Jesus' leadership was a leadership of humility. This act is strongly reminiscent of Luke 22:24-30, which Luke records as having taken place at the Last Supper. When a dispute arose about who should lead, Jesus told the disciples that their leader should become as a servant. Jesus showed His love by His voluntary service. This is what His followers should also do.

After Judas Iscariot had left the meal, Jesus stated explicitly what He wished of His disciples: " 'A new commandment I give to you, that you love one another, as I have loved you, so that you also might love each other. In this will all know that you are my disciples, if you have love for each other' " (John 13:34, 35). Here, then, is the heart of discipleship and the center of Christian community life—love, love like Jesus' love. Jesus, knowing full well that He was from God and would return there, took upon Himself the role of a servant. He showed His love by giving His life for us, that, in turn, we might love others. His disciples are not recognized by their morality, by their learning, by their correct doctrine, or by their careful organization, important though these things are. His disciples are recognized, above all, by their love for one another, a love that shows itself in service and a willingness to give all for each other. This, then, is the focus that the fourth Gospel places on the Last Supper.[4]

## JESUS, THE WAY TO THE FATHER (JOHN 14:1-14)

John 14:1-3 is one of the best-known passages in all of Scripture. This is as it should be, because this passage (vv. 1-14) is one that explicitly states things that are crucial for understanding the rest of he Gospel and that are only implicit there. It deals with the practical implications of Jesus' claim to be from the heavenly Father. This means that Jesus knows the way back to heaven. He will go back to the Father to prepare a place for His followers.

Thomas and Philip raise two important issues. Thomas asks how, without knowing where Jesus goes, it is possible to go there (v. 4). Jesus replies that He is the way, the truth, and the life. No one comes to the Father except through Him (v. 6). This, then, is the uniqueness of Christianity; Jesus is the true way to God.

In response to Philip's request, " 'Lord, show us the Father and we will be satisfied' " (v. 8), Jesus responds by pointing out that knowing Him is the same as knowing the Father. " 'I am in the Father, and the Father is in me' " (v. 10). In other words, if we know Jesus, then we know the Father. Again, this is an extraordinary claim—that the way to know God is to know Jesus. Jesus is not only the way to God, He fully and truly represents God. Herein lies His importance.

## THE PROMISE OF THE SPIRIT (JOHN 14:15-31; 16:5-15)

In further preparation for His coming separation from His disciples, Jesus promises to send them another "advocate" (Greek, *paraklētos*). The background of the Greek term *paraklētos* is that of a legal representative, a "lawyer" or "advocate," the individual who represents a defendant in a trial. It is clearly used in this way in 1 John 2:1: " 'My little children, I write these things to you so that you may not sin; but if any does sin, we have an *advocate* with the Father, Jesus Christ, the righteous.' " The language implies that Jesus represents us in the last judgment.

So, in John 14 Jesus is promising us an advocate. This advocate is His replacement, and the role of this advocate extends further than just that of a legal representative. This advocate is the Spirit of truth that will remain in the disciple of Jesus (v. 17). When Jesus goes back to His Father, He will not leave His disciples as orphans (v. 18). The advocate will teach the disciples all things and bring all things back to their remembrance (v. 26).

In a later chapter, Jesus returns to the subject of the advocate. The role of the advocate will be to convict the world of sin, righteousness, and judgment (John 16:8). The Spirit of truth will lead the disciples into all truth. He will speak only of what He hears, not of Himself.

Who, then, is this advocate? There is little doubt that Jesus is making reference to the Holy Spirit. In Jesus' absence, the Spirit will teach and guide His disciples and bring conviction to those who hear about Jesus. This is He whom Jesus will send. He will take the place of Jesus, to provide love and comfort, guidance and faith. In Jesus' absence, He will also take upon Himself the role of advocate, representing the disciple's case to God.

### THE VINE AND THE BRANCHES (JOHN 15)

Immediately after speaking about the Advocate for the first time, Jesus goes on to point out that the relationship between Himself and His disciples is as close as the relationship between a vine and its branches. A branch cannot produce fruit unless connected to the vine. If it does not produce fruit, it is cut off and burned with fire. The exact nature of the required "fruit" is not spelled out, but the context gives us some clues: If the disciples keep Jesus' commands, they will remain in His love (v. 10). So the bearing of fruit is somehow related to keeping Jesus' commands, especially the command to love one another as He has loved us. If disciples remain in Him and bear fruit, then whatever they will ask in the name of Jesus will be done (v. 16).

The link between loving Jesus and keeping His command (or word) is a continuous theme of these chapters (e.g., John 14:15, 21, 23, 24; 15:10). They do not spell out exactly what this word or command is, but the one new command Jesus does give is to love one another. This is the test of the true disciple. Thus, the one who keeps in touch with Jesus, the true vine, will be the one who bears the fruit of love for other disciples. Those who bear this kind of fruit will be heard by God.

### THE PRAYER OF THE ADVOCATE (JOHN 17)

This section of John concludes with a long prayer by Jesus. He deliberately prays this prayer so the disciples can hear. It is almost as though

Jesus is acting in His role of advocate—representing the disciples to God. His prayer contains several important themes.

First, His prayer celebrates the coming of His hour of glorification (vv. 1, 2). Ironically, this is also the hour of His suffering. Jesus is about to face the Cross, yet in some way that very cross is the way Jesus gains glory. By means of the Cross (and Resurrection, of course), Jesus will return to the Father to receive the glory He had with Him before the foundation of the world (v. 24). Jesus asks that His disciples be able to see this glory.

Second, in His prayer, Jesus commits the safekeeping of the disciples to God. While He had been with them, He had protected them. But now that He is leaving, it is God who will keep them safe (vv. 12-16). Jesus does not ask that they be taken from this world, only that they be kept safe from the evil one (v. 15). Just as the world has hated Jesus, so it will also hate them (vv. 13-16). Therefore, God's protection from the evil one will be badly needed.

Third, in two places in the prayer, Jesus prays for the unity of the disciples (vv. 11, 20-23). Just as Jesus and the Father are one, so also the disciples should be one.

Fourth, just as Jesus had been sent out from the Father, so also He was sending His disciples out to represent Him (v. 18).

Finally, Jesus prays not only for the disciples who can immediately hear Him, He prays for future disciples who will believe in Him through the witness of those who have known Him.

### Jesus' preparation of His disciples

In this way, Jesus prepares His disciples for the events that are about to overtake them. He warns them that He will be betrayed. Betrayal, fear, and the loss of Jesus is going to put great strains on the small group of disciples. But their response should be that of love. Although they will be faced with unremitting hostility, they will love both each other and those who hate them—as their Master did! This will be what distinguishes them as the disciples of Jesus. Jesus further points out the true source of their unity—that all His followers are as close to Him as are the branches of a vine to the vine itself. Jesus further prepares His disciples for His departure by promising them the comfort of one who, like Himself, will represent them to God and the world. The Spirit of truth will guide them into all truth. He will bring peace.

As Jesus Himself tells the disciples, only after the dramatic events of the Crucifixion and the Resurrection will they be able to look back at what He has been telling them and understand what He means (John 13:19; 14:29). But as Jesus calmly faces His destiny, He carefully makes preparations for the disciples, to help them through this difficult time and prepare them for their future task.

---

1. The KJV translates the Greek word *sēmeion* with two different English words, "sign" (John 2:18; 4:48; 6:30; 20:30) and "miracle" (John 2:11, 23; 3:2; 4:54; 6:2, 14, 26; 7:31; 9:16; 10:41; 11:47; 12:18, 37). Although "sign" is probably a slightly better translation, both "sign" and "miracle" are quite acceptable. But to use both options in the one translation is unfortunate because the meaning common to the one underlying Greek word is lost to the English reader. There are other Greek words that also can be translated "miracle" in the right context (e.g., *dunamis*, "act of power"; *teras*, "wonder"), but in every case where the KJV uses the word *miracle* in the Gospel of John, it translates the Greek word *sēmeion*.

2. Exactly 293 out of 879 verses.

3. In fact, in the fourth Gospel, the sacrifice of the Passover lamb coincides with Jesus' death on the cross (see, for example, the temporal note given in John 19:13, 14). This provides a problem for historians because the other three Gospels clearly identify the Last Supper as the Passover meal. The matter has already been discussed in chapter 18 in an extended endnote.

4. The command given in the other three Gospels to reenact the Last Supper in terms of bread and wine is not repeated in John. However, this does not mean that the use of the bread and wine by Christians to represent Jesus' body and blood is absent from John. It is placed instead in the heated controversy of John 6, where Jesus demands of His listeners that they eat His body and drink His blood.

CHAPTER TWENTY-SIX

# The Meaning Given to the Cross by John (John 18–20)

Jesus' cross and resurrection is the focus of the fourth Gospel.[1] In a sense, then, the early part of that Gospel serves to prepare the reader to understand these closing events. In this chapter, we will explore the meaning of the Cross in the fourth Gospel—some of which is shown by the way in which these events are portrayed, and some of which is made explicit in the earlier chapters of the Gospel.

## JESUS DELIBERATELY CHOSE DEATH ON THE CROSS

Each of the four Gospels has a unique perspective on the events surrounding Jesus' death. This is particularly true of John, and perhaps the most striking feature of the passion narrative in John's Gospel is that Jesus is in control of events and that His death is voluntary. For example, when Judas leads the soldiers, the Pharisees, and the armed servants of the high priest to arrest Jesus, He steps forward and asks them whom they seek. " 'Jesus, the Nazarene,' " they answer, to which Jesus responds, " 'I am He.' " At this self-revelation, the soldiers and servants fall backward to the ground. They are able to arrest Jesus only because He gives Himself into their hands (John 18:3-8).

Jesus is then taken to the high priest and after that to Pilate. In Pilate,

# The Four Faces of Jesus

Jesus meets the highest representative of earthly rule in Palestine, yet He meets him as an equal. When Pilate becomes exasperated by Jesus' attitude and exclaims, " 'Why do you not speak to me? Do you not know that I have the power to release you and the power to crucify you?' " Jesus calmly replies, " 'You have no power over me except that which is given to you from above' " (19:10, 11). Pilate's power has been granted to him, and Jesus voluntarily submits Himself to his jurisdiction.

Even on the cross Jesus remains in control of events. He places His mother in the care of the beloved disciple (19:26, 27), and after ensuring that a final detail of scriptural prophecy is fulfilled, He voluntarily dies (19:28-30).

While the four Gospels agree on the broad picture of the final events in Jesus' earthly life, it is clear that significant elements are found in the other three Gospels that are absent from John. For example, John notes that Jesus went to a garden (Gethsemane) on the Mount of Olives, where He was arrested by the soldiers and armed servants, but John has no record of Him praying, asking to be released from the task set before Him, or that Judas betrayed Him with a kiss. John likewise omits the fact that Jesus was not physically able to carry the cross and that Simon of Cyrene was pressed to carry it for Him. According to John 19:17, Jesus carried His own cross. In John, the crowd does not mock Jesus on the cross. Jesus does not cry out " 'My God, my God, why have you forsaken me?' " There is no reference to the darkening of the sun. The fourth Gospel is clearly independent of the three Synoptic Gospels, so there is no hard evidence that John has deliberately omitted these incidents from his account, but their absence certainly heightens the view that Jesus is in charge of events.

Summing up, then: In John, the crucifixion was not a tragic error or a blow of blind fate. It was something Jesus had foreknown and deliberately chosen. At every stage in the process, Jesus was in control of His destiny. He died because He deliberately chose the death of the cross.

## THE DEATH ON THE CROSS WAS ALSO GOD'S PREORDAINED WILL

Several times during the description of the events surrounding the crucifixion, John comments that what happened came about in order to fulfill prophecy. For example, at both 19:24 and 19:28 the actions of the soldiers and of Jesus are said to be in fulfillment of Scripture, while at 18:9 and 18:32 the betrayal by Judas and the sentence to death by crucifixion are said to be a fulfillment of the words of Jesus. If a thing is a fulfillment of prophecy, then it must have been preordained by God; that is to say, it was God's will that it happen.

## THE CROSS IS THE MOMENT OF GLORIFICATION

Paradoxically, in the fourth Gospel, Jesus' glorification and exaltation belong to His crucifixion. On at least three occasions, this link is made explicit. The first is found in John 12:23-32. In John 12:23 Jesus says, " 'The hour has come when the Son of Man is to be glorified,' " and then He goes on to speak of the necessity for a grain of wheat to die to give new life (v. 24). In some way, the hour of glorification is linked with Jesus' death. Jesus continues to talk about His "hour." He ponders whether or not He should ask the Father to save Him from "this hour," but He comments that this was the reason He came to the world (v. 27). He asks the Father to glorify His name, at which a voice from heaven says, " 'I glorified it, and will again glorify it' " (v. 28). It is in the context of the hour of glorification and judgment that Jesus says, " 'And I, if I be lifted up from the earth, will draw all men to me' " (v. 32). On the cross, as Jesus is lifted up from the earth, He is also lifted up to heaven. The Cross is an integral part of His glorification and exaltation.

Second, in His prayer recorded in chapter 17, Jesus again takes up the theme of His hour of glorification. " 'Father, the hour has come; glorify your son, so that the son might glorify you. . . . I glorified you on earth by finishing the work which you gave me to do; and now glorify me, Father, with your glory which I had with you before the world was' " (John 17:1-4). The hour of His glory is the hour of His suffering; on the cross He finishes the work that God gave Him (John 19:30).

Third, it is also interesting to note that it is not only *Jesus'* death that brings glory. John 21:19 notes that when Jesus tells Peter that he will also die by crucifixion, His words "signified the kind of death by which he [Peter] would glorify God."

The Four Faces of Jesus

In all three of these texts, there is an explicit link between the Cross and the glorification and exaltation of Jesus.

## THE CROSS IS THE ENTHRONEMENT OF JESUS AS KING

One of the stronger ironies of the crucifixion is that the charges against Jesus were both true and false. He was accused of being a king, and king He was. But not a king in rebellion against Rome, nor a king in any sense that Pilate could make out.

This theme of Jesus' kingship runs right through Pilate's dealings with Jesus (John 18:28–19:16). When Pilate asks if Jesus is King of the Jews, He assures Pilate that His kingdom is not of this world (18:36). When further pressed by Pilate, Jesus admits that He was born into the world for the purpose of being king (v. 37). Yet, it is after this that Pilate tells the crowd, " 'I find no crime in him' " (John 18:38). This is quite a remarkable statement to make of someone who has just admitted that He is a king of the Jews (in direct challenge to the Roman imperial will). The crowd demands Jesus' death, and Pilate hears that the people wish to kill Jesus because He claims to be God. This immediately makes Pilate fearful, and he asks the most important question of Jesus, " 'Whereabouts are you from?' " (John 19:9). This is the crucial question that has dominated much of the earlier chapters in John's Gospel. Jesus refuses to answer Pilate on this matter, at which Pilate tells Jesus, " 'Do you not know that I have the authority to release you and the authority to crucify you?' "

To this Jesus replies, " 'You have no authority over me except what is given you from above' " (John 19:11). Again Pilate seeks to release Jesus, by offering Him to the crowd as its king. They insist that Pilate would be going against Caesar to release Jesus. They also insist that they have no king but Caesar (John 19:12-15). Jesus is then crucified as "King of the Jews" (John 19:21). The supreme irony is that Pilate is convinced Jesus is the legitimate king of the Jews yet that He is no threat to the Roman state. Pilate desires to release Him. It is Jesus' own people, the Jews (through their leaders), who reject Him as king and accept the yoke of Rome instead.

# The Meaning Given to the Cross by John (John 18–20)

Pilate orders that a sign be made in three languages, "Jesus of Nazareth, King of the Jews" (19:19). Pilate continues to recognize Jesus' kingship over the nation, despite the opposition of "the high priests of the Jews" (John 19:21). In this way, Pilate announces the accession of Jesus to His throne. The charges are true: Jesus is king, but not the kind of king who should have been punished by crucifixion. He is king in yet another way—one that shows His style of kingship, a kingship of supreme love, as He offers Himself as a sacrifice on the cross. On the cross, Jesus is enthroned as king of the Jews.

## OTHER ASPECTS OF THE MEANING OF THE CROSS IN JOHN

Several other observations can be made about the meaning of the Cross in the fourth Gospel.

*Jesus dies as the Passover lamb.* Several times, John's Gospel notes the linkage of Jesus' death with the sacrifice of the Passover (John 18:28; 19:14; 19:31). Further, Caiaphas, the high priest (of all people) underlines the substitutionary nature of Jesus' death when he says it is better that one man die for the nation than for the whole nation to perish (John 11:50; 18:14). First John 2:2 and 4:10 make it even more explicit that Jesus' death is a sacrificial atonement, calling Jesus "the atonement."

*The Cross and the Resurrection are both essential parts of the one event.* The Cross is the moment that Jesus is lifted up, but this event has no meaning without His resurrection. Only by means of the Resurrection is Jesus able to go to the Father (John 20:17). Jesus is the One who came "from above," from the Father, and He returns to the Father. This He does subsequent to the Resurrection.

Most importantly, *the Cross shows the love of Jesus.* " 'There is no greater love than this, that somebody lay down his life for his friend. You are my friends' " (John 15:13, 14). This love is but a reflection of the love the Father had in giving His Son for us. " 'God so loved the world that he gave his only son' " (John 3:16). The Christian responds to this love of God and loves his fellow Christians with the same quality of love that Jesus showed in His death (John 15:12).

Finally, *the Cross is the completion of Jesus' mission.* Jesus' last words on

The Four Faces of Jesus

the cross are " 'It is finished' " (John 19:30). By His death on the cross Jesus accomplishes His mission to earth and finishes the task allotted to Him by His Father. The Cross is the culmination of what Jesus came to achieve and, together with His resurrection, reveals who Jesus is, where He came from, and the way to eternal life.

---

1. This is true of the other Gospels as well.

# CHAPTER TWENTY-SEVEN

# The Disturbing Jesus of the Fourth Gospel

## THE STARK CHOICE

The realization that the world is a very complicated place is a part of growing up. As children, we begin with clear and simple ideas of right and wrong. As part of our maturing process, we come to the distressing conclusion that these simple ideas just do not fit every situation. What began as black and white often becomes gray. The old certainties merge into probabilities. In most areas of life this is a good thing, a sign of mature thought.

The same thing can happen to our view of Jesus. With growing sophistication can come an erosion of earlier certainties. Jesus is very important, but is He really the center of history? Perhaps He is like other important spiritual leaders. Furthermore, He may have been important to us when we were children, but as adults it might be time to develop the maturity to stand apart from Him and develop our own philosophy of life.

In this way, our view of Jesus can develop over time. We can come to see Him as just one among other great religious leaders. This can be a very comfortable view of Jesus. At times He gives valuable insights into life, but generally speaking, His life and teachings have little impact on what we do from day to day.

But the Jesus we meet in the Gospel of John cuts right across this comfortable view. In point of fact, the Jesus of John is a downright disturbing individual. He deliberately provokes His hearers (and readers) by making extreme statements that are either true or false. If what He claims is true, then Jesus is not just another important religious leader, He is the center of history. But if these statements are wrong, then Jesus was merely deluded. There is no middle ground. There are no shades of gray.

Take, for example, some of the things Jesus says of Himself:

- Jesus often speaks of God as His Father in a way that implies a relationship unique to Himself. He also claims that the only way humans can approach God is through Himself. "Jesus said to him [Thomas], 'I am the way the truth and the life. No one comes to the Father, except by me' " (John 14:6).
- Jesus claims that He, and only He, has come from heaven, from God Himself. " 'And nobody has gone into heaven except the one who came down from heaven, the Son of Man' " (John 3:13). " 'Nobody has seen the Father except the one who was with God, he has seen the Father' " (John 6:46).
- When he says " 'I and my Father are one' " (John 10:30), Jesus claims nothing less than total unity with God. His listeners did not miss the implication of this claim and immediately picked up stones to stone Him for blasphemously claiming to be God (John 10:31-33).
- Jesus says that belief in Him is an essential prerequisite for receiving eternal life. Not only this, those who believe in Him will be raised from the dead by Jesus Himself. " 'For this is the will of my Father, that all who see the son and believe in him might have eternal life and I will raise him at the last day' " (John 6:40).
- Jesus claims that He is the judge of all men. " 'The Father judges no one, but has given all judgment to the Son' " (John 5:22).

# The Disturbing Jesus of the Fourth Gospel

- Jesus claims to have the power to give life to the dead. " 'For just as the Father raises the dead and makes alive, so the son makes alive who he wills' " (John 5:21).
- Jesus claims that He is as important to life as bread or light. " 'I am the bread of life' " (John 6:35). " 'I am the light of the world' " (John 8:12).

This is *not* a comfortable Jesus. This Jesus demands that we choose to believe His extraordinary claims or give up any belief in Him. There is no room left for the idea that Jesus is only an important spiritual leader. There is no room for understanding Jesus merely as a great teacher. There is only the frightening claim that a decision about Him is the most important decision facing any human being. Either He is right, and He is the center of human history and the hope of humanity, or He is deluded. He has left no possible middle ground.

Who Jesus is, then, is no trivial matter for the fourth Gospel. Indeed, according to John 20:31, one of the two central purposes of the Gospel is to explain who Jesus is. "These things have been written so that you might believe that Jesus is the Christ, the Son of God, and so that believing you might have life by his name." Most of the Gospel is taken up by this explanation, and in this chapter we will examine in greater depth how this picture of Jesus emerges—and some of its contours.

## TITLES

A large part of the fascination of John's Gospel is how it leads us into its unique world. The Gospel unfolds this world by introducing an idea and then coming back to it several times, adding a little information each time. The result is that the reader is led to a gradually developing understanding of what is intended. We have already met this process with the gradual introduction of the concept of "above and below" as a pattern by which to understand Jesus,[1] and it is true also of other aspects of the Gospel we will investigate in this chapter.

Take, for example, the titles applied to Jesus, which play such a vital role in the Gospel's explanation of who He is. Almost all the significant titles that are attributed to Jesus are introduced in the first chapter. Jesus is called the Messiah (1:17, 41), the Son of God (1:49), the Son of Man (1:51), the Lamb of God (1:29, 36), and the only-begotten (1:14, 18). When John the Baptist refuses the titles of Christ, Elijah, and Prophet (1:21), this further raises the expectation that the One who comes after John is the proper recipient of these titles.

Each of these titles has a background that grows out of both the Old Testament and popular understanding. In the first chapter of John, little is said of this background and how it relates to Jesus. In fact, little is said about these titles at all. Only in later chapters does the Gospel cleverly develop their meaning, often playing on these popular expectations and showing the reader how Jesus fulfills and transforms these titles. This can be well illustrated by the title "Messiah," which is what we will investigate next. After this, attention will be given to the titles "Son of God" and "Son of Man," and we will explore some of the implications these titles have for our understanding of Jesus.

## Jesus as Messiah

Four times, the first chapter of John's Gospel raises the expectation that Jesus is the Messiah—He is twice called the Messiah, once by the Gospel writer (v. 17) and once by Andrew (v. 41). And twice in the chapter (vv. 20, 25) John the Baptist denies that he himself is the Messiah, implying that Jesus is. But aside from giving the Greek meaning of the Hebrew term "the Messiah"—which means "Christ" (v. 41)—the chapter gives nothing of substance about the meaning of the title. The reader is led to think of Jesus as the Christ but is not challenged to think what that might mean. Neither do the next two occurrences of the title (John 3:28; 4:24-26) give much additional information, although we do find in John 4:24-26 that Jesus Himself says that He is the Christ.

It is only in chapter seven that real discussion of the title begins to take place. At the Feast of Tabernacles the crowd expresses amazement that Jesus is present, because the authorities are seeking to kill Him (John 7:25). In their astonishment, the people begin to debate whether or not

Jesus is the Messiah (vv. 25-31, 40-44). Their comments reveal some of their expectations of what the Messiah would be like and what He would do. The miracles Jesus worked indicated to them that He might be the Messiah (v. 31). But primary in their discussion was the question of where Jesus came from. They thought the Messiah would come from the town of Bethlehem (v. 42). The early readers of John's Gospel undoubtedly knew Jesus came from Bethlehem, but the Gospel never explicitly says this. In fact, Jesus challenges His listeners with their ignorance of where He comes from, because the view of John's Gospel is that although Jesus may have been born in Bethlehem, He certainly did not come from there. He was the One who came from heaven.

John 10:22-42 reveals a little more about what Jesus meant by calling Himself the Messiah. When He is directly challenged to say whether or not He is the Messiah (v. 24), He answers in terms of the relationship between Himself and God (whom He calls His Father). For Jesus, then, His Messiahship was tied up with where He came from (heaven) and who He was (the Son of God). Aside from a few unelaborated references to Jesus as the Messiah (9:22; 11:27; 21:31), this summarizes the direct discussion of the title in John, though, as we will see, it does not exhaust what the Gospel has to say about it.

From the clues given in the passages of the Gospel we have examined so far, it is reasonably clear that Jesus' listeners had a different conception of the Messiah and His function than Jesus did. A consideration of the Old Testament background might explain this difference. It appears that Jesus' listeners were equating the Messiah with the future conqueror who would arise from David's line. At several key places in Old Testament prophecies concerning Israel's future, there is the expectation that someone would arise from the lineage of David who would usher in a time of peace and triumph greater even than that experienced by those living in the time of David. For example:

> There shall come forth a shoot from the stump of Jesse, and
> a branch shall grow out of his roots. And the Spirit of the Lord
> shall rest upon him, the spirit of wisdom and understanding,

the spirit of counsel and might, the spirit of knowledge and the fear of the Lord. . . . The wolf will dwell with the lamb. . . . In that day the root of Jesse shall stand as an ensign to the peoples; him shall the nations seek, and his dwellings shall be glorious. In that day the Lord will extend his hand yet a second time to recover the remnant which is left of his people (Isa. 11:1-16).

David had been promised that his "house and . . . kingdom shall be made sure for ever before me [God]; . . . [his] throne would be established forever" (2 Sam 7:16). The prophecy in Isa. 11 takes up this promise and applies it to the future. Large sections of Zechariah and Ezekiel are given over to a description of this glorious future kingdom. The Davidic king was a key part of this glorious future, and it was this Davidic king whom those at the Feast of Tabernacles were expecting as the Messiah.

With this information, we can see that although the term *Messiah* is not used between John 12:34 and 20:31, the concept itself plays a crucial role in the crucifixion narrative. Jesus was crucified by the Romans because He was the king of the Jews! Now, if Jesus was claiming to be the kind of Messiah His listeners expected, then there would be a real basis for this charge. As the Davidic Messiah, His role would be to drive out the Romans and establish a kingdom greater than David's kingdom. In other words, He would have been advocating a revolt against Rome, something the Romans regarded as a capital crime. Pilate's examination of Jesus revolves around this very matter. He asks if Jesus is king of the Jews (John 18:33). Jesus admits that He is but goes on to explain that His kingship is quite different from that implied in Pilate's question. His kingship does not belong to this realm (v. 36). Jesus is mocked as king of the Jews, and on the cross a sign is placed, " 'Jesus, the Nazarene, king of the Jews' " (John 19:19). This is the supreme irony. Jesus, the Messiah, is indeed king of the Jews. But according to the fourth Gospel, His kingship is of a different order than was commonly anticipated for the Messiah. His kingdom revolves around where He has come from, His relationship with the Father, and where He is going. Because His kingdom is not of this world, His followers do not fight the kings of this world.

They look to join the kingdom above.

Even if they initially shared the military concept of the Messiah, careful readers of John's Gospel would have been gradually led to the point of clearly recognizing Jesus' understanding of Messiahship. Jesus has been presented as the Messiah from the beginning of the Gospel, but what kind of Messiah He is emerges only gradually as the clues developed in the Gospel fall into place. He might be a descendant of David and the king of the Jews. But this is not really as important as His kingship or Messiahship because it belongs to a different order than most of His contemporaries were expecting. His kingship is not of this world. He is the One who has come from the Father. He is the One who has come from heaven. His kingship transcends all earthly kingships.

## JESUS AS SON

The fourth Gospel develops the theme of sonship at some length. First, there are a number of important passages that speak of Jesus as the "Son" of His Father. For example, in John 5:19-30 Jesus states that His activities are dependent on what He sees the Father doing. The Father shows everything to the Son. Just as the Father judges and raises the dead, so also does the Son. In fact, the Father has given up His right of judgment and resurrection to the Son.

In a later passage (John 8:31-58) Jesus and His listeners ("the Jews," v. 31) discuss parenthood. The Jews claim Abraham as their father, and Jesus says that if that is so, then they should do the work of Abraham, which is to believe. If they believe in Him, then they will not die. The Jews answer that even Abraham died, at which Jesus goes on the attack and accuses His listeners of not knowing His Father, God. Abraham would have rejoiced to see Jesus, because before Abraham was born, "I am" (v. 58), Jesus says. Yet later in the Gospel, Jesus claims equality with the Father, at which His hearers make preparations to stone Him. When asked why, they say that Jesus has committed blasphemy, because although He is a man, He claims equality with God (John 10:30-39).

Finally, in John 14:1-14 Jesus tells His disciples that He is the way, the truth, the light, and the only way to the Father (v. 6). Philip asks that

Jesus show them the Father, and Jesus replies that if they have seen Him, they have seen the Father. In other words, the identity between Jesus and the Father is so close that to see Jesus is to see God.

To summarize, then, when Jesus speaks of God as His Father, He is speaking in a way that implies a much closer relationship than any other human has with God (although Jesus gives us all power to become the sons of God—John 1:12). The concept of sonship is present also in two titles of Jesus—"Son of God" and "Son of Man."

The title "Son of God" is used of Jesus in John 1:34 by John the Baptist; in 1:49 by Nathanael; in 3:18 by Jesus Himself in the context of unbelief that condemns in the final judgment; in 5:25 by Jesus in the context of raising the dead; in 6:69 by Peter; in 10:36 by Jesus in the context of claiming equality with the Father; in 11:4 by Jesus in the context of bringing glory to God, Father and Son, by the raising of Lazarus; in 19:7 as a charge made by the Jewish leadership against Jesus; and in 20:31 by John when he states his reason for writing the Gospel.[2] As can be seen, the title is mostly used in key situations and forms a summary of the unique relationship between Jesus and God. There is something otherworldly about Jesus. He belongs to the realm of the divine, not just the realm of the human. The title conveys such a close relationship with God that God and the Son are almost identical; their actions are so alike that Jesus does what God does and vice versa. The title "Son of God" is a claim to divinity.

"Son of Man" is another key title for Jesus in John's Gospel, drawing on the concept of sonship. As is the case in the other Gospels, the title is found exclusively on the lips of Jesus as a self-description. Within the fourth Gospel, the title "Son of Man" is found in John 1:51; 3:13, 14; 5:27; 6:27, 53, 62; 8:28; 9:35; 12:23, 34; 13:31. Like the title "Son of God," the title "Son of Man" occurs in contexts that point to the extraordinary nature of Jesus. In 1:51 Jesus tells Nathanael that he will see the angels of God ascending and descending on the Son of Man. In 3:13, 14 Jesus says the Son of Man is the only one who has descended from heaven and that the Son of Man has to be lifted up like the serpent in the wilderness so that those who believe in Him might have eternal life. In 5:27 Jesus is given authority to render judgment because He is the Son of Man (most likely a reference to Dan. 7:13, 26). In 6:27 Jesus tells His listeners to work for the bread that will give nourishment forever, which the Son of Man will give them. In 6:53 Jesus tells His listeners that they must eat the flesh and drink the blood of the Son of Man. In 6:62 Jesus asks what His listeners' reaction will be when they see the Son of Man returning to where He came from. John 8:27 speaks of the exaltation of the Son of Man. In 9:35 Jesus asks the man healed of blindness whether he believes in the Son of Man, meaning Himself. In 12:23 and 13:31 Jesus speaks of the arrival of the hour in which the Son of Man is to be glorified. And 12:34 makes yet another reference to the lifting up of the Son of Man.

Certain recurring themes are found in these references. The Son of Man will be lifted up—lifted up on the cross and exalted to heaven. Thus, this title reveals the union of suffering and glorification, humiliation and exaltation. It reveals, yet again, the close relationship between Jesus and the heavenly realm and His place there with God. It reveals His uniqueness as the arbiter of human destiny. It reveals that Jesus is the key to eternal life. These themes revolve around judgment, mediation, and suffering.

## EQUAL WITH, YET SUBORDINATE TO, THE FATHER

It is clear that the fourth Gospel attributes full divinity to Jesus. Jesus is twice called God (1:18;[3] 20:28). The second of these occurs when Thomas meets his risen Lord and confesses, " 'My Lord and my God' " (20:28). This is the confession of all who would follow Jesus. As Jesus tells Thomas at the time, " 'You believe me because you have seen me, blessed are those who even though they do not see me believe' " (John 20:29). Both the title "Son of God" and "Son of Man" convey the unique relationship Jesus has with the Father, a relationship that is so close that Jesus can say " 'I and my Father are one' " (10:30).

Yet, even though the fourth Gospel ascribes to Jesus full equality with God, it also contains the theme of voluntary subordination. Jesus is dependent on God for His message (7:16; 14:24), His life (5:26; 6:57),

His power (5:30), His authority to execute judgment and give life (5:21-29), His disciples (6:37, 44), and His glory (17:1).

## JESUS AS THE "I AM"

The use of the phrase or title "I am" is especially interesting in John's Gospel. It is a phrase that could be used in everyday language, and there are some examples of this use in the fourth Gospel. For example, the neighbors and onlookers of the man who received back his sight were debating whether or not he was the blind beggar. Some said he was; others said he wasn't, but was like him. The man identified himself by saying, "I am." This everyday use of the expression is used in other ways in the Gospel. In one set of references, the expression is used in different metaphors; in another, it takes on the characteristics of a title.

Jesus uses the phrase "I am" in the following metaphors:

" 'I am the bread of life' " (6:35, 48)
" 'I am the light of the world' " (8:12)
" 'I am the door' " (10:7, 9)
" 'I am the good shepherd' " (10:11, 14)
" 'I am the resurrection and the life' " (11:25)
" 'I am the way, the truth, and the life' " (14:6)
" 'I am the true vine' " (15:1, 5)

The imagery of these metaphors and the associated claims are relatively straightforward. Three of the images relate to how Jesus is necessary for eternal life. By saying that He is the bread of life, Jesus claims that He is as essential to humanity as food is to the body. Just as bread gives life, so Jesus gives eternal life. He also says that He is as important to humanity as the light (John 8:12) and embodies in Himself the principle of resurrection from the dead (John 11:25).

Two of the other metaphors relate to Jesus' claim that He is the only way to eternal life. When Jesus says that He is the way, the truth, and the life and that the only way to the Father is through Him (John 14:6), He is saying no more than He does when He describes Himself as the door to the sheepfold. There is only one way in—by belief in Jesus.

Two of the metaphors relate to community. Jesus is the shepherd of the flock—He is the protector and guide of the community of the saved. Jesus is the true vine—only by connection to Him can one be connected to the true community and to God.

Yet, there are a few usages of the phrase "I am" in which it becomes a title of great significance. One example of this usage is in John 8:24, where Jesus says " 'You will die in your sins unless you believe that "I am." ' " In John 8:58 He says, " 'Before Abraham was, "I am." ' " The phrase "I am" is therefore pregnant with meaning. One of the probable meanings flows from the Old Testament.

• "And Moses said to God, 'Behold, I will go to the sons of Israel and will say to them, "The God of your fathers sent me to you." They will ask me "What is his name?" What will I tell them?' And God said to Moses: 'I am the one who is.'[4] and he said, 'You will speak to the sons of Israel in this way, "The one who[5] is sent me to you." ' " (Exod. 3:13, 14, LXX; my translation).

• "The Lord God says, 'I am,[6] before me there is no other God, and with me there will never be [one]' " (Cf. Isa. 41:4; 51:12). (Isa. 43:10, LXX; my translation.)

In other words, "I am" is one of the titles of God in the Old Testament. Typical of most imagery in John, Jesus never quite directly claims to be the "I am" of the Old Testament, but He comes very close when He says "Before Abraham was I am" (8:58). The phrase becomes pregnant with meaning, so much so that when the soldiers and armed servants come to arrest Jesus and He identifies Himself as "I am," the everyday phrase has the power to throw them backward onto the ground (John 18:6). When Jesus is walking on the water, He also identifies himself as "I am" (John 6:20), at which moment the phrase also has an otherworldly ring about it.

## THE JESUS OF THE FOURTH GOSPEL IS FULLY DIVINE YET ALSO FULLY HUMAN

The fourth Gospel portrays Jesus as fully divine. It begins by announcing Him as the preexistent Word. It goes on to show Jesus claiming a special relationship with His Father. Jesus even calls Himself by titles that properly belong to Deity. When Thomas proclaims Him as " 'My Lord and my God' " (John 20:28), he is doing no more than stating the clear conclusion of the whole Gospel.

Yet, while the Jesus of the fourth Gospel is fully divine, He is also clearly portrayed as fully human. His earthly father, mother, and brothers are known (6:42; 7:2). He experiences human emotions such as love (11:5), anger (11:33), and sorrow (11:35). He can grow weary (4:6), and He bleeds (19:33, 34). Even His resurrection body has a form that can be touched (20:27). All of these are characteristics belonging to one who is fully human.

## SUMMING UP

John 3:36 echoes what is perhaps the dominant theme of the whole Gospel: " 'The one who believes in the Son has eternal life; the one who disobeys the Son will not see life, but the wrath of God remains on him.' " The Gospel revolves around who Jesus is. It claims that the destiny of every individual depends on who they believe Jesus to be. In this way, Jesus takes center stage as the most important being in the history of the world.

The Gospel leads the attentive reader to a gradual understanding of Jesus. There is something different about Him. His origins belong outside this world, even though He is human in every way. He has parents, experiences emotions, eats, and finally dies like every other human being. But He is also the divine Son of God, the embodiment of the great "I am" who was the God of Abraham and Moses, the Judge of the living and the dead, and the One who will give eternal life.

Not only does the Gospel present the reader with extraordinary claims as to who Jesus is, it demands a decision of the reader. It is he who *believes* in Jesus who already has eternal life. The reader who doesn't believe is already damned. Jesus is said to be more important than bread, water, or life itself. The Gospel demands that if we believe in Jesus, we believe His extraordinary claims. The Jesus we meet in the Gospel comes to us with disturbing questions. The Gospel urgently demands that we make a decision about whether we believe in Jesus.

---

1. See chapters 22 and 23.

2. It also occurs as a textual variant at 9:35.

3. There is a textual variant for John 1:18. The issue is whether the text should read "the only begotten *God* who is in the bosom of the father" or "the only begotten *son*. . . ." The fourth revised edition of the United Bible Societies' Greek New Testament gives this textual variant a rating of "B." In other words, the editors are reasonably sure that the text should read "only begotten God."

4. In Greek, *Ego eimi ho ōn.*

5. Greek, *ho ōn.*

6. Greek, *ego eimi.*

Part 6

# KEY GOSPEL THEMES

# CHAPTER TWENTY-EIGHT

# The Gospels' Witness to Jesus

## THE JESUS OF NICEA AND CHALCEDON

Nicea and Chalcedon are names of places that are significant to the church because of important meetings that were held in these locations. These meetings put in place the wisdom distilled from much controversy and thought regarding the nature of Jesus. The results of those meetings—the Nicene Creed and the Chalcedonian Definition—were the end products of long debate. To understand them we need to go back to find out the questions for which they provided answers.

The early church faced an extraordinary number of challenges. It was an illegal, often-persecuted organization. Its transition from a Jewish sect to a worldwide movement was particularly challenging. In moving from a Jewish background into the wider Roman world, the church moved into an intellectual environment dominated by Greek ideas. This immediately brought intellectual challenges to the church, some of which are reflected in the New Testament. One of these issues that dominated internal Christian debate for some centuries concerned the nature of Jesus. The New Testament, and indeed the early church, was adamant that Jesus was the Son of God.

Now, one thing the Greeks knew for sure was that God does not change. In technical language, they said God is impassible. This meant that He is above the vagaries of random events or emotions. How, then, could the church say that Jesus was God? Jesus lived as a human being. Humans are constantly changing. In fact, even becoming a human was an extraordinary change. As a human, Jesus became tired and thirsty (John 4:6; 19:28). Did this mean that God got tired and thirsty? Moreover, Jesus died! How could God die?

Even today, these are hard questions to answer. In fact, in any given Christian congregation one would no doubt find a wide variety of answers to these questions. What is interesting, though, is that most of the possible answers were already proposed long ago in the early church—and many of them proved to be inadequate.

One answer, popular early in the second century, was known as *Docetism.* Docetism solved the problem of the relationship of Jesus' divine and human natures by ignoring or playing down His human aspect. Yes, the Gospels describe Jesus as getting tired and thirsty, but according to the Docetists, Jesus never actually was tired or thirsty; He only *appeared*[1] to be. Jesus never actually suffered and died; He only *appeared* to suffer and die. In other words, the divine Jesus didn't change.

Docetism was expressed in a variety of ways, but perhaps its most important expression was in the ideas of the Gnostics, most of whom were docetic in some way. Now Gnosticism is a very complex phenomenon that is hard to summarize, but, essentially, it attempted to express Christianity in terms of Greek ideas. Greek thought placed great emphasis on the soul and despised the body. The concept of a bodily resurrection was repugnant to the Greeks (and to the Gnostics), so the concept that Jesus suffered and died was also repugnant to them.

Gnosticism was probably the greatest intellectual threat to Christianity in the second century. We contemporary Christians read about their ideas and think it strange that anyone would believe them, but that is because we do not share the Greek way of thinking that dominated that time period. Gnosticism was a very attractive way of understanding Jesus for many second-century Christians, but the church as a whole rejected it. In response, the church further developed the concept of orthodoxy and authority. Despite difficulties and setbacks, by this time the church was becoming better organized. Its leadership was slowly exerting more control over the churches—including what was taught. The leaders defined as orthodox the beliefs they wished to retain in the church and labeled any other beliefs as heresy. Gnosticism was perceived as heresy, and so Docetism, which was closely related to Gnosticism, also largely ceased to be a serious option for Christians. But this did not mean that the debate over the nature of Jesus had ceased.

Several disputes concerning the nature of Jesus continued to simmer in the church during this time, but the person at the center of the next crucial debate was Arius. Once again, the Greek idea of a supreme and distant God formed the starting point. For Arius, God was too wholly "other" to come into direct relation with men:

> We acknowledge one God, Who is alone ingenerate (ἀγέννητον i.e., self-existent,) alone eternal, alone without beginning (ἄναρχον,) alone true, alone possessing immortality, alone wise, alone good, alone sovereign, alone judge of all, [etc].[2]

As a consequence, Arius said that the Son must be a creature (something made or created). Furthermore, the Son must have had a beginning. Arius summarized this concept with his famous slogan, "There was when he was not." He said that the Son could have no communion with, and no direct knowledge of, His Father because He is distinct from God. Further, the Son must be liable to change and even sin. Then, in what sense could Arius call him the Son of God? Replied Arius: This was but a courtesy title which reflected His greatly superior status above all other creatures.

Arius and his followers proved to be masters of propaganda, and his ideas spread widely. So much so that when Constantine, the first emperor to adopt Christianity, took power, it looked as though there would be a split in the church over the matter. Constantine called a general council of the church to discuss the matter; the council met at Nicea in the year 325. The council rejected the position of Arius and issued a creed, called the Nicene Creed, which made this explicit.[3]

Nicea's condemnation of Arius did not bring an end to the discussion, however, although full-blown Arianism gradually lost support. Several more councils were held, but at Chalcedon in the year 451 a position on Jesus' nature was taken that was widely accepted thereafter. Known as the Chalcedonian Definition, this formulation distinguished between two natures in Jesus—He was "perfect in Godhead and perfect in Manhood, truly God and truly Man." Although He had two natures, He was only one person.[4]

All this has taken us a long way from the world of the Gospels. In many respects, the kind of questions the early church asked sprung from considerations alien to the world of early Christians. Yet these early Christians were struggling with real intellectual problems that cannot easily be brushed aside. Questions such as:

- If Jesus was God, did God die when Jesus died on the cross?
- If Jesus was fully human, surely He could have sinned. If He had sinned, then would God have sinned?
- Jesus was born a baby and learned what babies learn—to control His limbs, to sit up, to crawl, to walk, to talk. Jesus was fully human and shared the limitations of human knowledge. Although He knew some things not accessible to other humans, He did not know the exact time of the second advent (Matt. 24:36). But how can God have only partial knowledge?

Christians continue to struggle with such questions and generally end up close to the kind of answers given by Chalcedon—Jesus was fully God and fully man. He was one individual, however, not two beings coexisting together.

For many years, voices have been raised questioning whether or not the Chalcedonian Definition is still an adequate description of Jesus, and one would have to admit that some of the fine distinctions that rely on underlying Greek words and concepts do not work as well for us as they did for the church in the fifth century. But even today, the Chalcedonian Definition is still the understanding of Jesus' nature that most Christian groups follow.

## ARE THE GOSPELS ORTHODOX?

Now that we have been sensitized to some of these issues, there remains one very disturbing question: Are the Gospels orthodox? This question has been asked most urgently of the Gospel of John, which has been accused of being naively docetic.[5] Indeed, it is quite possible to read the Gospel of John from a docetic perspective, and for this reason it was a favorite of Gnostics. In fact, most of the early references we have to that Gospel come from Gnostic writers, and the very first commentary on John was written by a Gnostic writer.

But is John docetic? Only if the Gospel is read selectively. It is true that, of the four Gospels, John most clearly portrays Jesus' divine origins and nature. In John, Jesus is "from above" and returns there. His heavenly Father and He have a close relationship that can be described as one of equality and unity, although this needs to be balanced against those statements in the Gospel that carry within them an element of voluntary subordination. In John, Jesus says that knowing Him is the same as knowing God. He has knowledge not available to other humans. He says that knowing Him and believing where He comes from and who He is will lead to eternal life.[6] But this strong emphasis on Jesus' divinity is balanced by the fact that the fourth Gospel is also the Gospel that most clearly portrays Jesus' human nature. It is in this Gospel that we hear that Jesus gets tired (John 4:6). He experiences human emotions of love (11:5) and anger (11:33). He will weep at the graveside of a friend, even though He knows He is about to raise him from the dead (11:35). Although He can walk on water and miraculously appear in locked rooms, this is not His customary way of getting around in John's Gospel. Rather, Jesus normally walks from place to place. So He is portrayed as fully human. He goes about in real places and talks to real people. There is something more to Jesus than just His humanity, but He is fully human. Even after His resurrection, He retains His humanity—He can be touched

(20:27) and He eats with His disciples (21:9-13).

In summary, then, the Gospel of John shows that Jesus is both fully human and fully divine. The same may be said of the other Gospels. They know Jesus' human antecedents. He was born in Bethlehem and grew up in Nazareth. His mother, father, brothers, and sisters are all known. His trade was that of His father, a carpenter. He lived in real towns and among real historic personages. He traveled through Galilee and Judea. He met His death at Jerusalem. All these are experiences of a human.

In the three Synoptic Gospels, there is likewise something more than human about Jesus. He can walk on water. He multiplies a few loaves and fishes to feed a large crowd. He can heal the sick and even raise the dead. He is the Messiah, the Son of Man who will be coming back to earth to judge the living and the dead. Further, He is the one who is raised from the dead and who will return to raise all those who are dead. The Jesus of the Synoptic Gospels is likewise divine.

Yes, the four Gospels are orthodox, and this is just as well because if they weren't, something would have to be done about orthodoxy to bring it into closer agreement with the raw data. But even though the Gospels are orthodox, the Jesus of the Nicene Creed and the Chalcedonian Definition is not the same as the Jesus of the Gospels. The Jesus of the Gospels does not neatly fit anybody's theories!

The biggest difference between the Gospels and the creeds is the static nature of the creeds. The creeds focus on things that are almost peripheral to the concerns of the Gospel. The Gospels do reveal Jesus as fully human, but apart from recounting His appearances after the Resurrection, there is little concern to demonstrate this. There is more interest in showing that Jesus is more than human, but again, this is not done in the terms used by the creeds. It is done in a more dynamic way, a way that is more personally challenging. The Gospels want us to understand who Jesus is, but even that is not an end in itself. It is important only because Jesus comes to challenge our lives and demand our commitment.

Two major sections of this book have already been devoted to the

Gospels' portrayal of Jesus—a view of Jesus as seen from the perspective of one of the Synoptic Gospels is a major component of chapter 12, "The Message of Mark," and a whole chapter in part 5 was devoted to John's portrayal of Jesus.[7] In the overall assessment of the Gospel's witness to Jesus, there is no need to repeat what has already been said there. But there are two important features of the Gospel witness to Jesus that we have not yet explored in depth. These provide a suitable perspective from which to look at the Gospel's portrayal of Jesus. One is Jesus' favorite description of Himself; the other the way the disciples addressed their Master.

## JESUS AS THE SON OF MAN

The title "Son of Man" is used frequently in all four Gospels. It is unique, though, as a title that only Jesus uses, and as the one He uses most often. In the Gospel accounts, no individual other than Jesus calls Him the Son of Man, nor is the title a term the other writers of the New Testament use of Him.[8] It is a term that is well-nigh exclusive to Jesus and that conveys something about Himself He considers important.

What, then, is the background of this term? Within the Old Testament, it is most frequently found in Ezekiel, where it is used by God to refer to Ezekiel when He talks to the prophet (Ezek. 2:1, 3, 6, 8; 3:1, 3, 4, 10, 17, etc.). In Ezekiel, "Son of Man" is most likely used to emphasize the prophet's humanity in contrast to God. So confident are scholars of this that the NRSV translates this term consistently as "mortal."[9]

It is probably the usage in Daniel 7:13 that is more influential on the way the term is used by Jesus, though. Partway through the vision described in Daniel 7, Daniel looks into heaven and sees the Ancient of Days sitting on a throne. The court sits in judgment (Dan. 7:9, 10). To the Ancient of Days comes one like a Son of Man, who is "presented before him, and given dominion and glory and kingship. . . . His dominion is an everlasting dominion that shall not pass away, and his kingship is one that shall never be destroyed" (Dan. 7:13, 14). Thus, in Daniel 7 the Son of Man is a heavenly figure associated with the judgments of God and the everlasting kingdom.

# The Four Faces of Jesus

Outside the Old Testament, there is an interesting usage of the title "Son of Man" in 1 Enoch.[10] In a section of 1 Enoch called the similitudes, the Son of Man is a heavenly figure with characteristics not unlike that of the Son of Man in the Gospels. First Enoch was well known in the first century and is even quoted in the New Testament (Jude 14), but there has been a long debate among scholars whether the references to the Son of Man in the similitudes date prior to the time of Jesus or whether they are later additions to the work made by Christians.

Yet another relevant piece of information is that the Greek for "Son of Man" (*huios tou anthrōpou*) could be a translation of an Aramaic phrase (*bar [e]nasha*), which means "somebody," or "a man."

This background information shows that there is a wide variety of possible meanings that Jesus could have intended by the use of the title. As a result, the text of the Gospels themselves will need to be closely examined to find out exactly what the term means in them. To begin with, it appears unlikely that Jesus is using the term in the sense of "somebody," though there are several places where it could mean nothing more than "I" (Mark 11:19; Luke 7:34; Matt. 8:20; Luke 9:58; 22:48). These appear to be places where Jesus is talking about Himself and says "Son of Man" instead of "I." But this is much more specific than the more general meaning of "somebody."

Is Jesus wishing to emphasize His humanity by the term? This is the usage found in Ezekiel and in some other Old Testament references (Num. 23:19; Ps. 144:3). But in almost every use of the term, the Son of Man is involved in something that emphasizes the extraordinary nature of Jesus, not His humanity. This is not to deny that "Son of Man" is a designation that means "human." But it has a different emphasis. The title is mainly used to stress two distinctive things—the heavenly nature and importance of the Son of Man and His suffering.

*First, the Son of Man has extraordinary authority.* He is lord of the Sabbath (Matt. 12:8; Mark 2:27; Luke 6:5); He will come back in the glory of His Father and the holy angels (Matt. 16:27; Mark 8:38; Luke 9:26); He will be seen sitting at the right hand of power (Matt. 24:30; Mark 14:26; Luke 21:27); and He will sit on His glorious throne (Matt.

19:28). Jesus has been given authority to execute judgment because He is the Son of Man (John 5:27). In these passages, the Son of Man represents an extraordinary human who has powers and glory belonging to God Himself and who will come in the future to act as judge of mankind. Yet, there is another strongly emphasized aspect of the Son of Man in the Gospels.

*Second, the Son of Man is a figure of suffering.* Several times Jesus warns His disciples that, as the Son of Man, He must suffer (Mark 8:31; Luke 9:22; Matt.17:12; Mark 9:12). The Son of Man is one who is betrayed (Matt. 26:24; Mark 14:21; Luke 22:22; Matt. 26:45; Luke 11:30). He will die but rise again (Matt. 20:18; Mark 10:33; Luke 18:31).

The ambiguity resulting from the dual concepts of the suffering of the Son of Man and His future glory is nicely captured in the usage of the term found in the fourth Gospel. John 3:14, 15 says that the Son of Man must be lifted up like the snake in the wilderness. The lifting up of Jesus in the fourth Gospel is both His lifting up on the cross and His exaltation to heaven. As with the serpent, all who see Jesus lifted up will be saved. Both John 12:23 and 13:31 speak of the glorification of the Son of Man. This hour of glorification is also the hour of Jesus' death.

In summary, then, the term "Son of Man" is a term of self-description found often on Jesus' lips to convey the essence of who He is. He is indeed human. But He is an extraordinary human who has divine authority and who takes a crucial role in the dramatic events of the end of the world. Yet the way of the Son of Man lies through suffering. His importance lies in the fact that He is willing to serve and to suffer (Matt. 20:28; Mark 10:45).

## JESUS AS LORD

Although Jesus describes Himself as the Son of Man, His disciples call Him "Lord." This title is one that has a clear secular usage. It is used as one who owns something—in Mark 12:9 as the owner of a vineyard; in Luke 19:33 as the owners of an ass; in Matthew 15:27 as the owner of dogs. In particular, it is used as owners of slaves (Matt. 6:24; Luke 16:3) or as heads of a household (Mark 13:35). To call someone "Lord" could also be a very polite form of address used in the Gospels, somewhat similar to an English speaker addressing an important stranger as "Sir." Mary, for example, calls a stranger she has met "Lord" (John 20:15); the workers in the vineyard call their employer "Lord" (Luke 13:8); and the Pharisees call Pilate "Lord" (Matt. 27:63).

The New Testament also reflects another usage of "Lord," however. As they read the Scriptures aloud, the Jews were very reluctant to say the holy name "Yahweh"; instead, they substituted the term "Lord." In this way, "Lord" became a way to address God and, in fact, almost a name of God. This usage is also found in such places as Matthew 2:15, which says something happened "so that the word of the Lord through the prophets might be fulfilled" and goes on to quote from a prophecy in Jeremiah. Other examples of this kind of use are found in Matthew 3:3, Mark 12:29, Luke 1:9, etc. This usage could be combined with the more customary usage of "owner," as in Matthew 11:25 and Luke 10:21, for example. In these verses, Jesus prays to God as "Lord of heaven and earth." In other words, God is the ultimate owner and master over all heaven and earth.

Thus it is that the title "Lord," like that of Son of Man, has a certain ambiguity to it. It is a title used of deference, of masters and owners, but in addition, it is used as a title of divinity. So when the disciples address Jesus as "Lord," they are recognizing two things—that Jesus is their Master and that Jesus is God.

The Jesus who meets us in the Gospels is not One who presents Himself in the terms of an intellectual puzzle to be solved by the careful wording of a creed. He does not carefully lay out His full humanity and His claims to divinity. Instead, He confronts us with the claim that He is the master of life and death and insists that we make a decision to give our all to Him, to devote our entire life to His bidding. In a word, in the Gospels Jesus comes to us as our Lord.

---

1. The term *Docetism* is derived from *dokew*, a Greek word that means "to appear."
2. Cited J. N. D. Kelly, *Early Christian Doctrines* (New York: Harper & Row, 1978), 227.

3. "We believe in one God, the Father All Governing, creator of all things visible and invisible; And in one Lord Jesus Christ, the Son of God, begotten of the Father as only-begotten, that is, from the essence as the Father, God from God, Light from Light, true God of true God, begotten not created, of the same essence of the Father: through whom all things came into being, both in heaven and in earth: Who for us men and for our salvation came down and was incarnate, becoming human. He suffered and the third day he rose, and ascended into the heavens. And he will come again to judge both the living and the dead; and [we believe] in the Holy Spirit. But, those who say, Once he was not, or he was not before his generation, or he came to be out of nothing, or who assert that he, the Son of God, is of a different *hypostasis* or *ousia*, or that he is a creature, or changeable, or mutable, the Catholic and Apostolic Church anathematizes them." The Nicene Creed, as cited in John H. Leith, ed., *Creeds of the Churches*, 3d ed. (Atlanta: Knox, 1983), 30, 31.

4. "Following, then, the holy fathers, we unite in teaching all men to confess the one and only Son, our Lord Jesus Christ, at once perfect both in deity and also in human-ness; this selfsame one is also actually God and actually man, with a rational soul and body; of the same reality as God as far as his deity is concerned and of the same reality as we are ourselves as far as his human-ness is concerned; thus like us in all respects, sin only excepted. Before time began he was begotten of the Father, in respect to his deity, and now in these 'last days,' for us and on behalf of our salvation, this selfsame one was born of Mary the virgin, who is God-bearer in respect of his humanness. [We also teach] that we apprehend this one and only Christ—Son, Lord, only-begotten—in two natures, without transmuting one nature into the other, without dividing them into two separate categories, without contrasting them according to area or function. The distinctiveness of each nature is not nullified by the union. Instead, the 'properties' of each nature are conserved and both natures concur in one 'person' and in one *hypostasis*. They are not divided or cut into two *prosōpa*, but are together the one and only and only-begotten Logos of God, the Lord Jesus Christ. Thus have the prophets of old testified; thus the Lord Jesus Christ himself taught us; thus the Symbol of the Fathers has handed down to us." From the Chalcedon definition, as cited in Leith, *Creeds*, 35, 36.

5. Ernst Käsemann is the scholar who has urged this most cogently. He says: "We must ask: In what sense is he flesh, who walks on the water and through closed doors, who cannot be captured by his enemies, who at the well of Samaria is tired and desires a drink, yet has no need of drink and has food different from that which his disciples seek? He cannot be deceived by men, because he knows their innermost thoughts even before they speak. He debates with them from the vantage point of the infinite difference between heaven and earth. He has need neither of the witness of Moses nor of the Baptist. He dissociates himself from the Jews, as if they were not his own people, and he meets his mother as one who is her

Lord. He permits Lazarus to lie in the grave four days in order that the miracle of his resurrection may be more impressive. And in the end the Johannine Christ goes victoriously to his death of his own accord. . . . One can hardly fail to recognize the danger of the christology of glory, namely, the danger of docetism. It is present in a still naive, unreflected form and it has not yet been recognised by the community." *The Testament of Jesus* (London: SCM, 1968), 9, 26. Käsemann has been challenged by a large number of other scholars, but as can be seen from his own writing, he raises a question regarding the orthodoxy of the fourth Gospel that needs an answer.

6. These statements all grow out of what has been said of the fourth Gospel in part 5.

7. See chapter 27.

8. It does occurs outside the Gospels three times in visionary experiences involving the risen Christ, however. At the end of his long speech to the Sanhedrin, Stephen sees a vision of the Son of Man standing at the right hand of God (Acts 7:55, 56). This so enrages the court that they rush upon him, take him out of the city, and stone him. The title is also used twice in the visions in the book of Revelation to describe one "like the Son of Man" (Rev 1:13; 14:14).

9. E.g., Ezek. 2:1: "O mortal, stand up on your feet, and I will speak with you" (NRSV).

10. First Enoch is an interesting document, the bulk of which was composed in the period between the writing of the last part of the Old Testament and the first parts of the New Testament. It is composed of a collection of different things that Enoch, the one who had lived before the Flood, was supposed to have written. Included are visionary tours of the cosmos, as well as symbolic visions.

CHAPTER TWENTY-NINE

# The Kingdom of God

**THE IMPORTANCE OF THE KINGDOM IN THE SYNOPTIC GOSPELS**

All three of the Synoptic Gospels portray the announcement of the kingdom of God[1] as the essential component of Jesus' teaching and preaching (Matt. 4:17, 23; Mark 1:14, 15; Luke 4:43; 8:1; 9:11). Indeed, as will be seen, the kingdom is a major theme of Jesus' teachings as reported in the Synoptic Gospels. So much so that in this book, one chapter and significant parts of two others have already been devoted to the subject of the kingdom of God.[2] By any measurement, then, the kingdom of God is one of the key themes of the Synoptic Gospels.

Treatments of this theme in earlier chapters have focused on only one of the Gospels at a time. In this chapter we shall consider the wider picture that can be gained from the perspective of all three Synoptic Gospels considered together. In doing so, we will first examine the range of evidence and then examine the theme of the kingdom from four different perspectives—its nearness, its ethical implications, the kingdom's presence, and its future coming.

**THE RANGE OF EVIDENCE**

The word *kingdom* is found 162 times in the New Testament. Of these occurrences, fifty-five are in Matthew, forty-six in Luke, twenty in

# The Four Faces of Jesus

Mark, nine in Revelation, eight in Acts, five in John and in 1 Corinthians, and between one and three occurrences each in nine other books.[3] The expression "kingdom of God" is found sixty-seven times—thirty-two times in Luke, fourteen in Mark, five in Acts, five in Matthew, and three or less times in any other single book in the New Testament.[4] This does not mean that the concept is less prominent in Matthew than in Mark or Luke, because the equivalent expression "kingdom of heaven" is found in Matthew on thirty-two occasions and nowhere else in the New Testament.[5]

If nothing else, these statistics show that within the New Testament most of the material dealing with the kingdom of God is to be found in the three Synoptic Gospels. Indeed, significant proportions of these Gospels deal with this theme. For example, the following parables explicitly begin with the words "The kingdom of heaven is like . . .":

- a grain of mustard seed (Matt. 13:31, 32; Mark 4:30-32; Luke 13:18, 19)
- leaven hidden in a loaf of bread (Matt. 13:33; Luke 13:20, 21)
- a man who sowed good seed in his field but at night his enemy sowed weeds (Matt. 13:24-30, 36-43)
- treasure hidden in a field (Matt. 13:44)
- a merchant seeking beautiful pearls (Matt. 13:45, 46)
- a net thrown into the sea (Matt. 13:47-50)
- a king who wished to settle his accounts with his servants (parable of the unforgiving servant) (Matt. 18:23-35)
- a landowner who went out early to hire workers for his vineyard (Matt 20:1-16).
- a king who sent out invitations to his son's wedding (Matt. 22:1-14; cf. Luke 14:15-24, which also deals with the kingdom of God and has a similar theme)
- ten young maidens who, taking their lamps, went out to meet the bridegroom (Matt. 25:1-13)
- a man sowing seed in the earth (Mark 4:26-29)

# The Kingdom of God

As well as these, a number of parables explicitly mention the kingdom of heaven:

- The parable of the sheep and the goats (Matt. 25:31-46, especially v. 34)
- The parable of the sower (Matt. 13:3-9, 18-23, especially v. 18)
- The parable of the vineyard and the tenants (Matt. 21:33-46, especially v. 43)
- The parable of the ten minas (Luke 19:11-27; v. 11 says this parable was told specifically because some were expecting an immediate setting up of the kingdom)

These parables provide a rich source of information about the kingdom. They illustrate several different aspects of the kingdom. Some of them deal with the growth of the kingdom; others deal with the problem of the delay in the coming of the kingdom; others deal with the mixed nature of the kingdom; and yet others deal with the worth of the kingdom.[6]

Alongside of these parables, a good many of Jesus' *sayings* deal with the kingdom of God: it is possible to enter the kingdom (Matt. 18:3; 19:23, 24; 21:31; Luke 18:24, 25; 16:18); the kingdom is a place from which one can be thrown out (Matt. 13:41; Luke 13:28); the kingdom has keys (Matt. 16:19); it can be shut up against others (Matt. 23:13); yet it can be sought after (Matt. 6:33; Luke 12:31); it can be the subject of preaching (Matt. 9:35; Luke 4:43; 9:2); it is a gift that can be received (Luke 12:31); it has its own mysteries (Matt. 13:11; Mark 4:11; Luke 8:10); one can be a scribe instructed in the kingdom of heaven (Matt. 13:51); and it is something that will come (Luke 17:20).

There is no shortage in the Gospels of information regarding the kingdom of God. Quite the opposite, in fact. There are almost embarrassing riches in source material; it would take a small book to take even a preliminary look at each of these occurrences. So, in this chapter we will have to content ourselves by examining just the following issues—the ethics of the kingdom and the nearness, presence, and future coming of the kingdom.

# The Four Faces of Jesus

## THE KINGDOM NEAR

In both Matthew and Mark, the *nearness* of the kingdom of God is introduced at the outset of Jesus' public ministry as the essence of His teaching and preaching, and both Gospels repeat the idea of the nearness of the kingdom several times (Matt. 3:2; 4:17; 10:7; Mark 1:14, 15). In Luke's Gospel, this message is balanced, somewhat, by parables explicitly dealing with the possible delay of the coming kingdom (for example, the parable of the ten minas in Luke 19:11-27), but the same message is present and, moreover, is repeated (Luke 10:9-10; 21:31). Jesus is even cited as saying that some of those listening to Him will not taste death until they see the Son of Man coming in His kingdom (Matt. 16:28; cf. Mark 9:1; Luke 9:27). In summary, the three Synoptic Gospels are agreed that Jesus proclaimed the nearness of the kingdom. This has two consequences—one relating to the moral urgency this nearness brings, the other relating to the role Jesus Himself plays as the One who brings this future kingdom close. Let's look first at the issue of the moral urgency caused by the nearness of the kingdom.

## THE ETHICS OF THE KINGDOM

The message that the kingdom is near should bring transformation to the hearer (Matt. 3:2; 4:17; Mark 1:15). In fact, the matter of the kingdom is so urgent that it should be placed before every other matter (Matt. 6:33; Luke 12:31); it even takes priority over normal family relationships (Luke 18:29).

The message of the kingdom brings with it an expectation of high moral standards. The one who upholds God's law is called great in the kingdom (Matt. 5:19). In fact, only the one who does the will of the Father will enter into the kingdom. Those who have been "lawless" will be excluded (Matt. 7:21).

This strong ethical demand should not distract us from the central thrust of what the Gospels say about the relationship of Christians to the law. The law is fulfilled by those who love—those who love God and who love their fellows (Matt. 22:34-40; Mark 12:28-34; Luke 10:25-28). The key difference between the way Christians observe the law and the way Pharisees do so lies in the inner motivation. Jesus speaks about this in Matthew 5:17-48.[7] This may be the reason tax collectors and harlots are likely to enter the kingdom before the Pharisees, despite the latter's concern for upholding the law and despite the kingdom's requirement of high moral standards (Matt. 21:31).

Neither should the strong emphasis on the moral imperative lead the Christian to self-satisfaction or pride in his or her moral achievement. The one who is childlike is greatest in the kingdom of heaven (Matt. 18:1-4). Jesus insisted that children have access to Him, because the kingdom of God is made up of children and those who, like children, are trusting and spontaneous (Matt. 19:14; Mark 10:14; Luke 18:16). Furthermore, the kingdom belongs to the poor [in spirit] (Matt. 5:3; Luke 6:20) and those persecuted for the sake of righteousness (Matt. 5:10). In contrast, it is hard for the rich to enter the kingdom (Matt. 19:23, 24; Luke 18:24, 25).

### THE KINGDOM PRESENT

The close relationship between Jesus and the coming kingdom He announces reveals itself in the way the future kingdom has become present in Jesus' ministry. The clearest expression of this is in Luke's Gospel. In Luke 11:14-23, His enemies accuse Jesus of using the power of the prince of demons to cast out demons. After pointing out the logical fallacy of the charge, Jesus challenges His listeners with these words: " 'But if it is by the finger of God that I cast out the demons, then the kingdom of God has come upon you' " (v. 20). In other words, Jesus brought the kingdom of God into the present by casting out demons. The kingdom was present because He was present.

Jesus makes a similar statement in Luke 17:21 in responding to a question from some Pharisees concerning when the kingdom of God would come. Jesus said, " 'The kingdom of God is not coming with signs that can be observed; nor will they say, "Look, here it is!" or "There it is!" For, in fact, the kingdom of God is among[8] you.' " In what sense was the kingdom among them? Presumably, in the person of Jesus. This is not to say that the Gospel of Luke has eliminated references to the future kingdom (Luke 19:11; Acts 1:6). What we find, instead, is a phenomenon that has already been observed in the Gospel of John[9]—the future has come into the present in the person and ministry of Jesus. The kingdom of God belongs to the future and will be ushered in by the cataclysmic events associated with the end of the age. But this future blessing is present already in Jesus' activity.

References to a present and future kingdom—similar to those discovered in Luke and John—can also be found in Matthew's Gospel. Matthew 12:22-32 is the parallel passage to Luke 11:14-23 and conveys the same message—that the kingdom of God is present in Jesus' ministry. Furthermore, we have already observed that in Matthew the kingdom is closely associated with the activities of the community of believers, the church.[10] No doubt, this is because the church is carrying forward Jesus' mission and so, as it is faithful to that mission, the kingdom is present in its activities. The kingdom and the church are not identical, because until the end of the age the church is made up of those who are sons of the evil one as well as those who are sons of righteousness (Matt. 13:41-43).

All the Gospels, then, share the belief that the future kingdom has come into the present. But in each, the future kingdom is most important.

### THE END OF THE AGE AND THE KINGDOM FUTURE

A singular feature of what the Synoptic Gospels say about the future kingdom of God is that they give no description of what it will be like. One looks in vain for anything that corresponds to the last few chapters of the book of Revelation, for example. Instead, the Gospels direct our attention to the kingdom's nearness, our attitude toward this nearness, and the moral consequences that this has in our lives. All three Gospels give an account of the signs by which we can ascertain the nearness of the kingdom (Matt. 24, 25; Mark 13; Luke 17:20-37). Furthermore, it is clear that the coming of the kingdom corresponds with the end of this age and the event associated with the end—such as the last judgment (Matt. 25:31-46, esp. vv. 34, 46).

# The Kingdom of God

The Gospels also pay considerable attention to how we should understand the nearness of the kingdom. In an earlier chapter, on Matthew 24, 25,[11] we noted the pair of parables in Matthew 24:45–25:13. All the characters in these two parables expected the coming of their lord. The difference between them was how they reacted to this belief. The wicked servant lived his life on the assumption that the lord's coming would be delayed, so he was caught unprepared when the lord returned sooner than he expected. The faithful servant remained ready for his lord's appearance at any time. This same parable is found in Luke 12:41-48, where it likewise emphasizes that the servant must be prepared for his lord to come at any time. In Matthew 25:1-13, the ten maidens also expected the bridegroom. The contrast between the wise and foolish maidens in this parable lies in the fact that the wise prepared for the possibility of delay. The foolish maidens lived their life on the assumption that the coming would be very soon. This proved not to be the case. In Luke's Gospel, the parable of the ten minas (Luke 19:11-27) makes a similar point. Jesus told this parable in the context of those who were thinking that the kingdom might come immediately. This parable carried the strong message that there would be an intervening time and that the servants of Jesus would be responsible for how productive they had been while He was away.

In other words, the message of the coming kingdom is a message that affects the disciple's present life. There is a moral urgency concerning his or her behavior. The disciple lives in the expectation that the Lord can return at any time. But the disciple must also be ready for the possibility of delay, and wise disciples use that time productively for their Lord. On the other hand, even though signs are given to help us work out the times in which we live, Jesus' coming will catch everyone by surprise. Our responsibility is to be ready, for He may come at any time.

---

1. In place of the "kingdom of God," the Gospel of Matthew has a preference for the description, "kingdom of heaven." The fact that "kingdom of heaven" and "kingdom of God" are synonymous in that Gospel is shown by two things—the parallelism between the two terms in Matthew 19:23, 24 and the frequent occa-

# The Four Faces of Jesus

sions in which Matthew has the term "kingdom of heaven" where the other Gospels have "kingdom of God" (cf. Matt. 4:17 and Mark 1:15; Matt. 13:31-33 and Mark 4:30-32, Luke 13:18-20). This chapter will follow the usage of Mark and Luke.

2. See earlier chapters 6, 12, 17.

3. Romans, Galatians, Ephesians, Colossians, 1 & 2 Thessalonians, 2 Timothy, Titus, and 2 Peter.

4. Three times in 1 Corinthians, twice in John, and once in Romans, Galatians, Colossians, 2 Thessalonians, and Revelation.

5. The statistics in this paragraph are those produced by the analysis of the twenty-sixth edition of the Nestle-Aland Greek New Testament by the Gramcord program.

6. *Growth:* the grain of mustard seed, Matt. 13:31, 32; Mark 4:30-32; Luke 13:18, 19; the leaven hidden in a loaf of bread, Matt. 13:33; Luke 13:20, 21; the seed, Mark 4:26-29; *delay:* the ten maidens, Matt. 25:1-13; the parable of the ten minas, Luke 19:11-27; *mixed nature:* the wheat and the weeds, Matt. 13:24-30, 36-43; the net, Matt. 13:47-50; *worth:* the hidden treasure, Matt. 13:44; the pearl of great price, Matt. 13:45, 46.

7. This passage is discussed at some length in chapter 2.

8. There is considerable debate regarding exactly how the Greek preposition *entos* should be translated in this verse. The word is only used twice in the New Testament. In other usage, it normally conveys the concept of "within." It does sometimes mean "among" (i.e., within a group), and the NRSV has followed this usage. While one could imagine Jesus telling His disciples that the kingdom was within them, it is hard to imagine Him saying the same to His opponents, so the translation "among" is probably correct.

9. See chapter 22.

10. See chapter 6.

11. See chapter 8.

CHAPTER THIRTY

# Salvation

## HOW SALVATION IS PRESENTED IN THE GOSPELS

It is hard to overestimate the importance of the subject of this chapter. The concept of salvation embodies the essence of the way Christians understand reality and their claim that the Christian religion adequately solves the problems inherent in human existence. Furthermore, according to the New Testament, nothing less than our personal eternal destiny hangs on our reaction to the salvation wrought by Jesus.

Unlike those parts of the New Testament that explicitly explore how salvation has come about, the four Gospels present the topic of salvation in their narration of the events of Jesus' life, death, and resurrection. Even John's Gospel recounts these events with very little accompanying interpretation. Nevertheless, the way the Gospels emphasize the implicit meanings of these events, and the context they provide for them, give the reader clear guidance to their meaning. In addition, much of Jesus' teaching, as recorded in the Gospels, deals with the concept of salvation in one way or another.

In this chapter, we will first consider what the Gospels—both the Synoptic Gospels and John—say and imply concerning salvation; then we will move on to discuss the centrality and meaning of the Cross, before finishing the chapter with a personal anecdote.

# The Four Faces of Jesus

## SALVATION AS PRESENTED BY THE SYNOPTIC GOSPELS

What, then, do the three Synoptic Gospels tell us about salvation?

*First, they tell us that humans need salvation because they are sinners by nature.* Indeed, in the Gospels, the recognition of that need appears to be the basic starting point from which the sinner's salvation must begin. For example, it is not the Pharisee, who prays and tells God about his good deeds, who is justified. Rather, it is the tax collector, who could say only, " 'God, be merciful to me, a sinner,' " who went home justified (Luke 18:13). Further, it is those who hunger and thirst for righteousness who will be filled (Matt. 5:6), not those who consider themselves righteous. Thus, there appears to be nothing inherent within us that can recommend us to God. Nor is there anything external that would so recommend us—certainly not wealth. The rich young ruler, convinced that he deserved eternal life because he had observed God's law from childhood, left Jesus sorrowfully because Jesus challenged him to give away all his wealth (Matt. 19:16-22).

What we *do* has no part to play in our salvation, either. This is the strong implication of a second aspect of the Gospel's understanding of salvation—*salvation is a free gift; it is not earned.* The parable of the workers in the vineyard is perhaps the best illustration of the fact that salvation is a gift (Matt. 20:1-16). This parable compares the kingdom of heaven to a landowner who hires laborers to work in his vineyard. He hires the first group of laborers early in the morning and agrees to pay them a wage of one denarius.[1] After this, he goes out several times during the day and hires more laborers. The last group, he hires just prior to the end of the day. No wages are agreed upon; the landowner simply promises to pay them whatever is "just." When it comes to the end of the day, those who were hired last are paid first. To their amazement, they receive a denarius, the wage for a full day's work! This turns out to be exactly the same amount paid to those who have worked all day. Those who have worked all day complain, but the landowner points out to them that they agreed to work for this amount and that he should not be criticized for showing his goodness to the others.

In what way is this parable to be related to the kingdom?

302

In the parable, all get the same reward, no matter how much work each has done. Thus it is with the kingdom. Salvation in God's kingdom is a gift, given independently of how much we have done—or not done. Mind you, the fact that heaven is a free gift does not mean that it is without cost. It cost the merchant all he owned to buy the pearl (Matt. 13:46). It cost the farm laborer all he owned to buy the land in which the treasure was hidden (Matt. 13:44). And Jesus asked the rich young man to give away everything he had (Matt. 19:21, 22; Mark 10:21, 22; Luke 18:22, 23). But what we *do* does not *earn* us a right to heaven. God, in His goodness, gives us a right to heaven. The parable of the lost son(s)[2] also illustrates this point. The prodigal son would like to work as one of his father's hired servants, but the father freely accepts him back into the family, rejoicing that his lost son is now found. The son did not have to *do* anything to be accepted by the father.

The parable of the lost son(s) also illustrates another aspect of salvation the Gospels assert repeatedly: *Salvation is based on the love both Jesus and His Father have for the lost.* The very ministry and death of Jesus is evidence of this love. In the Gospel account, Jesus is conscious that His death is necessary for the forgiveness of sin (Matt. 26:38). Despite His distress at the prospect of dying, leading Him to petition His Father to release Him from the obligation (Matt. 26:39, 42, 44, and parallels), He is prepared to die to enable this forgiveness to become available to sinners, who by definition are unworthy of His self-sacrifice.

In fact, many times in the Gospel accounts Jesus is moved with pity for those with whom He comes in contact—the crowds because they were harassed and helpless (Matt. 9:36); for the 5,000 because they had sick among them (Matt. 14:14); for the 4,000 because they had run out of food (Matt. 15:32); and for the widow whose only son had recently died (Luke 7:13). Furthermore, by His actions, Jesus shows His acceptance and friendship of the marginalized elements of society. He is notorious as a friend of sinners!

Fourth, the actions of Jesus clearly demonstrate *that by His life and ministry He gained the victory over the demonic forces.* Matthew and Luke both describe in detail how the devil himself, immediately after Jesus' baptism, personally tempted Jesus to abandon His ministry. All three of the Synoptic Gospels describe several occasions when Jesus speaks to demons[3] and overcomes them by His command. These very demons recognize Jesus as the Son of God (Mark 5:7) and are subject to His authority. When the seventy disciples return to report to Jesus that even the demons submitted to them, Jesus replies, "I watched Satan fall from heaven like a flash of lightning" (Luke 10:18).

Fifth, by His actions, *Jesus brings cleansing from uncleanness.* Contrary to all previous religious expectations, when Jesus touches the unclean, they do not make Jesus also unclean. Rather, Jesus makes the unclean clean. This is true of the woman with the flow of blood and of the dead child in Mark 5.[4] This is also true of the leper whom Jesus cleansed with a touch (Matt. 8:3). This cleansing is represented by baptism, which becomes the door into the community of believers.

Sixth, the *healing miracles themselves are paradigms of salvation.* This is because of the double meaning of the Greek word *sōzō.* This word means both "to heal" and "to save." Thus, in the Gospels, every time Jesus "heals," the person reading or hearing the Greek would automatically make the linkage between healing and salvation. Thus, the faith of the woman with the flow of blood both "heals" and "saves" her.[5]

These are but six of the different facets of salvation as presented in the Synoptic Gospels. What of the fourth Gospel? Because so much of John's Gospel is unique to itself, perhaps its presentation of salvation is different from the picture that emerges from the Synoptic Gospels. We will turn now to the Gospel of John to discover its particular viewpoint and to ask how it compares with the Synoptic Gospels.

## SALVATION IN THE FOURTH GOSPEL

Salvation in the fourth Gospel is expressed in terms of possessing eternal life. Those who possess eternal life are characterized by belief and love. First, the one who is saved *believes in Jesus.* Note that this Gospel does not talk of a belief *about* Jesus; rather, it regularly speaks of a belief *in* Jesus. A belief *in* Jesus has something added to the regular content of belief. Certainly, there is content to this belief, and part 5 of this book devoted several chapters to what John's Gospel had to say about Jesus—although fully human, He was divine; He had come from God and would go to God, etc. Yet such knowledge needs to lead the believer to a personal connection to Jesus. The language of "believing *in* Jesus" is the language of relationship.

The Jesus of the fourth Gospel confronts us with His extraordinary nature and His claims on our lives, and asks "Do you believe?" This confrontation grows more intense as the Gospel develops. It reaches a climax in the dialogue between Jesus and Martha (John 11). Martha's brother has died and is in the tomb. She has just come from a household full of those who are mourning his passing. Jesus looks at her and says, " 'I am the resurrection and the life; anyone who believes in me, even if they die, they will live, and all who live and believe in me will not die forever. Do you believe this?' " Jesus demands of Martha a belief that is stronger than death itself. This extraordinary demand is made both of Martha and of the reader of the Gospel because if we, the readers, believe in Jesus, then we, too, can have eternal life (John 3:16; 20:31).

In addition to *belief,* the other word closely associated with the one who has eternal life is *love.* This love is both a response to God's love (expressed through the gift of His son, Jesus—John 3:16), and also a response to the love that Jesus Himself has given us. The ultimate expression of this love is Jesus' voluntary death for us. As John 15:9, 12-14 says: " 'Just as the father loved me I also love you; remain in my love . . . this is my command, that you love one another as I have loved you. No one has greater love than this, that they lay down their life for their friends. You are my friends . . .' " Jesus showed His love for us by dying for us. In return, if we are His disciples, we will love each other with the love that Jesus has for us. In fact, this kind of love will identify the true disciples of Jesus—they love one another (13:35). It is noteworthy that both "believing in" and "love" imply a relational response.

How does this concept of salvation compare with the picture found in the Synoptic Gospels?

There are similarities and differences. For example, both give full evidence of God's love and of our need for a love response. Both give priority to the necessity of faith. Although expressed in different terms, most of the themes mentioned in connection with the Synoptic Gospels are also found in John, with one exception—demons, prominent as they are in the three Synoptic Gospels, are virtually absent from the fourth Gospel.[6]

## CENTRALITY AND MEANING OF THE CROSS

The events surrounding the Cross and Jesus' resurrection are the focus of all four Gospels. They form the largest connected narrative and a significant proportion of the whole story. The Gospels provide few editorial comments on the meaning of the Cross, but enough clues are present to give some guidance to how these events should be understood.

Within the three Synoptic Gospels, two series of comments and one report stand out in this regard. The first of these are the comments relating to *the necessity of suffering*. In all three Synoptic Gospels, Jesus tells His disciples no less than three times that the Son of Man is to suffer and die and rise on the third day (Matt. 16:21-24; 17:22, 23; 20:17-19; Mark 8:31-34; 9:30, 31; 10:32-34; Luke 9:21-23; 9:43-45; 18:31-34). Furthermore, this suffering and death *is necessary.* When Peter tries to remonstrate with Him about it, Jesus strongly rebukes him (Matt. 16:22, 23; Mark 8:32, 33). This incident is missing from Luke's Gospel, but the necessity of the Cross is emphasized in an incident unique to that Gospel. After His resurrection, Jesus explains from Scripture to two disciples that His death was necessary (Luke 24:26). In fact, it might be safely said that we can measure the adequacy of any Christian presentation of salvation by how well it shows that the Cross was necessary and by how central the Cross is to that presentation.

Probably the passage that most reveals the meaning that should be attached to the Cross is Jesus' remark as He is celebrating the Passover with His disciples the night before He is betrayed. He picks up the wine glass and says, " 'This is the blood of the new covenant which is poured out for many [for the forgiveness of sins]' " (Matt. 26:28; Mark 14:24; Luke 22:20). Together with what Jesus said about the bread, this action *links Jesus' death to the Passover sacrifice.* In some way, His death is analogous to the death of the Passover lamb. The phrase "for the forgiveness of sins," unique to Matthew, heightens this linkage. Jesus' death thereby becomes analogous to sacrificial atonement. The Old Testament background of the concept of sacrificial atonement is found in the sacrifices made at the temple, many of which had the effect of forgiving sins. The death of the animal "atoned" for the sin. It is this concept of sacrificial atonement that appears to be the background of Jesus' statement.[7] The sinner deserves death. But just as the sacrificial animal died in the place of the sinner, so Jesus has died in our place.

The third indication of meaning is the fact that the veil in the temple was ripped at the moment of Jesus' death. All three Gospels record this event (Matt. 27:50-52; Mark 15:38; Luke 24:45). They give no explanation or interpretation for what happened. And we should be careful not to import the whole theology of the book of Hebrews into this one text. But the basic thrust of Hebrews fits this incident nicely. In other words, the tearing of the veil suggests *the replacement of the temple sacrifices as the principal means of access to God.*

The fourth Gospel, like the Synoptic Gospels, stresses the linkage of the death of the Passover lamb with Jesus' death (John 18:28; 19:14, 31). In addition, it stresses one further aspect of the meaning of the Cross: *the Cross is an expression of the deep love that Jesus has for us.* " 'There is no greater love than this, that somebody lay down his life for his friend. You are my friends' " (John 15:13, 14). Such human self-sacrificing love is still but a reflection of the love that the Father had in giving His Son for us. " 'God so loved the world that he gave his only son' " (John 3:16). The Christian responds to God's love by loving his fellow Christians with the same quality of love that Jesus showed in His death (John 15:12).

### THE ROLE OF FAITH AND A PERSONAL NOTE

One theme that has reoccurred in several of the previous chapters is the centrality of faith as the appropriate human response to salvation. God's goodness and grace is the basis of our salvation. Our response is to accept the salvation that has been provided at such great cost. To put it bluntly, salvation is available on the basis of faith alone. For example, in the Gospel of Matthew we have seen that the accounts of the healing miracles in Matthew 8, 9 are presented in a way that highlights the centrality of faith.[8] When looking at Mark 5, we also noted that Jesus deliberately spoke to the woman who had been healed of her long-standing problem of a flow of blood. Likewise, this was to highlight the necessity of faith. Furthermore, earlier in this chapter, we noted that faith "in Jesus" is at the core of John's presentation of salvation. There is no need to repeat the evidence from these earlier chapters that salvation is on the basis of faith alone. But neither should we overlook some of the practical implications of this concept because, not only is faith the basis for our participation in salvation, it is at the heart of the individual Christian's experience. This becomes a matter that greatly affects what it is like to be a Christian.

Christians generally recognize that there is a difference between faith and knowledge. Now, Christian faith is not something that is divorced from evidence. The evidence is there—Jesus lived, died, and rose again; He challenges us to make a decision for Him, and He tells us that this decision has eternal consequences. But, like so many other important choices in life, this decision has to be made before all the facts are known for sure. A decision has to be made nevertheless—a decision whether or not to believe in what Jesus says about Himself.

This was brought home to me a few years ago at my mother's funeral. Mum had been very ill for some time, but even so, it was a painful and numbing break when she died. Her death took place in the middle of a teaching semester, so I traveled from Australia to New Zealand and back in one weekend. I met family and old friends whom I hadn't seen for years. I was so busy there was hardly any time to think. But there was one moment for meditation. During the funeral service, I remember clearly thinking that the preacher had really got to know Mum quite well, because his sermon exactly fitted her beliefs. He spoke of the great comfort there was in knowing that when Jesus returned we would all be reunited. He quoted all the texts dealing with this topic and spoke warmly of the salvation available through Jesus.

At the time, I had only recently finished my Ph.D. I suppose you could say that I had spent a major part of my life up to that moment in an increasingly sophisticated study of the Gospels. Now here I was, sitting in the church I had attended as a child and teenager. Since that time I had learned four languages and could read the Gospels in Greek. I had explored the issues and reached greater sophistication in all areas of my Christian understanding. But the central issue had not changed for me since my childhood: "On the basis of the evidence I have now, do I believe that Jesus' death and resurrection made such a difference in history that I can be saved? Do I believe Jesus will return to raise the dead and transform the living?"

My study had provided answers to some of the questions that had been troubling me, but it had also raised further questions for which I still seek answers. Whether or not I believe is a decision I still have to make on the balance of evidence, knowing that I still have some unanswered questions. Yet I have to make a decision—What will I do with Jesus? My salvation depends on the answer to that question. And that answer can only be the answer of faith. Salvation is indeed based on faith, not knowledge.

---

1. A denarius was a silver coin about the size of an American dime. It is hard to estimate a comparative value in modern currency; one would have to estimate what amount of money would be equivalent to a day's agricultural labor (Matt. 20:2) or, perhaps, what would buy bread to feed twenty-five individuals (Mark 6:37). Two denarii would pay for accommodation at an inn for a period of some days (Luke 10:35).
2. This parable, in Luke 15:11-32, is more fully explained in chapter 16.
3. The KJV consistently translates *daimonon* as devil (plural, devils). Most modern translators use "demon" to translate this word and reserve the word "devil" for translating the Greek word *diabolos*, which is used in the New Testament almost exclusively of the prince of demons, the devil himself (Matt. 4:1; 25:41; Luke 4:2; John 8:44; Eph. 6:11; and Rev. 12:9). John 6:70 is an exception.
4. See chapter 10, where this concept is developed more fully.
5. See further on this woman in chapter 10.
6. Demons appear in John mainly in accusations that Jesus Himself is acting as

their agent (8:48, 52). The devil appears as an actor a few times, particularly as the one who incites Judas to betray Jesus (John 13:2, 27). But compared to the Synoptic Gospels there is a lot less interest in this aspect of Jesus' ministry.

7. The concept of atonement is found less frequently in the New Testament than in the Old. The word *atonement* itself is found only three times in the New Testament—Rom. 3:25; 1 John 2:2; 4:10.

8. See chapter 3.

CHAPTER THIRTY-ONE

# Community, Discipleship, and Mission

**WHERE THE RUBBER MEETS THE ROAD**

This chapter deals with those aspects of Christianity that have the most practical impact on the individual believer. It begins with a consideration of the community in which Christians find themselves; that is, it looks at what the New Testament has to say about the church. This is a topic of lively debate in almost all circles of the contemporary church—from those who are seeking to reform the particular organizational structure in which they find themselves, down to some of the church's youth who wish to rebel against what they perceive to be the suffocating closeness of the Christian community. From there, this chapter considers the individual Christian, understood as a disciple. The last section of the chapter deals with the mission of the believer and the community.

## *COMMUNITY*

**THE GOSPELS AS COMMUNITY DOCUMENTS**

It is possible to use the Gospels to discover community organization only because they represent the beliefs and values of the community as much as they represent those of their individual writers. This is because the Gospel writers were more closely linked to their community than are modern writers. This conclusion is based on two separate lines of evidence—the anonymity of the Gospels and insights from sociologists.

A curious feature of all four Gospels is that they are anonymous. The text of neither Matthew nor Mark identifies the author in any way. This identification was provided by the early church at a later time.[1] Luke and Acts have an individual author, as is evident from the prologue to both the Gospel and Acts. Further, because several of the chapters in Acts are written in the first person ("We left . . . we arrived," etc.), it appears that the writer was a companion of Paul. But even so, which of Paul's companions actually did the writing is not explicitly stated.

The place the fourth Gospel gives to the "beloved" disciple marks it as somewhat different, in that the beloved disciple is the witness who is said to authenticate the truthfulness of the whole. Yet it is the fourth Gospel that gives us the strongest clue about the community nature of the Gospels. This clue is found in John 21:24: "[The beloved disciple] is the disciple who witnesses concerning these things, and who writes these things, and *we* know that his witness is true" (emphasis supplied). Only one person can write at any one time, so why does he say "*We* know these things are true" instead of "I know these things are true"? Clearly because there is a larger group that is also taking responsibility for what is written in the fourth Gospel. In other words, the Gospel is the product of a community of believers gathered around the beloved disciple.

This is the most likely reason the other three Gospels are anonymous too—they were not considered to be the product of just one author but rather belonged to a larger group gathered around the individual responsible for writing.

The findings of sociologists throw an unexpected light on this matter. In their study of different societies in different time periods, sociologists have pointed out that most societies have been based around stronger group attachments than are modern Western societies. This is certainly true of New Testament times, and we can see the evidence of it reflected in the New Testament itself. Even Paul, perhaps the most "rugged individualist" of any writer in the New Testament, is never alone. He is surrounded by such individuals as Barnabas, Titus, Timothy, Luke, and Demas; when visiting a new city, he lives in close proximity to those there whom he already knows.

All this has been leading to one conclusion—It was inconceivable to the writers of the New Testament that a Christian would not immediately become a member of the community. They expressed this in the very language they used. Christians were baptized *into* Christ (Rom. 6:2). They considered their fellow believers as their family and used family terms to address each other. Favorite among these was the description "brother" (Acts 7:2; Rom. 1:13; 10:1; 1 Cor. 1:10; Gal. 3:15; Eph. 6:10; Col. 4:15; 1 Thess. 1:4, etc.). Further, each of the Gospel writers lived in close proximity to his own community. It is impossible to describe with certainty the exact relationship between the writer and his community, but that it was close is guaranteed. Thus the Gospels not only represent the individual writer but also the community in which he worshiped.

### THREE DIFFERENT ORGANIZATIONAL MODELS PRESENTED IN THE GOSPELS

Given that the Gospels reflect the community of its writer, and given that it was inconceivable that a new Christian would not immediately become a member of a community, do the Gospels give any indications of how these communities were organized?

In fact, the four Gospels actually represent three different types of community organization. The clearest of these is found in Luke and Acts, particularly in Acts. The Christian communities in Acts appear to have been under the leadership of a board of elders (Acts 14:23; 20:17, etc.). Those who formed the earliest Christian groups had had prior association with synagogues, and synagogues were governed by a board of elders. So this form of community government was most likely based on the synagogue model of organization. Elsewhere in the New Testament we find that these elders were appointed by the community (Tit. 1:5).

Early in Acts we find a second title for church leaders—deacons—who were likewise appointed by the community. Initially, these were given lesser roles than those of the apostles (Acts 6:1-6), but later in Acts they are shown in leadership roles (Acts 6:8–7:60; 8:4-8, 26-40).

The apostles are another important group visible in both Acts and the Epistles. Eleven of these had belonged to the group of Jesus' twelve disciples. One of the first items of business the early community undertook was to replace Judas Iscariot so that there would again be twelve of these apostles (Acts 1:15-26).[2] Some of these apostles remained very important in the early church, particularly Peter and John. Others, although not part of the initial circle of twelve, became equally important. Two notable examples are James, the brother of Jesus, and Paul. What happened to the other apostles is lost in the mists of time. Numerous legends abound, but few have credibility.

The book of Acts records one other significant event related to the matter of community organization—the church council, in Acts 15. When a significant doctrinal dispute arose, the communities involved sent representatives to Jerusalem so the rights and wrongs of the matter could be discussed. Thus, while each community appears to have been largely autonomous under the leadership of its board of elders, some overarching matters of concern were dealt with by wider consultation under the leadership of those closest to Jesus.

The community organization visible in the fourth Gospel and in John's Epistles is quite distinct from the pattern in Acts. In the Epistles we find the logical outworking of what John's Gospel says about the guidance of the Comforter. It appears that at the time John's Epistles were written, the Johannine community was under threat by a group teaching a docetic Christology (1 John 2:18, 19, 26).[3] Yet the community made no appeal to the authority of a board of elders in response to this threat. Instead, there was a strong reiteration of the adequacy of leadership by the Holy Spirit: "As for you, the anointing that you received from him abides in you, and so you do not need anyone to teach you" (1 John 2:26). Third John 9 makes it evident that there is some authority within the community, but this authority is based squarely in the leadership and testimony of the Holy Spirit. If ever there was a spirit-led community, it was the Johannine community.

Matthew's Gospel reveals a community organization somewhat between the two outlined above. A previous chapter[4] has outlined the evidence for its organization, so only the conclusions need to be given here. The community has taken responsibility for its own self-governance. Ultimate authority lies with the entire community. Elders are not mentioned. Some are taking leadership roles in the community that, within Judaism, would entitle them to the title "rabbi" or "father" or "teacher," but they were prohibited from taking these titles because of a basic egalitarianism within the community—all were equal under Christ.

It is a historical fact that the Christian communities developed over time, but how the three different types of community organization described above should be related to that historical development is problematical. What is evident, though, is that in the second century, the organization model, reflected in Acts, Timothy, and Titus, emerged as the dominant organizational model. After all, it had long-term stability and was the one best equipped to handle the threat of heresy. In later centuries, separation between the clergy and the laity developed, along with a three-tiered leadership model of bishops, elders, and deacons.

Each particular religion and denomination struggles with the issue of organization. Those that begin with a sincere effort to have no organization quickly discover it is not possible to have long-term stability and growth without some kind of structure. Those that begin with a strong emphasis on authority and clear structure soon find that if they are not to become stagnant they need to find ways to allow flexibility and input from their "grass roots." From the Gospels and Acts, it is evident that the early Christian communities approached these issues in various ways. Moreover, their willingness to invent a new type of organizational structure (by appointing deacons) showed that they were prepared to adapt organization and structure to their changing needs. This does not mean that the Gospels give no guidance about the future organization of the community, but this guidance dealt with the attitudes of church leaders rather than in the form of exact organizational models.

### PRINCIPLES OF COMMUNITY LEADERSHIP

According to Jesus' words in Luke 22:25-27, there was to be a big difference between the type of leadership exercised over Christian communities and that exercised in other types of organizations. Christian leadership was to be characterized by service. Unlike the public benefactors of the Roman Empire, Christian leaders should not seek authority but rather should act as servants. In this manner, they are to follow the example of their Master, who came as One who serves. This attitude is reinforced by the sayings in Matthew 23:1-12 that criticize the attitudes of the scribes and Pharisees. Their love of the place of honor at banquets, the best seats in the synagogues, greetings in the marketplace, and the title "rabbi" should not be repeated among Christians. Instead, Christians are to remember that Jesus is their Teacher and Master. The greatest in the community should become a servant.

The incident described in Matthew 16 is also instructive for Christian leaders and those they lead. Within the one chapter, Jesus commends Peter by telling him he will be the foundation on which He will build His church (vv. 17, 18) and condemns Peter by calling him Satan (v. 23). Jesus commends Peter for his insight that Jesus is the Christ (v. 16), but He condemns him because he refuses to contemplate that Jesus must suffer (v. 22). Peter indeed turned out to be a leader in the early Christian community, but this does not mean that everything he did was automatically right. On one occasion, Paul reports that he found it necessary to resist Peter to his face (Gal. 2:11). Thus, it appears that Christian leaders are not to be followed blindly. If they are acting in a way consistent with their confession, then they deserve due respect. But if not, then although they should still be treated with Christian courtesy, they must be resisted—sometimes as strongly as one would resist the devil himself!

Thus it is that Christians will find themselves as part of a wider family, the family of believers. This community will have structured itself in a way that meets its organizational needs, but its leadership will not act from a desire for power and control. Christian leaders will act from motives of love and a desire to serve others. This much the Gospels tell us about our community and the responsibilities of its leaders. But what do they have to say to us individually concerning our personal life? The answer to this question is found in the concept of discipleship.

# Community, Discipleship, and Mission

## *Discipleship*

### The call

All four Gospels portray Jesus as calling disciples to Himself. Typically, Jesus finds individuals at his everyday tasks and says, " 'Come, follow Me.' " This call becomes an analogy for becoming a Christian; a Christian is one who follows Jesus.

The invitation comes without reservation. The previous chapter stressed that salvation is a free gift from God through Jesus. There is nothing in ourselves that warrants such a gift. It is given because God and His Son, Jesus, love us and have, at the great cost of the Cross, made eternal life available to us.

Matthew 22:1-14 compares this process to an invitation to a wedding feast.[5] The wedding of a king's son would be an important occasion, but when the invitation arrived, it was ignored. When more servants were sent, they were killed. The king became angry and destroyed the murderers and their village. But because the feast was already prepared, he invited everybody whom his servants could find, both the evil and the good (v. 10). The invitation to participate in the kingdom is a joyous event extended to everyone, both good and bad. It is given by someone of great importance, and to refuse would be as churlish as a refusal to accept an invitation to the wedding feast of the king's son.

### Cost

Although membership in the kingdom is a freely given gift, it is not received without cost. It's acceptance requires total commitment. Jesus tells His listeners:

> " 'Whoever comes to me and does not hate father and mother, wife and children, brothers and sisters, yes, and even life itself, cannot be my disciple. Whoever does not carry the cross and follow me cannot be my disciple. . . . So therefore, none of you can become my disciple if you do not give up all your possessions' " (Luke 14:26, 27, 33).

The kingdom is to take priority over family ties, wealth, or even life itself. Following Jesus brings great benefits—a close family relationship with other believers, forgiveness, the kingdom of heaven. But it also carries a cost. When disciples follow Jesus, it means that they also must be prepared to follow Him to Calvary, if necessary.

## ETHICS OF THE KINGDOM

The gift of salvation is just that, a gift. It is not earned. So, the disciple of Jesus does not produce good works in order to be saved. But there is a response to the gift of salvation that exerts a tangible influence on behavior and motivation. The Christian responds to the love of Jesus and in return acts in a loving way to others. The heart of Christian ethics is love of God and loving one's neighbor as oneself (Matt. 22:36-40; Mark 12:29-31). In the parable of the good Samaritan (Luke 10:25-37), we discover that our neighbor is anyone who is in need, even if that person is a hated enemy. In Matthew 5:43-48 we discover that in this respect we need to be like God, loving both the good and the bad. In this is found Christian perfection.

The Sermon on the Mount also highlights another fundamental feature of the ethics of the kingdom. The essence of the law is preserved, even though it is transformed, by the Christ event. This means that Christians will not only refrain from adultery but also avoid lustful thoughts. Christians will not murder, but further, they will not hate. The ethics of the kingdom make greater demands on the lives of Christians than even those made by the Pharisaic interpretation of the law. The Christian keeps the transformed law of God by pure motives.

Finally, Christians treat others as God has treated them. They are forgiving of others. Because they have been forgiven much, they will forgive much (Luke 7:47). The other side of this coin is the frightening threat that if we do not forgive, then God will not forgive us in turn (Matt. 18:35).

## PRAYER AND TRUST

The life of the disciple is characterized by prayer and trust. Jesus tells His disciples not to worry about food and clothing. God looks after the birds and the grass, and He will provide for those who are His (Matt.

# Community, Discipleship, and Mission

6:25-34). The disciples have only to ask, and it will be given to them; only to seek, and they will find; only to knock, and it will be opened to them (Matt. 7:7-12; Luke 11:9, 10). If we, who are evil, know how to give good gifts to our children, how much more, then, will God, who is good, give good gifts to His children (Matt. 7:11).

## MISSION

Both Jesus' followers and their community inherit the mission of Jesus. In both Matthew and Luke, the group of disciples is given a commission to take the message of Jesus into all the world:

> And when Jesus came to him he said, "All power in heaven and on earth is given to me. Therefore, go and make disciples of all the nations, baptizing them in the name of the Father, and the Son, and the Holy Spirit, teaching them to observe all that I have commanded you" (Matt. 28:18-20; cf. Acts 1:8).

During His ministry, Jesus sends His disciples to preach that the kingdom of heaven is near, to heal the sick, raise the dead, cleanse lepers, and cast out demons (Matt. 10:6). In fact, His disciples are to carry on the ministry in which Jesus had been involved; He also had been healing the sick and preaching that the kingdom was near (Matt 4:23; 9:35). In Luke's Gospel, a second set of disciples, seventy in number, were also sent out on a similar mission (Luke 10:1-12). They also proclaimed the nearness of the kingdom (v. 9). Following Jesus' resurrection and ascension, His followers were to take over this task of proclaiming the nearness of the kingdom. They were to continue Jesus' mission.

Carrying on the mission of Jesus means that, like Him, Christians will seek the lost, be a friend to sinners, and seek the good of all. Their lives will be lived in self-sacrificing love as they care for those who are sick and warn everyone that the kingdom of heaven is at hand.

## A FINAL WORD

This completes our introductory study of the four Gospels. They are

# The Four Faces of Jesus

fascinating and stimulating in many ways and will richly repay further study. In our investigation, we have looked at all kinds of information—historical, archaeological, lexical, and theological. We have studied the Gospels from the different perspectives offered by a detailed examination of their constituent parts. And we have taken time to look at the big picture. Throughout all this, though, one thing has been a constant—the witness that these Gospels make concerning Christ. This is a disturbing witness to a disturbing individual. The Gospels claim that although Jesus was God, He became man and died for our sins. They do not present this as interesting information. Rather, they present this as a life-changing decision that they force on our attention. In the Gospels, Jesus is the One who comes to us where we are working and demands, " 'Come, follow Me.' " The Gospels also say that eternal consequences are determined by our response to that demand. The question they ask, then, is: "What will *you* do with Jesus?"

---

1. For further information on this, see endnote 1, in chapter 1 and endnote 2 in chapter 22.
2. The title "apostle" was not reserved only for these twelve. Paul and Barnabas are also called apostles (e.g., Acts 14:14).
3. The docetic nature of the Christology espoused by the "antichrists" who "would deceive you" is evident in such passages as 1 John 2:22; 4:2; 2 John 7. Docetism is discussed further in chapter 28.
4. See chapter 7.
5. There is a similar parable in Luke 14:15-24 that also revolves around the theme of an important invitation turned down for inappropriate reasons, though there are also large differences between the parables. Several explanations have been given as to how these differences may have come about. Some have suggested the differences could be explained in terms of translation from an underlying Aramaic original ("marriage feast" and "banquet" are two possible meanings of the one Aramaic word, to give just one example of how translation might account for the differences). Others suggest that a similar theme of invitation and rude rejection might have given rise to two different parables. In any event, the fact that there are two similar parables does not detract from the point being made—that the call to membership in the kingdom is like an invitation to an important banquet. Moreover, this concept finds expression in both Matthew and Luke.